OXFORD TEXTUAL PERSPECTIVES

Literature and the Great War 1914–1918

GENERAL EDITORS

Elaine Treharne   Greg Walker

Literature and the Great War
1914–1918

RANDALL STEVENSON

OXFORD
UNIVERSITY PRESS

OXFORD

UNIVERSITY PRESS

Great Clarendon Street, Oxford, OX2 6DP,
United Kingdom

Oxford University Press is a department of the University of Oxford.
It furthers the University's objective of excellence in research, scholarship,
and education by publishing worldwide. Oxford is a registered trade mark of
Oxford University Press in the UK and in certain other countries

First Edition published in 2013

Impression: 1

British Library Cataloguing in Publication Data

Data available

ISBN 978-0-19-959644-7 (Hbk)
978-0-19-959645-4 (Pbk)

Printed in Great Britain by the
MPG Printgroup, UK

SERIES EDITORS' PREFACE

Oxford Textual Perspectives is a new series of informative and provocative studies focused upon texts (conceived of in the broadest sense of that term) and the technologies, cultures, and communities that produce, inform, and receive them. It provides fresh interpretations of fundamental works, images, and artefacts, and of the vital and challenging issues emerging in English literary studies. By engaging with the contexts and materiality of the text, its production, transmission, and reception history, and by frequently testing and exploring the boundaries of the notions of text and meaning themselves, the volumes in the series question conventional frameworks and provide innovative interpretations of both canonical and less well-known works. These books will offer new perspectives, and challenge familiar ones, both on and through texts and textual communities. While they focus on specific authors, periods, and issues, they nonetheless scan wider horizons, addressing themes and provoking questions that have a more general application to literary studies and cultural history as a whole. Each is designed to be as accessible to the non-specialist reader as it is fresh and rewarding for the specialist, combining an informative orientation in a landscape with detailed analysis of the territory and suggestions for further travel.

Elaine Treharne and *Greg Walker*

PREFACE

Early in 2010, the Commonwealth War Graves Commission reinterred the bodies of 250 British and Australian soldiers, twenty miles or so south of Ypres, close to France's border with Belgium. Their remains had been discovered the previous year, still in mass burial pits, dug hastily for the thousands of casualties of the Battle of Fromelles, fought one summer evening in 1916, during the Somme campaign. Their discovery is typical of ways the dead and the debris of the battles of 1914–18 continue to resurface nearly a century later, in the fields of France and Flanders, and in other war zones around the world. The Great War, in general, likewise refuses to remain buried in the past. Armistice days, poppies, war memorials in every town and village in Europe—perhaps above all, the writing the conflict produced—have kept the Great War firmly present in the mind and memory of later decades. Yet it has been remembered variously. Its lengthening shadow has been repeatedly reshaped, as Chapter 4 considers, by the changing cultural landscapes across which it has fallen. Great War literature has likewise been variously evaluated, with views continuing to evolve since influential critical studies began to be published late in the twentieth century. Assessments have moved on even since Samuel Hynes's comprehensive *A War Imagined* appeared in 1990, and more extensively since Paul Fussell published a still more influential analysis, *The Great War and Modern Memory*, in 1975.

Had Fussell been writing thirty years or so later, he might have considered 'The Great War and *Post*modern Memory' as a title. Early pages of his study quote a letter Henry James wrote on 5 August 1914, the day after the beginning of the war. James reflects that 'the plunge of civilization into this abyss of blood and darkness . . . is a thing that so gives away the whole long age during which we have supposed the world to be, with whatever abatement, gradually bettering'. Thomas Hardy also reflects on the demise of 'bettering' in a poem about the war's ending, in the signing of the armistice on 11 November 1918. By that date, Hardy considers, 'old hopes that earth was bettering slowly, | Were dead and damned'.[1] The end of a long age of supposed 'bettering' became a central interest of postmodern criticism late in the twentieth century. Much of it envisaged the Second World War terminating faiths in progress, modernity, and rational systems of thought which had been sustained ever since the Enlightenment in the eighteenth century. Yet in the lengthening perspectives of the twenty-first century, the faltering of these faiths seems readily retraceable, much as Hardy and James suggest, to origins in the Great War.

A new century offers further evidence for this extension of Fussell's views. *The Great War and Modern Memory* concludes with reference to Thomas Pynchon's *Gravity's Rainbow* (1973). It is naturally a more recent Pynchon novel, *Against the Day* (2006), which now seems to offer more to understanding of the Great War. In particular, *Against the Day* envisages technology and supposed progress contributing, by the early twentieth century, not to 'bettering' but instead to world-wide foreclosure, mechanization, and loss of opportunity, culminating in the irreversible destruction of 1914–18. One of Pynchon's characters straightforwardly concludes that 'the world came to an end in 1914', and that its inhabitants have 'been in Hell ever since that terrible August'.[2] As he suggests, if the Great War refuses to remain buried in the past, it is because the shock, disillusion, and fractured faiths of that first, fundamental modern crisis have so long continued to shape the world in the present, from 1914 all the way to a postmodern age.

Commentators on *The Great War and Modern Memory* have suggested revisions of other kinds, sometimes complaining that Fussell concentrates too much on poetry, and on the Western Front, and too exclusively on writing by educated, usually middle-class officers—invariably, of course, male. Drawing on the many studies appearing in the intervening years, Samuel Hynes offers a broader view in *A War Imagined*, assessing women authors as well as literature from other war zones and from the Home Front. Hynes also warns against narrowing of another sort—the steady settling of memories into what he describes as a 'collective narrative' or simplified 'Myth of the War'.[3] Since he wrote, this tendency has been

[1] Henry James, Letter of 4/5 August 1914 to Howard Sturgis, *The Letters of Henry James*, ed. Percy Lubbock (London: Macmillan, 1920), II: 398; Thomas Hardy, ' "And There Was a Great Calm" ', *The Complete Poems of Thomas Hardy*, ed. James Gibson (1976; rpt. London: Macmillan, 1991), 589.

[2] Thomas Pynchon, *Against the Day* (London: Jonathan Cape, 2006), 1077.

[3] See Chapter 4, p. 195.

criticized more fiercely by another generation of commentators. For these revisionist historians, collective narratives have tended less towards myth than simple misrepresentation, obscuring historical realities in unrestrained regret and in complacent convictions about the Great War's futility and mismanagement. Chapter 4 suggests that their views are more likely to qualify than replace the general conclusions Hynes outlines. In this way, though, they can be genuinely useful, contributing to reconsideration of long-held views of the war, and to recognition of a fuller range of perspectives in the literature it produced—a recognition also encouraged by new anthologies of Great War poetry appearing early in the twenty-first century.[4] Reconsideration and recognition of this kind are main aims of the present study, intended to reappraise Great War literature in the light of all the evolving ideas mentioned above. It also seeks to diversify these still further, in two principal ways. The first of these involves fuller consideration of Great War narrative than criticism often offers, much of it finding poetry more rewarding. This preference may well be justifiable, but it is worth exploring further. Difficulties the Great War imposed on narrative writers, considered in Chapter 2, usefully indicate its effects on contemporary imagination more generally, and may also help account for the particular strengths of poetry, assessed in Chapter 3.

Difficulties the war imposed on drama left it the least successful of the three main literary genres, or at any rate one often passed over in later assessments. In September 1914, the playwright and novelist Gilbert Cannan was already asking 'with London striving to become a military camp and, in its effort, turning into one vast music-hall, where shall the drama rear its head?'[5] Some answers to his question did emerge as the war went on. The Old Vic continued to present seasons of innovatively staged Shakespearean and classic drama. But censorship, public opinion, and the preference for light entertainment Cannan mentions—also an irritant to George Bernard Shaw[6]—created difficulties still greater than those encountered by poetry or narrative in

---

[4] Vivien Noakes (ed.), *Voices of Silence: The Alternative Book of First World War Poetry* (Stroud: Sutton, 2006); Dominic Hibberd and John Onions (eds), *The Winter of the World: Poems of the First World War* (London: Constable, 2008).

[5] Gilbert Cannan, 'The Drama: A Note in War Time', *Poetry and Drama* (September 1914), 2(7), 307–8.

[6] See 'Heartbreak House and Horseback Hall', his introduction to *Heartbreak House* (1919).

FIG 1   The Royal Flying Corps Kite and Balloon Section Concert Party (the 'Tonics') rehearse *Cinderella*, in January 1918, amid the ruins of Bapaume.

© Imperial War Museums (Q 8378)

presenting any genuine account of the war. Plays attempting to do so, such as Miles Malleson's *'D' Company* and *Black 'Ell* (1916), were regularly banned. Other forms of theatre, including those presented in actual military camps, did continue to thrive. Around the Western Front, and in other combat zones, theatrical and concert companies were widely employed to entertain the soldiers, who regularly put on shows of their own during rest periods away from the front line (Fig. 1). This activity, and those war plays that were produced, deserve fuller critical attention, as commentators such as Heinz Kosok have argued. But such attention is inevitably limited in a study of the *literature* of the Great War—mostly of written or published material, and of work, in Kosok's definition, 'with at least a limited degree of literary aspirations'.[7]

[7] Heinz Kosok, *The Theatre of War: The First World War in British and Irish Drama* (London: Palgrave Macmillan, 2007), 198.

Dramatic literature is considered at appropriate points throughout, but war plays, with regret, are denied a separate chapter to themselves.

This leaves more scope for another aim—a second aspect of the broadening of critical perspectives mentioned above. Most studies of Great War literature concentrate, obviously, on writing by combatants or former combatants, or by direct witnesses of the conflict, or of life on the Home Front. Some also discuss this writing's relations with modernist initiatives gathering pace in the 1920s, or with the evolution of literature in later decades. A few consider its relations with the work of an older, established generation of authors—writers such as Arnold Bennett, or Robert Bridges, in many cases drawn into producing propaganda during the war, as Chapter 1 describes. It is more unusual to find critical studies which assess all three of these areas. *Literature and the Great War* attempts to do so, tracing war writing's reciprocal relations with broader developments in the literature and culture of its time, and with the changing expectations of readers, as these evolved during and after the war.

This broad approach facilitates exploration of a central interest throughout—in ways the Great War's challenges to established systems of thought particularly focused on language and representation. Concerned in August 1914 about the failure of 'bettering', Henry James went on to worry early the following year that the war had also 'overstrained' and 'weakened' any resources available to represent it.[8] As he suggests, if the Great War did not end the world—as Pynchon's character feared—it radically challenged the ways words could be related to it. Chapter 1 outlines the sharp divisions it opened up between public and private discourse, between official accounts of events and eyewitnesses' views of them, and between the outlooks of established writers and those of a younger, emerging generation of solider-authors. The new and almost unimaginably violent experience of the war also profoundly challenged the capacities of conventional literary forms, and ultimately of language itself, to represent the life and death of the times. Though such challenges particularly confronted war authors, shifts in something as fundamental as the role or surety of language also remained influential on the innovative, modernist writing emerging alongside their work in the 1920s.

---

[8] See Chapter 1, p. 49.

Analysis of these challenges naturally focuses mostly on published fiction, poetry, autobiography, and memoir. But in assessing the encounter of words with a violent world, there is good reason to examine more immediate, unrevised forms of writing in diaries, letters, and journals. Where possible, reference is made to published, generally available material of this kind, though there is obviously much to be learned from writing *not* suited or intended for publication in any form, and examples of this are incorporated where appropriate. In general, the focus is on writing in English, especially on British and occasionally on US literature. Reference is also made to non-Anglophone authors for comparison or contrast, or in instances—such as Henri Barbusse's work, or Erich Maria Remarque's—where this was strongly influential on the British context.

Within these fields, chapters that follow assess most of the literary texts that deal directly and influentially with the Great War. They also show how influentially the Great War dealt with text—with language and its representation of the world—and with what effects for literary form and imagination at the time and later. These aims are particularly appropriate to the Oxford Textual Perspectives series, and I'm very grateful to Greg Walker for his invitation to write for it, and for his generous, thoughtful support throughout the writing. In Oxford University Press, Jacqueline Baker, Ariane Petit, Rachel Platt, and Charles Lauder, Jr, looked after the project encouragingly and efficiently throughout. I'm also grateful to many others, from the 1990s and beyond. I'm fortunate to work in an English Literature department as clever, collaborative, and supportive as the University of Edinburgh's, and particularly indebted to several of its members: to Sarah Carpenter, Paul Crosthwaite, Simon Malpas, and Andrew Taylor, and to Jonathan Wild, whose knowledge of the period and sustained encouragement greatly enhanced the project overall. For information, advice, and help with particular aspects, I'm also grateful to David Denby, Nina Engelhardt, Pam King, Rick Rylance, Roger Savage, Anna Stevenson, and Elaine Treharne. Some of the material of Chapter 1 previously appeared in *The Edinburgh Companion to Twentieth-Century Literatures in English* (2006), and I'm grateful to Edinburgh University Press, and to my fellow editor of that volume, Brian McHale, for permission to redeploy this here.

The study was assisted by academic leave granted by the University of Edinburgh's School of Literatures, Languages and Cultures during

2009–10. I'm grateful for grants from the same source, and from the British Academy, which contributed towards the cost of illustrations. The Imperial War Museum was helpful in advising about these, and in providing reproductions. For further help with illustrations, and with many other matters, thanks to the National Library of Scotland's staff—in particular to Alison Metcalfe, whose assistance with manuscripts was invaluable. For permission to quote from these—from the journals of LCPL George Ramage, from letters to Lt. Nigel Trotter's family, and from the papers of FM Earl Haig—acknowledgement is gratefully made to the Trustees of the National Library of Scotland.

CONTENTS

LIST OF ILLUSTRATIONS

Unspeakable War

A *Times* correspondent describes as follows a scene on the Western Front, early on a summer morning, looking out over the rivers Somme and Ancre and the ruined church at Albert:

> The night mists still hung heavy, and the herbage was soaking with dew…immediately within view was the valley of the Ancre, and the town of Albert…It was a lovely summer morning, the sun, still low, shining directly in our faces…Albert was almost hidden in mist, except that the church tower, with the wonderful spectacle of the leaning figure of the Virgin, stood clear above the white bank below and gleamed golden in the sun…
>
> A beautiful summer day, with promise of great heat…The sky above is clear blue, flecked with dazzling white islands of cloud.

That summery scene soon darkened. It was the morning of 1 July 1916, the first day of the Battle of the Somme. A huge artillery bombardment abruptly ceased, and at 7.30am the British infantry struggled out of their trenches, shouldering heavy packs as they clambered over the top. Around four hours later, 60,000 of them were casualties, nearly 20,000 killed outright. The wounded could be heard crying out, in the No Man's Land between the trenches, for days afterwards.

This was the worst day's loss in British military history, and the worst endured by any army during the Great War. Losses continued on an almost equivalent scale in the weeks that followed. By the time the Somme offensive petered out, late in 1916, it had left more than a million casualties overall, 420,000 of them on the British side. Many were men who had volunteered enthusiastically at the very start of the war, on 4 August 1914, or responded to the call for more troops—for a 'first hundred thousand'— made a few days later by the Secretary of State for War, Lord Kitchener. In his poem 'MCMXIV' (1964), Phillip Larkin looks back on the huge crowds that turned up outside recruiting offices, familiar from contemporary photographs of 'long uneven lines' of men, 'grinning as if it were all | An August Bank Holiday lark'.[1] Recruits responding to Kitchener had gradually formed a replacement for the Regular Army. The core of the British Expeditionary Force (BEF), strengthened by Reservists and Territorials, this army had been beaten back from Mons to the Marne, along with its French allies, by the German offensive in the late summer and autumn of 1914. Its numbers were depleted further by the brief counter-offensive which followed, then by the settling of the conflict into the attrition and stalemate, throughout many months of trench warfare, which the Battle of the Somme was confidently expected to end.

When the long uneven lines of Kitchener's new army were destroyed by German artillery and machine guns on the Somme, something more seemed to have been lost than life, manpower, or the expectation of military breakthrough. For R. H. Mottram, in his *Spanish Farm* novel sequence (1924–7), the Somme destroyed 'perhaps the greatest voluntary army of history', and one that could not be replaced in the same way.[2] For some time even before the Somme, it had been clear that volunteers alone would never be enough to replace the loss of life on the Western Front, and in other failed initiatives such as the attack on the Turks in Gallipoli throughout 1915. The Military Service Act became law, in its final form, five weeks before the Battle of the Somme, obliging all men under the age of 41 to serve unless specifically exempt. Over three million men were eventually conscripted in this way, helping to form another, third, British army. This endured further slaughter on the Western Front, particularly at Passchendaele in 1917, survived the

[1] Philip Larkin, *The Whitsun Weddings* (London: Faber and Faber, 1964), 28.
[2] R. H. Mottram, *The Spanish Farm Trilogy* (New York: The Dial Press, 1927), 257.

German offensive in the spring of 1918, then, successfully counter-attacking, and with the help of increasing numbers of US troops, saw the war through to the armistice on 11 November 1918.

Even in victory this army could hardly reproduce the idealism of Kitchener's recruits of 1914. In the judgement of one of their number, the novelist and journalist C. E. Montague, these were 'men of handsome and boundless illusions...all the air was ringing with rousing assurances. France to be saved, Belgium righted, freedom and civilisation re-won'. In the view of another former soldier, the poet David Jones, after the Somme 'things hardened into a more relentless, mechanical affair'—a feeling also shared among the German armies. In his war memoir *Storm of Steel* (*In Stahlgewittern*, 1920), Ernst Jünger recalls that 'the Battle of the Somme...marked the end of the first and mildest part of the war; thereafter, it was like embarking on a different one altogether'. For many later commentators, the change was still more far-reaching. The Great War historian John Keegan considered that the Somme 'marked the end of an age of vital optimism in British life that has never been recovered'. Henry Williamson—a combatant throughout the Great War—uses terms still more epochal in his novel sequence *A Chronicle of Ancient Sunlight* (1951–69). *The Golden Virgin* (1957) describes 'the watershed of the Somme...the fragmentation of steel and flesh and the dust of detonated village hanging in the sun' marking 'not only the end of the old order, but the end of ideas that had endured a thousand years'.[3]

Faith in the reliability of language figured among these doomed ideas. A watershed in the war, even in modern history generally, the Somme was also a decisive moment in the failure, evident since 1914 or earlier, of an 'old order' of ways that life—and death, on a new scale—could be communicated, imagined, or rendered into language and text. Changes and challenges concerned are immediately apparent in the first edition of *The Times* to report the battle. As that sunny first of July was a Saturday, much reporting in the newspapers was delayed until Monday 3 July: the account of the 'lovely summer morning', above, comes from *The Times*

---

[3] C. E. Montague, *Disenchantment* (London: Chatto and Windus, 1922), 2–3; David Jones, *In Parenthesis* (1937; rpt. London: Faber and Faber, 1963), ix; Ernst Jünger, *Storm of Steel* (1920/1961/1978), trans. Michael Hofmann (Harmondsworth: Penguin, 2004), 69; John Keegan, *The First World War* (London: Hutchinson, 1998), 321; Henry Williamson, *The Golden Virgin* (1957; rpt. Stroud: Alan Sutton, 1996), 340.

that day.[4] Three of its main news pages are devoted to what a headline describes as 'The Great Battle: "Biggest British Offensive"'. But there is also space for other war news, and for an incidental but significant indication of new influences on the communication of this news, and on the public's engagement with it.

Words, Films, Myths

On page 8 of *The Times*, a column describing the French Army's 'glorious' recovery of the 'rubbish-heap of ruins which once was Thiaumont' offers a typical example of newspapers' rhetorical reshaping of ruin and destruction into glory. This is further considered later in this chapter. There is a still more immediate irony simply in this column's positioning on the page. This irony appears in the juxtaposition of the report's headline, 'Good News from Other Theatres', alongside a column of advertisements, almost all of which are for current theatre productions on the London stage. The two exceptions are adverts for D. W. Griffith's film of *Macbeth*, showing at His Majesty's, and for the Scala. The latter offers 'special films' of the life of Lord Kitchener (who had drowned on his way to Russia, in early June, when HMS *Hampshire* struck a mine) and of 'the British Empire's Forces AT THE FRONT'. The Scala continued as a principal venue for war films, which attracted growing audiences as the war went on. A month or so later, it launched the immensely popular documentary *The Battle of the Somme*, quickly produced and on general release by 21 August 1916. It was booked by a thousand picture houses and village halls throughout Britain, and seen within six weeks by around twenty million people—perhaps as much as 80 per cent of the adult population. Many of them must have shared the experience of Rebecca West's heroine in *The Return of the Soldier* (1918), who finds she relies on war films for her imagination—even for her dreams—of a loved one's life at the Front. She particularly recalls a moment—unforgettably realistic for most civilians who saw *The Battle of the Somme*, though it was actually faked by the film-makers—when soldiers shot while going over the top 'slip down . . . softly from the trench parapet'. Many of the film's spectators were soldiers themselves, some of them survivors of the battle.

---

[4] 'Beginning of the Attack', *The Times*, 3 July 1916, 9–10.

A fictional version of their experience appears in Williamson's *Chronicle of Ancient Sunlight*, his hero seeing *The Battle of the Somme* while on leave from the Front. As an alternative to memories it provokes, he finds that he 'forgot himself in the hilarity of a Charlie Chaplin film' (Fig. 2).[5]

Growing numbers of civilians, and soldiers, shared something of his experience. *The Battle of the Somme* was unusually popular, but by 1916 around 30 per cent of city dwellers attended the cinema weekly. From the early days of the war, 'cinematograph marquees' in base camps and picture houses in towns close to the Front allowed soldiers to attend as regularly, when not on active duty. By 1918, according to one account, there was 'a picture show on every street corner' in Arras. Cinema more and more shaped combatants' imagination of death as well as life: like Rebecca West, Siegfried Sassoon later recalled a 'dream cinematograph' in which his dead comrades returned to him in sleep.[6] For novelists such as May Sinclair and Hugh Walpole, cinema likewise provided a metaphor for the rapid wartime procession of events and impressions across the mind. Cinema's capacity for realistic representation of wartime events was sometimes a source of disquiet as well as approval. Several correspondents wrote to *The Times* to suggest that *The Battle of the Somme* showed events too awful to be made into public spectacle, though the film was also vigorously defended. One correspondent suggested that 'it did more to bring home to my mind the realization of what war is...than all the sermons I have heard or books I have read'.[7] The same claim was made for earlier war films in that *Times* advertisement on 3 July. This included views expressed by the Earl of Derby when speaking at the Scala: that the 'interesting spectacle' war films offered 'will bring home to the people more than it has ever been brought home to them before what our men are doing'. A newspaper might have found such claims prejudicial to appreciation of its own war reporting. The owner of *The Times*, Lord Northcliffe, nevertheless acknowledged that 'not everyone reads the newspapers, and those who do forget what they have read, but no one can forget what he has seen happen on screen'—

[5] Rebecca West, *The Return of the Soldier* (1918; rpt. London: Virago, 2004), 14; Henry Williamson, *Love and the Loveless* (1958; rpt. Stroud: Alan Sutton, 1997), 63.

[6] Stuart Chapman, *Home in Time For Breakfast: A First World War Diary* (London: Athena Press, 2007), 111; Siegfried Sassoon, *Siegfried's Journey: 1916–1920* (London: Faber and Faber, 1945), 70.

[7] James P. Cooper, letter to *The Times*, 2 Sept. 1916, 3.

FIG 2 Charlie Chaplin's films were popular throughout the war. *Shoulder Arms* (1918) shows him training with the new US army and dreaming of serving in the trenches, capturing the Kaiser, and establishing 'Peace on Earth'.

Getty Images.

though adding that 'speaking as a newspaperman', this was something he hated to admit.[8]

The Battle of the Somme, in other words, highlighted the cinema's capacity to provide more than popular entertainment. Films were not only providing entertainment, but nudging print media out of long-standing leading roles in reporting and representing the world—in 'bringing it home' to the mind. This development might alone have been enough to provoke change or crisis in contemporary appreciation of literature, language, and text. Yet challenges to the representative powers of language also had other sources, of longer and more diverse provenance. These can be seen in European thinking predating the war, sometimes evident before the invention of cinematography in the 1890s. In 1880, Friedrich Nietzsche claimed that 'mankind set up in language a separate world beside the other world', realizing only in his own age that 'this belief in language...propagated a tremendous error'. This 'error' widely concerned turn-of-the century epistemology. Similar scepticism figures in the work of Henry James's brother, the philosopher William James, convinced that 'language works against our perception of the truth'. In a study published a year earlier, in 1889, Henri Bergson likewise found 'no common measure between mind and language'. Confidence in language was further questioned by Sigmund Freud's emphasis on pre-verbal mental activity in studies such as *The Interpretation of Dreams* (1899). By the early years of the twentieth century, linguisticians themselves were introducing comparable doubts into their field of study. These were summarized in Ferdinand de Saussure's *Cours de linguistique générale*, especially in his influential conclusion that 'the link between signal and signification is arbitrary...*the linguistic sign is arbitrary*'.[9]

Saussure's study was published posthumously, in Lausanne and Paris, in 1916. Soldiers might have come across copies in Paris bookshops when on leave from the Somme, and might have found particularly good reason, in their recent experience, to agree with Saussure's conclusions.

---

[8] Quoted in Cate Haste, *Keep the Home Fires Burning: Propaganda in the First World War* (London: Allen Lane, 1977), 45.

[9] Friedrich Nietzsche, *Human, All Too Human: A Book for Free Spirits* (1880), trans. R. J. Hollingdale (Cambridge: Cambridge University Press, 1986), 16; William James, *The Principles of Psychology* (London: Macmillan, 1890), I: 241; Henri Bergson, *Time and Free Will: An Essay on the Immediate Data of Consciousness* (1889), trans. F. L. Pogson (London: George Allen and Unwin, 1971), 165; F. de Saussure, *Course in General Linguistics* (1916), trans. Roy Harris (London: Duckworth, 1983), 67.

New technologies, new media, and newish philosophies were all challenging textual representation by 1916, but these challenges were greatly deepened and diversified by factors specific to the Great War. Principal among these was the wilder, stranger, almost unimaginable world language had to represent—far beyond familiar experience for serving soldiers, but also for an entire population, long unused to military conflict on any substantial scale. By 1914, Britain had enjoyed almost a century of generally sustained peace. Military campaigns were mostly safely distanced from the domestic population: in the Crimea in the 1850s, then—though with serious implications for Britain's imperial confidence—in the Boer War in South Africa at the turn of the century. There were further alarms throughout the early years of the twentieth century, some precautionary military planning in secret, and, eventually, obviously ominous consequences developing from the assassination of Archduke Franz Ferdinand in Sarajevo on 28 June 1914. Yet the declaration of a European war seemed astonishing, to much of the population, when it finally occurred on 4 August. An almost blue sky in foreign affairs was still being confidently described, even in mid-July, by the Chancellor of the Exchequer, Lloyd George—later, from 1916, Prime Minister. Until the beginning of August, there had seemed more risk of civil war in Ireland than of European conflict. For C. E. Montague, in his memoir *Disenchantment* (1922), this conflict remained throughout its early stages 'outlandish...an unimagined war'—one that 'did not conform to the proper text-books as it ought to have done'. For Mottram, in *The Spanish Farm*, the war came as 'one great catastrophic surprise'. Writing shortly after its outbreak in *Boon* (1915), H. G. Wells likewise records 'habitual disregard...of war as a probability' in May or June 1914—even though he had partly anticipated its nature in a novel serialized at the time, *The World Set Free* (1914). 'For some days after the declaration of war against Germany', *Boon* continues, 'the whole business seemed a vast burlesque. It was incredible.'[10]

In another wartime novel, *Mr. Britling Sees It Through* (1916), Wells further emphasizes the incredulity marking this period. 'Things that had seemed solid for ever were visibly in flux', he remarks, contributing to 'a phase of imaginative release...one of the first effects of the war on many

---

[10] Montague, *Disenchantment*, 44–5; Mottram, *Spanish Farm*, 139; H. G. Wells, *Boon* (1915; rpt. London: T. Fisher Unwin, 1920), 244–5.

educated minds.'[11] War's outbreak moved beyond the familiar suddenly enough to pitch the whole population beyond ordinary experience and almost into the domain of myth. Though as thoroughly educated as anyone, the novelist Henry James eagerly shared the widespread belief that trainloads of Russian soldiers were being transported through Britain to assist in France. Their origin was often said to be confirmed by traces of snow on their boots, apparently surviving even the unusually warm weather of August 1914. In a letter of 1 September, James was still offering to 'eat the biggest pair of moujik boots in the collection' if the story was false. Two days later, he regretfully recognized that it must be, and that it had been a product only of what he describes as 'hallucination, misconception, fantastication' spreading rapidly through British life at the time.[12]

Further evidence of this atmosphere soon appeared in accounts of the BEF's first major encounter with the enemy: the Battle of Mons, fought on 23 and 24 August. In the light of the long retreat that followed, Mons seemed an unusual, almost miraculous success. Experienced and well-prepared, the Regular Army could direct rifle fire very rapidly, managing to inflict casualties heavy enough to halt the German advance temporarily. Before long, though—following the publication of Arthur Machen's short story 'The Bowmen' in the *Evening News* in late September—Mons began to be considered a genuine miracle, and the BEF the beneficiary of angelic intervention. Rather than rapid rifle fire, the Germans were said to have been halted by volleys of arrows, aimed by angels from above the battlefield. Though Machen explained that his story was merely war-worried wish-fulfilment, belief in the Angels of Mons was widespread and long-standing, turning up regularly in later fiction and memoirs (Fig. 3). Arnold Bennett's novel *The Pretty Lady* (1918) mentions a soldier still asking himself in 1916 'just after Mons…was it an angel I saw'. More prosaically, in A. D. Gristwood's autobiographical novel *The Somme* (1927), a soldier bereft of cigarettes remarks that 'if the Angels of Mons should appear to him that moment, the only manna he would ask would be a "Woodbine"'.[13]

---

[11] H. G. Wells, *Mr. Britling Sees It Through* (London: Cassell, 1916), 197–8.

[12] Henry James, Letters to Edith Wharton, *The Letters of Henry James*, ed. Percy Lubbock (London: Macmillan, 1920), 414, 419.

[13] Arnold Bennett, *The Pretty Lady* (1918; rpt. Leek, Staffordshire: Churnet Valley Books, 2009), 130–1; A. D. Gristwood, *The Somme: Including Also The Coward* (1927; rpt. Columbia: University of South Carolina Press, 2006), 73.

From the painting by W. H. Margetson

"THE ANGELS OF MONS."

FIG 3 A postcard depicting the Angels of Mons, based on a painting by W. H. Margetson.

Getty Images.

Any sense of fantastication felt on the Home Front, early in the war, was inevitably expanded hugely by experience of the Western Front, or of any other theatre of conflict. Two pages after that cinema advertisement in *The Times*, a report of one of the Somme's engagements makes what seems another odd admission for a newspaper when it talks of fighting 'of the most desperate character... fierce beyond description'. Yet the acknowledgement of the war as 'beyond description' was regularly repeated by war correspondents, Philip Gibbs later remarking even of an early phase of the conflict that 'no code of words... would convey the picture of that wild agony'.[14] If war correspondents—at a safe distance, with a full view of operations, and fully briefed about the purpose of the battle—found the fighting 'beyond description', there was much more reason why it should seem so to those immediately involved. Then and later, war seemed to them not only beyond description, but almost beyond imagination itself—beyond all boundaries of known experience. On the German side, Ernst Jünger describes the trenches as like 'an enormous dump somewhere off the edge of the charted world'.[15] For soldiers on all sides, bombardment, sudden death, mutilation, men blown to pieces—even just the depths of sodden drudgery experienced during quieter periods in the line—likewise seemed beyond anything that could be represented in conventional language or charted through established narrative form.

Many memoirists and diarists comment directly on this difficulty, much in the terms employed by that *Times* reporter. 'The most practised pen cannot convey a real notion of the life at the Front, as the words to describe war do not exist', remarked Vernon Bartlett, later a journalist and politician, in 1917. The journal Pte Len Smith kept during the war, eventually published as *Drawing Fire* (2009), explains that 'a bombardment is beyond my description', adding that the 'miles and miles of churned up ground' around the trenches exhibited a wretchedness that 'no amount of clever writing could adequately describe'. Skills in drawing helped Smith escape some of the constraints of writing, but not the sense that there were things that not only could not but *should* not be described. For Smith, a murderous attack on the trenches seemed simply 'a ghastly unprintable affair'. When dealing

---

[14] 'The Devil's Cauldron of Thiepval', *The Times*, 3 July 1916, 10; Philip Gibbs, *Realities of War* (London: William Heinemann, 1920), 4.

[15] Jünger, *Storm of Steel*, 114.

with a roomful of corpses, one of whose intestines are spilling out of his belly, Jünger likewise records that it may be futile to 'waste words over something like this'.[16] 'I can write nothing', Ford Madox Ford remarks of the battlefields in his essay 'A Day of Battle' (1916), finding himself unable even to 'evoke pictures of the Somme…as for putting them—into words! No: the mind stops dead, and something in the brain stops and shuts down.'[17]

Difficulties in communicating war experience—or imagining it at all—are emphasized throughout Henri Barbusse's *Under Fire* (*Le Feu*, 1916), one of the earliest and most influential novels attempting to describe combat, selling over 200,000 copies by the end of the war. They are discussed at length by his central characters:

> Paradis, his back bowed under carpets of mould and clay, was trying to describe his feeling that war is unimaginable and immeasurable in time and space.
>
> 'When you talk about the war, he said, meditating aloud, it's as though you didn't say anything. It stifles words. We are here, looking at this, like blind men'…
>
> 'No, you can't imagine it'…
>
> 'To begin with, how could anyone imagine this, without having been here?'
>
> 'You'd have to be mad!'…
>
> '…whatever you tell them they won't believe you…they just won't be able…Nobody's going to know. Just you.'
>
> 'No, not even us! Not even us!' someone shouted…
>
> 'We've seen too much of it!'
>
> 'And everything we've seen is too much. We're not built to take all this in.'[18]

Barbusse's soldiers identify a crisis in communication, during the Great War, which can be considered in two aspects. The first and most obvious of these, assessed throughout the chapters that follow, concerns events impossible to 'take in'—ones threatening to overwhelm literary genres, prece-

[16] Vernon Bartlett, *Mud and Khaki: Sketches from Flanders and France* (London: Simpkin, Marshall, Hamilton, Kent, 1917), 12; Private Len Smith, *Drawing Fire: The Diary of a Great War Soldier and Artist* (London: Collins, 2009), no page numbers; Jünger, *Storm of Steel*, 136.

[17] Ford Madox Ford, 'A Day of Battle: Arms and the Mind' (1916), rpt. in *The Ford Madox Ford Reader*, ed. Sondra J. Stang (London: Paladin, 1987), 456. Ford retained his original surname, 'Hueffer', until 1919.

[18] Henri Barbusse, *Under Fire* (1916), trans. Robin Buss (Harmondsworth: Penguin, 2003), 303–4.

dents, and imagination, or words themselves, leaving combatants 'like blind men', even in reporting what they had seen. A second aspect, assessed in this chapter, concerns other difficulties the Great War imposed on communication and language use—ones also deeply influential on accounts of it, and on literature in the years that followed, and in contemporary society generally. Some of these difficulties arose from the demands Barbusse identifies from 'them'—friends, families, or the general public who had not 'been there', yet were naturally keen to know what was going on. As that huge film audience for *The Battle of the Somme* confirmed, there was more demand for knowledge of this kind than in any previous war, or any earlier phase of history: from anxious civilians, seeking like Rebecca West's heroine to imagine what was happening to loved ones abroad. Huge numbers of men, during the war—millions, in the end, along with many women— found themselves distant from home and obliged to provide information not face to face, as they might otherwise have done all their lives, but in writing, in letters or postcards. This need to wrestle with the written word, on a scale new in history, added significantly to the challenges the Great War imposed on both soldiers and civilians.

Language and Letters

'Wrestling' was sometimes almost literally what was required. Barbusse records one of his French soldiers struggling in vain with his spelling, while 'down on all fours working on an envelope with a pencil'.[19] Among British soldiers, improvements initiated by Education Acts in the 1870s ensured much more general literacy than in previous wars, but this did not always extend into practised familiarity with written communication. On the contrary, in an otherwise mostly affirmative account of the training of Kitchener's army, *The First Hundred Thousand* (1915), Ian Hay records the limitation of most army letters to a few reassuring but empty phrases:

> *It is with the greatest of pleasure that I take up my pen—*
> It is invariably a pencil, and a blunt one at that...
> *We are all in the pink...having no more to say, I will now draw to a close.*[20]

---

[19] Ibid. 161.
[20] Ian Hay, *The First Hundred Thousand* (1915; rpt. London: Corgi, 1976), 192–3.

'In the pink' became a stock phrase in letters and conversation, its ubiquitous use sometimes parodied in the trench journals which were often produced close to the Front. Hundreds of these survive in the Imperial War Museum. In one of the most successful, *The Wipers Times*—printed at one stage within 700 yards of the front line—'Intha Pink' even features as a character in a series of Sherlock Holmes parodies. Another kind of near-parody, though unintentional, appeared in the form of the Field Service Postcard, which avoided the need for personal expression by offering a set of straightforward assertions—'I am quite well', 'I have been admitted into hospital', etc.—to be deleted as appropriate (Fig. 4). One of its early printings, in November 1914, ran to a million copies. Minimal but functional, the postcard was both symptom and solution for difficulties encountered in communicating war experience. These were obviously compounded by the conditions under which letters often had to be produced—'sordid, noisy, terrifying, wretched and utterly uncongenial to clear thought and orderly writing', according to Private Smith in *Drawing Fire*. The urge to go on writing was nevertheless strong enough to encourage difficulties to be ignored. Over eight million army letters were going to and from the Western Front, weekly, by 1917. Among hundreds written to his home by Lt Col E. W. Hermon, for example, are several which remain admirably lucid and thoughtful, even though completed in the front lines shortly after an attack.

Letter-writing was only one of many linguistic challenges confronting soldiers. 'You can hardly understand some of the men', Hermon records when taking command of troops from the North of England, '[they] talk a foreign language all right.'[21] Though recruiting was often locally based, this did not always ensure dialectal uniformity within units, and inevitably amplified differences between them. No broadcast media existed at the time to familiarize the population with accents other than their own local ones. Prior to enlistment, in the quiescent years of the early twentieth century, many recruits had scarcely travelled beyond their home areas. They therefore encountered with some surprise, during training or service abroad, different and sometimes

---

[21] Lieutenant Colonel E. W. Hermon, *For Love and Courage: The Letters of Lieutenant Colonel E. W. Hermon from the Western Front 1914–1917*, ed. Anne Nason (London: Preface, 2009), 266.

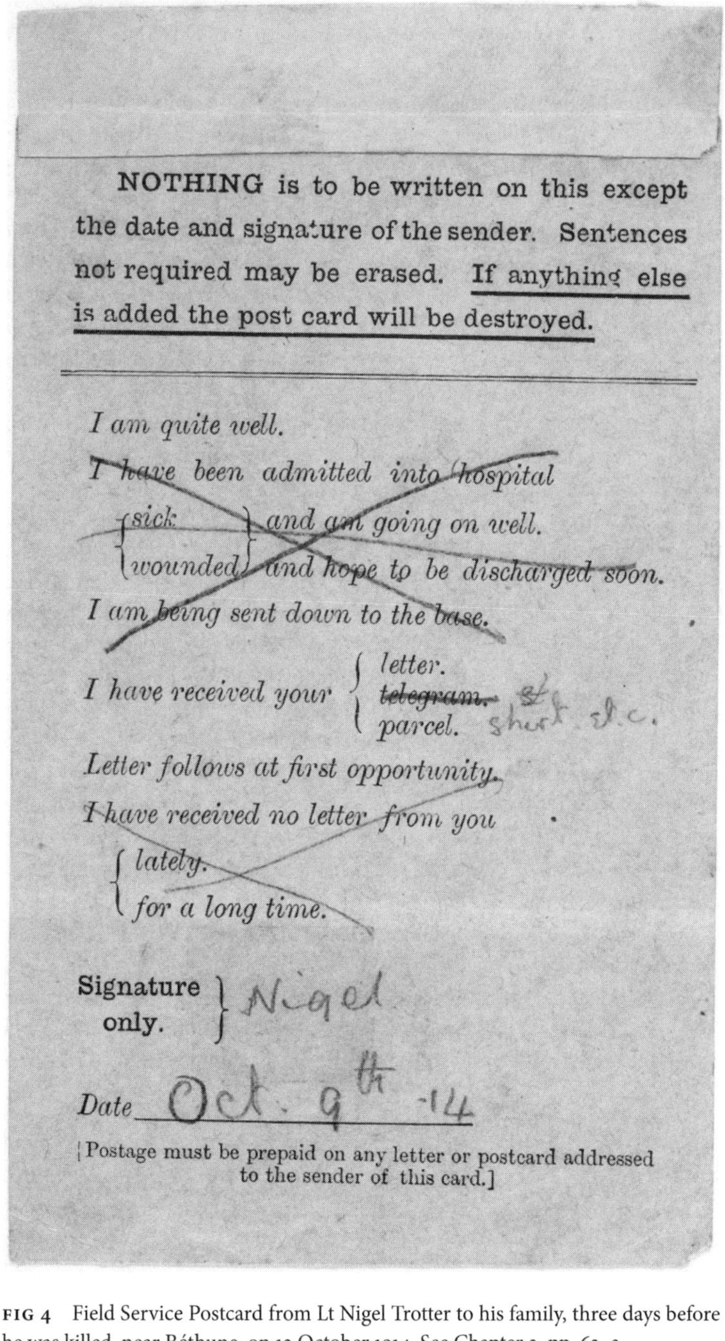

NOTHING is to be written on this except the date and signature of the sender. Sentences not required may be erased. If anything else is added the post card will be destroyed.

I am quite well.

~~I have been admitted into hospital~~

~~{ sick }~~ ~~and am going on well.~~
~~{ wounded }~~ ~~and hope to be discharged soon.~~

~~I am being sent down to the base.~~

I have received your { letter.
~~telegram.~~ *shirt etc.*
parcel. }

Letter follows at first opportunity.

~~I have received no letter from you~~

~~{ lately. }~~
~~{ for a long time. }~~

Signature only. } *Nigel*

Date __*Oct. 9th -14*__

[Postage must be prepaid on any letter or postcard addressed to the sender of this card.]

FIG 4   Field Service Postcard from Lt Nigel Trotter to his family, three days before he was killed, near Béthune, on 12 October 1914. See Chapter 2, pp. 62–3.

barely intelligible dialects from elsewhere in Britain or overseas. A greater challenge accompanied encounters—still likelier to be unprecedented, for the great majority of them—with genuinely foreign languages. Dealing with daily existence around the Western Front, or accessing such pleasures as were available to the troops, obviously proved more difficult without some knowledge of French. 'We feel our linguistic deficiencies', LCPL George Ramage remarked, a day or so after arriving in France in 1915, also recording in his (unpublished) journal the dreamlike strangeness of being wakened, on his first morning abroad, by the unintelligible voices of newspaper-sellers.[22]

Much ingenuity was devoted to overcoming these deficiencies, with much new vocabulary the result. '"Oofs!! Compree, eggs?" | Will you e'er forget the jargon?', a poem in the *Wipers Times* asked in November 1918. Much was compreed—sometimes 'by some miracle', as Ian Hay describes— through an evolving jargon of Franglais. This could even incorporate the dialectal divergences described above, Private Smith remarking at one point in his journal, in fluent Franglécossais, 'why we halted so long we "didna ken pas"'.[23] Similar inventiveness cheerfully transformed place names troops encountered near the trenches—Auchonvillers into 'Ocean Villas', Fonquevillers into 'Funky Villas', Ypres into 'Wipers', and so on. 'Lingua Franca-Britannica', as Lieutenant Colonel Hermon called it, was also taken up by the French, sometimes with sad succinctness. '"Ah, no bon!"', villagers murmur to passing troops, headed for the Somme, in Frederic Manning's novel *The Middle Part of Fortune* (1929). Perhaps inevitably, the most regular adaptation was 'Na pooh', from 'il n'y a plus'—frequently used, Hay explains, because it came to mean '"done for," "finished," and in extreme cases, "dead"', and could even work as a verb: '"Poor Bill got napoohed by a rifle-grenade yesterday"'.[24]

A good deal of genuine French came to be employed, too, alongside inventive Franglais. '"Ici nous sommes encore!"', the *Wipers Times* cheerfully remarked to its soldier audience in November 1918, though

[22] George Ramage, 'The rather tame war experiences in Flanders 1915 of Lance Corporal George Ramage, 1st Battalion Gordon Highlanders', National Library of Scotland MS944-7, I, 12, 19.

[23] Patrick Beaver (ed.), *The Wipers Times: A Complete Facsimile* (London: Macmillan, 1973), 309; Hay, *First Hundred Thousand*, 197; Smith, *Drawing Fire*.

[24] Hermon, *For Love and Courage*, 248; Frederic Manning, *The Middle Parts of Fortune: Somme and Ancre, 1916* (1929; rpt. London: Peter Davies, 1977), 140; Hay, *First Hundred Thousand*, 197.

also launching a spoof language course, warning that 'there are quite a number of nouns…but each one means something different'.[25] For some soldiers, differences encountered or linguistic deficiencies overcome left a long-lasting trace in imagination. Fiction about the war occasionally reproduces elements of French not only in dialogue, but embedded in descriptive passages. R. H. Mottram's *Spanish Farm* sequence often echoes French expressions, appropriately enough in its account of the work of a French-speaking English officer. Description of a character who 'supported the war very badly' suggests the endurance implied by French '*supporter*', rather than the usual significance of the English verb. Characters who regret 'deranging' another by asking for food, explaining that they 'had the hunger of a wolf', likewise echo French '*déranger*' and '*faim de loup*'.[26]

Echoes of this kind continued to resound after the war. Recent experience abroad encouraged forms of linguistic eclecticism, and porousness to foreign terms, to spread through Anglophone culture in the 1920s and later, not only among British writers. Authors brought from the USA to Europe by the conflict—such as Ernest Hemingway, John Dos Passos, and E. E. Cummings—readily incorporate foreign voices and idioms into their writing, directly or more subtly. Cummings uses so many of them in *The Enormous Room* (1922)—often changing language in mid-sentence—that most editions of his novel include an extensive glossary. Longer term US émigrés, Ezra Pound and T. S. Eliot, have less to say, directly, about a conflict each experienced at a safe distance. But the linguistic and cultural diversity of their poetry seemed more accessible, even natural, to a post-war audience. Snatches of partly understood foreign tongues—as well as domestic dialects—punctuating *The Waste Land* (1922) seemed less unexpected after the war than in 1914, particularly to returning soldiers. In this way, the Great War eventually added flexibility to writing in English, and a wider use of the vernacular, even though, at the time, it did more to impress those involved with the difficulties and slipperiness of language itself. Any British soldier who happened to pick up Saussure's new study in 1916 might have been particularly ready to accept evidence it adduces for the arbitrariness of the linguistic sign—that

---

[25] Beaver (ed.), *Wipers Tines*, 303, 326.
[26] Mottram, *Spanish Farm*, 29, 9.

there is no internal connexion, for example, between the idea 'sister' and the French sequence of sounds $s - \ddot{o} - r$ ... The same idea might as well be represented by any other sequence of sounds. This is demonstrated by differences between languages, and even by the existence of different languages.[27]

Between 1914 and 1918, such differences were experienced on a scale, and with a daily immediacy, Saussure could scarcely have anticipated during the first decade of the twentieth century, when much of the work that became *Cours de linguistique générale* was undertaken.

Differences and 'linguistic deficiencies' were not always cheerfully overcome. In Manning's *The Middle Parts of Fortune*, an unfortunate corporal's remark to the hostess in his billets—'Cushy avec mademoiselle'—communicates to French ears a sexual proposition very different to the simple appreciation he seeks to express. An interpreter explains hastily that '"Cushy" est un mot d'argot militaire qui veut dire doux, confortable' ('Cushy' is a term in military slang meaning agreeable and comfortable). The corporal regrets his lack of French: the interpreter tells him to refrain from mixing 'the little you do know with Hindustani'.[28] As the incident suggests, soldiers struggling with French also had to deal with military slang, a good deal of which—terms such as 'cushy', 'blighty', or 'dekko'—was indeed Hindi or Urdu in origin, adopted during the British Army's long sojourn in India. Older army officers were even known to use Hindi in telephone conversations, hoping to escape decipherment by any enemy listeners. George Ramage—a well-educated lance corporal, and a teacher in civilian life—records lists of military slang and their translations in his journal, to be learned almost as vocabulary homework during his service in France. Nor was this the only new vocabulary required. New recruits and those newly posted abroad had to deal with crossword complexities of military acronyms and jargon, as well as the army's habit, based on quartermasters' inventorying, of regularly inverting adjective and noun. This was a source of much mirth in the *Wipers Times*. It describes 'Quartermasters with books, note, one, and pencil, copying... arguing the point re boots, gum, thigh'. The same issue, in March 1916, defines a 'Master Quarter, one' as 'a bird of strange habits:—when attacked covers itself with indents and talks backwards'.[29]

[27] Saussure, *Course in General Linguistics*, 67–8.
[28] Manning, *Middle Parts of Fortune*, 104–5.
[29] Beaver (ed.), *Wipers Times*, 44–5.

These and other strange habits required the learning of a kind of military code. Actual codes, official or otherwise, added further to challenges involved. Heliograph, flag, and Morse codes, as well as phonetic alphabets for use on the field telephone, all had to be learned by signallers, and often by other soldiers. Many of them, Wilfred Owen included, worked out further codes of their own—patterns of deletion on Field Service Postcards which could communicate to their families more than the bare messages on offer. In her autobiography *Testament of Youth* (1933), Vera Brittain describes coded phrases used to communicate with her fiancé and her brother at the Front: the latter even resorted to writing to her in Latin. Genuine military codes figure in Robert Graves's memoir *Goodbye to All That* (1929), which describes using the supposedly secret term 'accessory' whenever referring to equipment for dispersing poison gas. In *The Middle Parts of Fortune*, Manning's protagonist finds the word 'rats' endowed with the same esoteric significance, and also learns that 'pepper and salt were code words for two battalions in the Brigade'.[30] Increasingly, between 1914 and 1918, language departed from convention, often threatening to carry meanings quite other to normal usage. In one way, this offered literary potential. John Buchan's popular spy novel *Greenmantle* (1916) begins with a challenge to its hero Richard Hannay—and its readers— to decipher a fragment of code, one which remains a key plot device throughout. But codes also added elements of puzzle and paranoia to contemporary life—aptly indicated, on the Home Front, by the decision in April 1916 to stop newspapers publishing chess problems, in case these were covertly employed to send information to the enemy.[31] In the trenches, even raising eyes heavenward offered soldiers no relief from marauding sign-systems. Many wartime journals and letters explain encounters with the system of markings—roundels and gothic crosses—used for the first time during the war to distinguish the flying machines droning in increasing numbers over the battlefield (Fig. 5).

Soldiers might therefore have experienced unfamiliarity not only with letter-writing, but with aspects of language itself, pressured into many challenging new usages. Yet neither difficulty was necessarily the

---

[30] Robert Graves, *Goodbye to All That*, rev edn (1957; rpt. Harmondsworth: Penguin, 2000), 123; Manning, *Middle Parts of Fortune*, 67.

[31] See Haste, *Keep the Home Fires Burning*, 31.

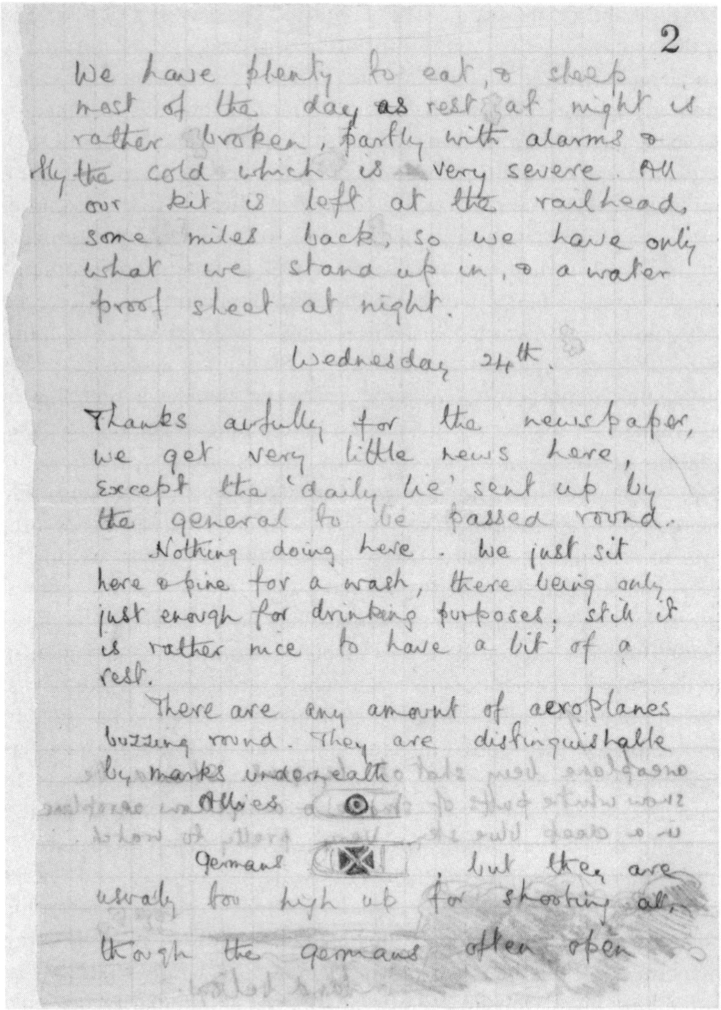

We have plenty to eat, & sleep
most of the day as rest at night is
rather broken, partly with alarms &
the cold which is very severe. All
our kit is left at the railhead,
some miles back, so we have only
what we stand up in, & a water
proof sheet at night.

Wednesday 24th.

Thanks awfully for the newspaper,
we get very little news here,
except the 'daily lie' sent up by
the general to be passed round.
Nothing doing here. We just sit
here & pine for a wash, there being only
just enough for drinking purposes; still it
is rather nice to have a bit of a
rest.
There are any amount of aeroplanes
buzzing round. They are distinguishable
by marks underneath [...]
[...] Allies [...]
[...]
German [...], but they are
usually too high up for shooting at,
though the germans often open
[...]

FIG 5   Letter of 24 September 1914 from Lt Nigel Trotter to his family, illustrating aircraft markings and complaining of a lack of news and the unreliability of army briefings.

prime obstacle to communication. A more serious one arose from wariness about what could appropriately be said—from a need, also experienced while on leave, not to shock or depress family or friends at home. An early example of such reticence appeared in 1914 in Florence Barclay's romantic war novella *My Heart's Right There*. Barclay's hero explains to his wife, 'I should never forgive myself—if, to ease my own mind by sharing them, I passed on to you the ghastly things I've been forced to know and to see'. Siegfried Sassoon's memoirs emphasize a similar need to maintain 'a polite pretence' when talking to civilians about the war. His poem 'Remorse' confirms that 'there's things in war one dare not tell | Poor father sitting safe at home, who reads | Of dying heroes and their deathless deeds'. 'You *had* to lie', the hero concludes in Vernon Bartlett's novel *No Man's Land* (1930), recalling his mother's question about what it is 'really like out there' and his reassurance that things are 'not half bad...topping fellows, and we don't get much shelling'.[32] Such economy with the truth was evident at all levels of the Army. The Commander-in-Chief of the BEF, Sir Douglas Haig, received information about the casualties on the Somme—albeit underestimated by a third—on 2 July 1916. Yet letters to his wife during the first week of the battle reported that 'things are going quite satisfactorily for us here' (3 July) and that 'the situation looks most favourable' (4 July), suggesting nothing worse than that 'it will be a hard struggle' (6 July).[33]

A greater obstacle to communication—though not one much affecting Haig—was the constraint of military censorship, requiring all letters to be scrutinized by company officers before dispatch. Especially in dealing with officers' own letters, the system was often less than fully enforced, though like much else in the war, it became more stringent around the time of the Somme offensive, whose planning had proved a very poorly kept secret. Its exigencies are recorded widely in soldiers' wartime journals, and in their letters themselves. Lt Nigel Trotter, for example, remarked tantalizingly in a letter to his family in September 1914 that 'the only things I have to tell you I am not allowed to say', inviting them in

---

[32] Florence Barclay, *My Heart's Right There* (1914; rpt. London: G. P. Putnam's Sons, 1916), 48; Sassoon, *Siegfried's Journey*, 14, and *Collected Poems: 1908–1956* (London: Faber and Faber, 1961), 91; Vernon Bartlett, *No Man's Land* (London: George Allen and Unwin, 1930), 238.

[33] Papers, *c.*1859–195?, of Field Marshall Earl Haig, National Library of Scotland, Acc. 3155, no. 144.

another to note his 'good example in not sending any war news'. George Ramage's journal records his irritation on finding a letter has failed to pass the censor on the grounds that its mention of 'lice, bully beef, biscuits, excessive wire entanglements' and generally defensive army tactics might 'alarm the people at home'. He concludes that they are 'not worth fighting for if they are so easily alarmed'.[34] He also records omitting all details of dates, places, and regimental movements from his journal, to be filled in later. This was in partial accord with another official constraint—discouragement of keeping journals or diaries at the Front, on account of military information these might offer the enemy if the writer were captured. Bartlett's *No Man's Land* describes a soldier whose chief concern, even when lying gravely wounded between the trenches, is the destruction of an illicit journal whose discovery might aid the Germans or cause difficulties with his own superiors.

Concerns about censorship also feature in Manning's account in *The Middle Parts of Fortune* of the 'laborious business' of letter-writing:

> 'What would our folks think,' he said, 'if they could see us poor buggers sittin' 'ere writin' all manner o' bloody lies to 'em?'
> 'I'm not writin' any bloody lies,' said Madeley. 'I'm tellin' 'em I'm in the pink, an' so I am.'...
> 'Nothin' but the bloody truth, eh? "Dear Mother, by the time you get this I'll be dead."'
> 'If you do write the truth they rub it out in th' orderly-room,' said Martlow; 'so you might just as well write cheerful. Me mother told me the first letters I sent 'ome was all rubbed out wi' indelible pencil, so as she couldn't read anythin', 'cept that it were rainin'.'

In the *Spanish Farm* sequence, R. H. Mottram's central figure, Skene, falls foul of several of the factors outlined above when trying to reply honestly to an uncle who 'had asked for some idea of what the life was like'. The life concerned proves too violent, new, and strange to describe easily. Any convincing or accurate attempt to do so might 'give them the horrors' at home, or fail to pass the censor, particularly if 'information as to names or positions of units is put on paper'. Skene tears up two detailed, vivid letters and instead writes only that the weather is tolerable and that the army is 'winning fast'.[35]

---

[34] Lt Nigel Trotter, letters of 13 and of 6 or 8 Sept. 1916, National Library of Scotland, Acc. 6614; Ramage, journal, II: 13.

[35] Manning, *Middle Parts of Fortune*, 192–3; Mottram, *Spanish Farm*, 186, 188, 189.

Press and Propaganda

Newspapers might have been expected to provide any interested uncle—or any member of the public—with more than sufficient information about the experience and progress of the war. This was copiously reported throughout the hostilities, some newspapers bringing out as many as four editions daily. Hay's *The First Hundred Thousand* even suggests that it might be 'far easier to follow the course of events from home, where newspapers [were] more plentiful' than at the Front. A character in R. C. Sherriff's play *Journey's End* (1929) likewise mentions that he knows 'what's going on' only thanks to letters from his wife, who 'reads the papers every morning'.[36] Another look at *The Times* of 3 July 1916 indicates a more complicated picture. 'For the first time since the outbreak of war', an editorial remarks, 'our people are able to watch in spirit the exploits of their countrymen, to thrill with pride at the spectacle of their valour'. *The Times* also passes on to General Haig and the War Office 'the thanks of the public for the steady stream of news which has been permitted to flow since the battle began...far greater than on any previous occasion, and completely justify[ing] the long pressure for reform'.[37] These comments are more confident than ones quoted earlier about the potential of print to describe 'exploits' and 'spectacle'. Yet they also indicate how thoroughly any such potential had been curtailed. The press's expanding powers had been immediately recognized and carefully controlled from the very first days of the war. Though Lord Northcliffe worried that 'not everyone reads the newspapers', the introduction of cheaper rotary presses and mechanical typesetting—along with widening literacy since the 1870s—ensured greatly advancing circulation by the early years of the twentieth century. *The Times* sold fewer than 50,000 copies in the 1880s, but this figure had almost quadrupled by 1914. By then another of Northcliffe's papers, the *Daily Mail*, was selling nearly a million. Despite occasional price increases, sales of many popular and tabloid newspapers expanded substantially during the war—the *Daily Express* doubling its circulation between 1914 and 1918, when it was selling around 600,000 copies daily.

---

[36] Hay, *First Hundred Thousand*, 132; R. C. Sherriff, *Journey's End* (1929; rpt. Harmondsworth: Penguin, 2000), 25.
[37] 'The Battle of the Somme', *The Times*, 3 July 1916, 9.

As early as 6 August 1914, a Press Bureau had been established to control this widening influence, censoring articles submitted by newspapers to ensure they matched the terms of the Defence of the Realm Act, likewise hastily introduced at the time. The Press Bureau was also responsible for channelling information from the War Office and the Admiralty—for some time, almost all that newspapers had available, as their own correspondents were banned from the Front. After the 'long pressure' *The Times* mentions, this ban was lifted by mid-1915. Five accredited correspondents were allowed on the Western Front: for *The Times*, the nature-loving Percy Robinson, whose despatches favoured details of herbage and mists such as appear in the report quoted at the start of this chapter. These correspondents' despatches were carefully censored by the army. As another of them, Philip Gibbs, recalled, military censorship eliminated 'any allusion to dead or dying men, to the ghastly failures of distinguished generals, or to the filth and horror of the battle-fields'.[38] Though well controlled, correspondents were also well looked after by a military hierarchy very sensitive to their influence. Their preferential treatment irritated Lloyd George, perhaps the first British Prime Minister to be fully aware of the media's powers, and of ways they could be manipulated. He later remarked that 'G.H.Q. could not capture the Passchendaele ridge, but it was determined to storm Fleet Street, and here strategy and tactics were superb'. His memoirs go on to complain that the army command conspired with war correspondents—including Philip Gibbs, one of the more honest among them—in 'suppressing every check or repulse, and exaggerating with unbridled extravagance every trifling advance purchased at a terrible cost (the latter also suppressed)'.[39]

Censorship and suppression by the military and the Press Bureau, along with often-bellicose patriotism in newspapers, scarcely allowed readers 'to watch in spirit the exploits of their countrymen'. Instead, newspapers offered only a carefully sanitized description of these exploits, usually delivered through the rhetoric of 'deathless deeds' Sassoon warns against. It is hard to imagine anything more misleading than the version of the Battle of the Somme which appeared in *The Times* and other newspapers on 3 July 1916. In response to the British

---

[38] Gibbs, *Realities of War*, 7.

[39] David Lloyd George, *War Memoirs* (1934; rpt. London: Odhams Press, 1938), II: 1318, 1320.

army's worst-ever day's losses, *The Times* recorded that 'Sir Douglas Haig telegraphed last night that the general situation was favourable'— much the same blandly reassuring message he sent to his wife. Other reports affirmed 'a good beginning', that 'everything has gone well', that the British army was 'winning new glory', that the troops were 'in good spirits', and that 'we got our first thrust well home, and there is every reason to be most sanguine as to the result'. Any reader finding 'sanguine' a worrying word choice would have been reassured to read in another report that 'as far as can be ascertained our casualties have not been heavy'.[40] Anyone anywhere near the Somme, on the other hand— and within a few months, as news spread by word of mouth, almost anyone in the British army—could not fail to be appalled by these reports and others like them. C. E. Montague records the effects of this kind of reporting, immediate and longer term, in *Disenchantment*:

> most of the men had, all their lives, been accepting 'what it says 'ere in the paper' as being presumptively true...now, in the biggest event of their lives, hundreds of thousands of men were able to check for themselves the truth of that workaday Bible... The most bloody defeat in the history of Britain...might occur on the Ancre on July 1, 1916, and our Press come out bland and copious and graphic, with nothing to show that we had not had quite a good day—a victory really. Men who had lived through the massacre read the stuff open-mouthed. Anything, then, could figure as anything else in the Press—as its own opposite even. Black was only an aspect of white...the fighting soldier gave the Press up.[41]

'Giving up' on the press may have been less complete than Montague concludes. Though knowledge of the war's overall progress may have been scarce—as Hay and Sherriff indicate—among soldiers at the Front, newspapers were more plentiful than they suggest. *The Times* and other newspapers were often available by 5 or 6pm on the day of publication, close to the front line. 'Even under shellfire', Frank Richards records in *Old Soldiers Never Die* (1933), French newsboys often brought the day's papers as far as the communication trenches which led forward into the battle zone. They were as readily available on the German side. Another memoir, Wyndham Lewis's *Blasting and Bombardiering* (1937), recalls finding a

[40] *The Times*, 3 July 1916, 8, 9, 10.
[41] Montague, *Disenchantment*, 98.

German trench 'profusely lined with fresh corpses', in the aftermath of an attack, and that 'newspapers in Gothic type were a feature of this scene'. Troops were understandably interested in accounts of their own exploits: Private Smith was one of many soldiers who looked for reports of recent engagements involving his regiment. He mentions 'cheery news cuttings… making note of our activities', and retains one of these, from the *News of the World*, in his journal.[42]

Generally, though, despite cheery qualities—or rather because of them—newspapers offered too sharp a contrast, as Montague suggests, 'between the daily events that men saw and the daily accounts that were printed'.[43] Suspicion of the press is a repeated theme of Great War writing. Manning's central figure in *The Middle Parts of Fortune* looks sceptically 'at his newspaper, in the hope of learning something about the war… the spirit of the troops was excellent, the possibility of defeat was incredible… Bourne only glanced hastily at all the solemn empty phrases'. In *The Somme*, Gristwood's protagonist expresses distaste for 'the rhetoric of a thousand journalists… howling chauvinist newspapers… brainless ineptitudes put into his mouth by cheerful Special Correspondents'. In *Memoirs of an Infantry Officer* (1930), Siegfried Sassoon is scathing about the 'intolerable twaddle' of correspondents and the 'camouflage War which was manufactured by the press'. Frank Richards thought war correspondents should be awarded a special medal, 'For Distinguished Lying Off the Field' and for writing 'the biggest B.S.'.[44] They were also a target for the *Wipers Times*, which parodied in particular the *Daily Mail* correspondent W. Beach Thomas, whom it found guilty not only of glorifying the fighting but of an advanced and appalling addiction to alliteration. A similar spirit of parody figures in *Under Fire*, when a soldier pretends to read a newspaper's confident report that 'the Kronprinz is mad, after being killed at the start of the campaign and, meanwhile, he has every illness you can think of. Kaiser Wilhelm will die this evening and again tomorrow. The Germans have no munitions left and are eating wood'.[45]

[42] Frank Richards, *Old Soldiers Never Die* (1933; rpt. London: Faber and Faber, 1964), 133; Wyndham Lewis, *Blasting and Bombardiering* (1937; rpt. London: John Calder, 1982), 133; Smith, *Drawing Fire*.

[43] Montague, *Disenchantment*, 193.

[44] Manning, *Middle Parts of Fortune*, 42; Gristwood, *The Somme*, 146–9; Siegfried Sassoon, *The Complete Memoirs of George Sherston* (1937; rpt; London: Faber and Faber, 1972), 464; Richards, *Old Soldiers Never Die*, 134.

[45] Barbusse, *Under Fire*, 34.

In Wilfred Owen's 'Smile, Smile, Smile' (1918), wounded soldiers just view the press resignedly:

> Head to limp head, the sunk-eyed wounded scanned
> Yesterday's *Mail*; the casualties (typed small)
> And (large) Vast Booty from our Latest Haul
> ....
> ...the half-limbed readers did not chafe
> But smiled at one another curiously[46]

Scepticism was shared on the German side. *The Times* fulminated regularly, and apparently unselfconsciously, against what it described as 'German official misrepresentations of the facts of the fighting', and 'falsification of battle news—the lie as a buttress of moral'.[47] German combatants' memoirs show that they were generally as aware of this falsification as their British counterparts. Some of them nevertheless remained innocent enough, during the informal Christmas Truce of 1914, to offer British soldiers food and cigars in return for a copy of the *Daily Mail*, hoping that it might bring them nearer to the truth. A lasting memento of gaps between newspapers and the truth, and between the trenches and reports read at home, appears in the title of the outstanding war novel on the German side—Erich Maria Remarque's *All Quiet on the Western Front* (*Im Westen Nichts Neues*, 1929). Remarque describes the experience of soldiers whose deaths, occurring independently of any specific battle, offer '*nichts neues*'—no news. On the Western Front, on both sides, there were sometimes as many as a thousand such casualties daily. These were referred to by the military as 'wastage'. Unworthy of headlines, they reached the newspapers only, eventually, as further 'casualties typed small'.

In criticizing the German press, those comments in *The Times* of course offer reasons for newspaper falsifications, and for their appeal. A public widely prepared to accept stories of the Angels of Mons was not necessarily ready for accurate accounts of enormous casualties, or even daily 'wastage', and potentially grateful instead for 'the lie as buttress of moral'. Henry Williamson illustrates war reporting in this role in his novel *The Patriot's Progress* (1930), which moves without comment

---

[46] *Wilfred Owen: The Complete Poems and Fragments*, ed. Jon Stallworthy (London: Chatto and Windus, Hogarth Press, and Oxford University Press, 1983), I: 190.

[47] 'What the Germans are Told' and 'The Lie Factory', *The Times*, 18 Aug. 1917, 6.

between the blasted wilderness of Ypres and an old couple comfortably consoled at home by inflated accounts of heroism. In *Mr. Britling Sees It Through*, Wells considers a comparable role for 'columns in the white windows of the newspapers through which those who lived in the securities of England looked out upon the world'. The price for sustaining these securities was nevertheless high, both at the time and in the longer term. In *The Great War and Modern Memory* (1975), Paul Fussell suggests that

> public euphemism. . . . can be said to originate in the years 1914-18. It was perhaps the first time in history that official policy produced events so shocking, bizarre, and stomach-turning that the events had to be tidied up for presentation to a highly literate mass population.
>
> A lifelong suspicion of the press was one lasting result of the ordinary man's experience of the war. It might even be said that the current devaluation of letterpress and even of language itself dates from the Great War.[48]

Mobilizing Authors

Newspapers were only one of the outlets for public euphemism and tidied information, also influentially disseminated through several forms of propaganda. Some of these had strong literary involvements, and some predated the war. Early in the century, several novels had focused attention on the threat of Germany, the need to continue the 'Dreadnought' race of battleship-building, or the advantages of conscription. One of the most accomplished appeared as early as 1903—*The Riddle of the Sands*, Erskine Childers's story of English yachtsmen happening upon an invasion fleet lurking in the Frisian Islands, off Germany's north-east coast. Illustrated with maps and charts, and subtitled *A Record of Secret Service Recently Achieved*—ostensibly only edited by Erskine Childers—*The Riddle of the Sands* carried a strong suggestion of authenticity. This added urgency to its concluding question: 'is it not becoming patent that the time has come for training all Englishmen

---

[48] Wells, *Mr. Britling Sees It Through*, 160; Paul Fussell, *The Great War and Modern Memory* (Oxford: Oxford University Press, 1975), 178, 316.

systematically either for the sea or for the rifle?'[49] The same kind of question was reiterated in an introductory letter provided by the former Commander-in-Chief of the army, Field Marshall Earl Roberts, for William Le Queux's *The Invasion of 1910* (1906). Like Childers, Le Queux sought a sense of authenticity, offering in his subtitle a *Full Account of the Siege of London* and providing numerous maps and plans. To maximize the effect, particularly for serialization in Northcliffe's *Daily Mail*, Le Queux ensured his 'invasion' passed through as many centres of population as possible. Later episodes were advertised in London by files of men dressed in German uniforms. Questions were asked in Parliament, the circulation of the *Daily Mail* increased, and sales of a million copies were secured for the novel—promptly translated into six European languages, including, intriguingly, German.

Despite such warnings, war broke out in August 1914 with an apparent suddenness, discussed earlier, which left a measure of public bewilderment, not least about its causes and aims. Worried that sufficient reason for waging war might not be apparent in the immediate cause of its declaration—German infringement of Belgian neutrality—H. G. Wells explored numerous other motives in a series of newspaper articles, quickly collected as *The War That Will End War* and published in September 1914. His concern about public understanding and commitment was shared by the government. Late in August, it had established a War Propaganda Bureau at Wellington House under C. F. G. Masterman, a cabinet minister and former literary editor. One of its first and most influential initiatives was the publication in May 1915, in thirty languages, of the Bryce Report— the work of a government committee of enquiry, set up under the chairmanship of a former British ambassador to the United States. The report supposedly authenticated rumours current at the time, rarely more than partially reliable, suggesting that the Germans had violated much more than Belgian neutrality. In the view of the report, they had also violated, in the grossest manner, the lives and decencies of its people, through numerous atrocities including rapes, the murder and mutilation of women and children, and the use of civilians as human shields for advancing troops.

The report offered a foundation for what proved lasting assumptions about the moral justification of the war. Well before its publication,

[49] Erskine Childers, *The Riddle of the Sands: A Record of Secret Service Recently Achieved* (London: Smith, Elder, 1903), 336.

though, the Propaganda Bureau had already been active. It probably intervened in September 1914 to help spread rumours about the Angels of Mons. It had certainly recognized, by that early stage of the war, the value of stories, imagination, and myth. Later described by C. E. Montague as an 'Angel of Delusion', the Bureau began on 2 September an extensive recruitment of imaginative writers to assist in the propagation of war ideals. That afternoon—one of melancholy late-summer sunshine, Thomas Hardy later remembered[50]—Masterman called a secret meeting of leading authors. Twenty-five attended, including—as well as Hardy—J. M. Barrie, Arnold Bennett, the Poet Laureate Robert Bridges, G. K. Chesterton, Sir Arthur Conan Doyle, John Galsworthy, John Masefield, and H. G. Wells. Rudyard Kipling sent apologies but promised his services. Ford Madox Ford was soon involved, attacking 'the rat of Prussianism' in *When Blood Is Their Argument* (1915), a study seeking to demonstrate that German culture and education lead to 'the death of clear thinking'.[51] Others—John Buchan, Ian Hay, and Hugh Walpole—became involved later, sometimes as members of the Bureau's staff.

Probably never previously in history had literature been considered influential enough to justify the co-option of so many authors—almost all of those well-known or successful at the time—directly into the affairs of state. Its chances of ever being so considered again had already begun to diminish by 1916, when another of the Propaganda Bureau's initiatives—that film of the Battle of the Somme, carefully sanitized and affirmative—demonstrated the huge potentials of cinema and image in reaching the public. These potentials were exploited more widely in propaganda thereafter, though several of Masterman's authors maintained leading roles in the Bureau and successor institutions. In February 1917, John Buchan became director of a Department of Information, incorporating the Bureau's work alongside propaganda initiatives previously undertaken by the Admiralty and the War Office. In the last months of the war, after Lord Beaverbrook's resignation, Arnold Bennett found himself—perhaps as a reward for the four hundred articles on the war he had published since its outbreak—briefly in charge of the entire operation. Since early in 1918, this had

[50] Montague, *Disenchantment*, 113; see Philip Waller, *Writers, Readers and Reputations: Literary Life in Britain 1870–1918* (Oxford: Oxford University Press, 2008), 932.

[51] Ford Madox Ford, *When Blood Is Their Argument: An Analysis of Prussian Culture* (London: Hodder and Stoughton, 1915), xi, 296.

been centred in a new Ministry of Information, further expanding the work of Buchan's department.

Wells's *The War That Will End War* defined the conflict, even in its early stages, as one—for the first time in history—'not of soldiers but of whole peoples'.[52] Propaganda inevitably had a growing role in such a conflict. Unlike most continental countries, Britain still had no conscription in 1914, making propaganda crucial in encouraging enlistment, as well as supporting morale more generally. New opportunities were also available for influencing the enemy. 'Thanks to the aeroplane', C. E. Montague remarked, 'you can circularize the enemy's troops'. Ernst Jünger duly records finding—though delivered by balloon—'propaganda leaflets which the enemy had taken to dropping in ever greater numbers as morale bombs', some using Schiller's poetry to help convey their message.[53] The efforts of British writers, though, were mostly directed towards encouraging enlistment and buttressing resolve on the Home Front, or drawing in support from potential allies abroad—in particular, the United States. Twenty-eight further authors—including Rider Haggard, May Sinclair, Jerome K. Jerome, and Rudyard Kipling—joined those who had attended Masterman's meeting in signing a letter simultaneously published in *The Times* and the *New York Times* in September 1914. This supported Britain's entry into the war, regretted 'terror in Belgium', and deplored the 'dangerous and insane' views of the Germans and their allegiance to 'the rule of "Blood and Iron"'.[54] Several of the signatories continued to be employed by the Propaganda Bureau in producing small books or pamphlets. In order to minimize evidence of government involvement, these were placed discreetly with established publishers—including Oxford University Press. A fee of around £5 was usually offered, with a further £5 contributing to advertising—welcome assistance for publishers, faced with a fivefold increase in the cost of paper by 1916. Like the declaration in *The Times*, the publications concerned generally stressed the justice of the British cause, the monstrosity of the enemy, and the cheerful goodwill of the British soldier—particularly lauded in Hay's *The First Hundred Thousand*.

[52] H. G. Wells, *The War That Will End War* (London: Frank and Cecil Palmer, 1914), 8.

[53] Montague, *Disenchantment*, 111; Jünger, *Storm of Steel*, 275.

[54] 'Britain's Destiny and Duty: Declaration by Authors', *The Times*, 18 Sept. 1914, 3.

Wells's *The War That Will End War* showed a similar determination to focus idealism and optimism in the early days of the war. Like Ford in *When Blood Is Their Argument*, Wells is vitriolic about the 'evil system of government' of Germany's Prussian rulers, and about the propaganda they had used to deceive a fundamentally decent population. But he is also full of optimistic plans for future peace, post-war settlement, and the 'opportunity of Liberalism' which might result. There is an obvious irony in Wells's criticism of propaganda, but a free admission that he is using it himself, and a measure of restraint in the way he does. This also appears in the novel which soon followed, *Boon*, scathing about the 'belligerent lustfulness' of newspapers such as the *Morning Post*, and anxious to distance its own views from more strident ones expressed in the press at the time.[55] Similar restraint extends into much of the work fellow authors produced for the Propaganda Bureau. After the embargo on war correspondents had been lifted, several recorded impressions of trips to the Front—trips which were of course judiciously monitored and escorted by the military. Arnold Bennett's *Over There: War Scenes on the Western Front* (1915) is typical of the result. In the form of an engaging travelogue, Bennett subtly takes for granted the monstrosity of Germany's attack on civilization, carefully fosters admiration for French allies, and reports that the Front is 'the most cheerful, confident, high-spirited place I had seen in France, or in England either'.[56] Bennett nevertheless vividly records some of the dangers it presented, describing brief encounters with shelling, and with bits of corpses—German ones—protruding from a trench wall.

A measure of restraint—or of opinion rather different to those expressed in their propaganda—also appears in fiction written during the war by the authors Masterman had gathered at Wellington House. In John Buchan's *Greenmantle*, when Hannay contrives to meet the Kaiser during his desperate flight across Germany, he finds him 'no common man'—certainly not the monster of many propaganda publications—and even feels 'in his presence...an attraction'. This soon extends to the German people generally, Hannay finding an earlier wish to give 'the Huns some of their own medicine' dispelled by an idyllic

[55] Wells, *War That Will End War*, 8, 55; Wells, *Boon*, 262.
[56] Arnold Bennett, *Over There: War Scenes on the Western Front* (London: Methuen, 1915), 66.

period of convalescence in a woodcutter's cottage.[57] In *Mr. Britling Sees It Through*, Wells likewise includes an engaging German character, and criticizes opinions resembling his own in *The War That Will End War*. John Galsworthy also repents his earlier commitments in *The Burning Spear*, originally published under a pseudonym in 1919. His novel is a fable describing a man who 'has no knowledge of anything save what is recorded in the papers' and attempts in a series of ludicrous episodes to advance the work of the 'Ministry of Propagation'. Realizing this work is 'corroding the vitals and impairing the sanity of [his] countrymen', he eventually tries to immolate himself on a pyre of newspapers and journals, among which Horatio Bottomley's notoriously jingoistic *John Bull* is most prominent.[58] Similar sentiments might even be covertly at work in a short story ending in another conflagration, Rudyard Kipling's 'Mary Postgate' (1915). Mary ends as Galsworthy's hero begins—as an unswerving believer in the bellicose patriotism wartime newspapers propagated, and in the propagandist caricatures of the enemy they often offered. Her treatment of a fallen German airman seems to act on such views, though also—in its extreme cruelty, in which she takes profound pleasure—to suggest some implicit criticism of them. Reservations Kipling could not express in his propaganda work may have been redirected—consciously or unconsciously—into this puzzling story instead.

Criticism is more explicit in Bennett's *The Pretty Lady*, often sceptical of British attitudes and institutions. Bennett's vivid account of a Zeppelin raid, describing a child's severed hand left lying in the street, would hardly have allayed contemporary readers' anxieties. Nor would the attitudes of some of his characters. His central figure, the businessman G. J. Hoape, thinks the raids 'marvellous...terrible but exquisite'. An aristocratic friend finds them thrilling enough to insist on watching from the roof of her London mansion, where she is killed by a shrapnel splinter. Her insouciant end is typical of her circle's self-indulgent pursuit of new amusements during the war. Hoape admits to himself that 'morally, he was profiting by the war. Nay, more, in a deep sense he was enjoying it.

---

[57] John Buchan, *Greenmantle* (1916; rpt. Oxford: Oxford University Press, 1993), 76, 99.

[58] John Galsworthy, *The Burning Spear: Being the Experiences of Mr. John Lavender in Time of War: Recorded by A.R. P-M* (London: Chatto and Windus, 1919), 191, 7, 243.

The immensity of it, the terror of it, the idiocy of it, the splendour of it, its unique grandeur as an illustration of human nature, thrilled the spectator in him'. Other members of London's fashionable circles likewise find themselves on a society occasion 'comfortably conscious of... helping to support two renowned hospitals where at that very moment dissevered legs and arms were being thrown into buckets'.[59] Bennett's vision of a ruling class—responsible for allowing the war to occur, yet complacent about its continuation—resembles several other literary assessments of the Home Front. It even shares details. Self-indulgent yet self-destructive relish of air raids also figures in Galsworthy's *Saint's Progress* (1919), and in George Bernard Shaw's play *Heartbreak House* (1919). Shaw was one of the few well-known authors Masterman had not been able to draw into propaganda work at Wellington House. An anti-war stance is evident in his work twenty years earlier, in his play *Arms and the Man* (1894), and Shaw extended it in his pamphlet *Common Sense about the War* (1914), equating British militarism with its Prussian counterpart. He quickly found himself a target of patriotic opprobrium as a result. By the time of writing *Heartbreak House*, in 1916–17, he had relented into reluctant support for the war. Yet his play resumes earlier criticisms just as fiercely, if in a different mode, suggesting that Britain's ship of state had sailed into the war while captained and crewed as a ship of fools.

At the time and later, many other writers questioned a society whose governing institutions and classes had failed to prevent the outbreak of war in 1914. 'Poor old ship! Poor old England!', C. E. Montague laments in his novel *Rough Justice* (1924), describing institutions ranging from the University of Oxford to the government decaying in a pre-war doldrum, their dullness extended into the running of the war.[60] Elsewhere in Europe, the war provoked similar scepticism about a languid, ailing pre-war society—in Thomas Mann's *The Magic Mountain* (*Der Zauberberg*, 1924), for example. Seclusion in a mountain sanatorium allows Mann's self-obsessed bourgeois circle to overlook, almost literally, violence impending throughout the wider life of their times. This is encountered all the more shockingly when Mann's central figure finds himself caught up in a barrage and infantry attack in the novel's closing pages. Comparable criticisms are implied in Robert Musil's *The Man Without*

[59] Bennett, *Pretty Lady*, 205, 195, 141.
[60] C. E. Montague, *Rough Justice* (1926; rpt. Chatto and Windus, 1969), 78.

Qualities (*Der Mann ohne Eigenschafften, 1930–42*). Its setting in 'stirring times, round about the end of 1913 and the beginning of 1914' highlights the confused, porous optimism still sustaining the ruling class during the last days of the Austro-Hungarian Empire.[61]

Negative views of the war were not altogether omitted even from propaganda published by Masterman's authors, but instead carefully subordinated within affirmative accounts of its progress. The occluded honesty informing Bennett's *Over There* reappears in the history of the Somme which John Buchan quickly produced late in 1916. This passes over neither the losses incurred in the battle nor their impact on Kitchener's volunteer army, described as 'the very flower of Britain'. Yet Buchan is carefully reticent about their scale, and about the small extent of ground gained. He claims instead a greater gain: that through their deaths these 'bronzed, steel-hatted warriors' have become 'the shining spires of that City to which we travel'. Though he also praises 'the happy gift of the British soldier' for turning 'the ghastly business of war into something homely and familiar', this is not a gift he much seeks to share.[62] On the contrary, his history of the Somme eventually elevates the dead into worthy familiars of the Angels of Mons. The rhetoric of such writing—as in those reports of the battle in *The Times* of 3 July—seeks to make even a 'rubbish-heap of ruins' glorious, and the war itself, if not reassuringly 'homely and familiar', a matter of noble, spiritual, or idealistic aspiration instead.

Further discussed in Chapter 3, rhetoric of this kind was employed particularly widely during the early, more idealistic days of the war, not necessarily appearing artificial or inflated at that time—nor, among civilians, even later. A. D. Gristwood confirms that serving soldiers were generally more sceptical, especially after mid-1916. In *The Somme*, Gristwood especially objects to

> the tale of the wounded man…invariably he professes regret at 'missing the fun,' and seeks to convey the impression that bayonet fighting is much like a football match, and even more gloriously exciting. It was such trash that drugged men's minds to the reality of war…patriots at

[61] Robert Musil, *The Man Without Qualities* (1930–42), trans. Eithne Wilkins and Ernst Kaiser (1954; rpt. London: Picador, 1979), II: 67.

[62] John Buchan, *The Battle of the Somme: First Phase* (London: Thomas Nelson, 1916), 108, 39, 109, 24.

home urged that 'it was necessary to keep up the nation's spirit...', but a people that must be doped to perseverance with lies is in an evil case.[63]

Though combatants were resistant to such drugging and doping, it often took time for this immunity to develop, or for idealism imbued from recruitment campaigns to wear off. In his autobiographical *Flax of Dream* novel sequence (1921-8), Henry Williamson's central figure experiences genuine surprise on discovering, during the Christmas Truce of 1914, clear contradictions to the notion propagated by 'nearly all English newspapers... that the Germans were all brutes'. In *Goodbye to All That*, Robert Graves recalls he did not register 'direct experience of official lying' until May 1915. Looking back on his enlistment in the first days of the war, motivated partly by disgust at reports of German actions in Belgium, he explains that although he 'discounted perhaps twenty per cent of the atrocity details as wartime exaggeration, that was not, of course, sufficient'.[64] George Ramage's journal suggests a comparable transition. During a station stop at Bailleul, journeying towards the Front in April 1915, it records that 'a wounded Tommy lying in a cot exchanged bright smiles with us—his calm friendly encouraging smile seemed to express his pleasure that we gallant chaps were going to carry on the good work which he could not now share in'. These comments appear on one of the recto pages Ramage uses for most of his journal writing. Opposite, on the left-hand page, usually blank, he records a pencilled afterthought: 'in describing this Tommy's smile I am perhaps unconsciously adopting the damned cant of the newspapers that one and all make Tommy a burning patriotic Mars—perhaps his smile was an enigmatic Mona Lisa smile— perhaps an ordinary friendly smile' (Fig. 6). Risks of adopting 'damned cant' continue to concern Ramage—sometimes justifiably, as he seems ready himself, in later pages, to find a 'suggestion of brutality' in the features of every one of the German prisoners he encounters.[65]

Perhaps the most thorough rejection of 'damned cant' later appeared in Compton Mackenzie's *Gallipoli Memories* (1929). Mackenzie considers that a worrying 'insight into the state of mind set up by modern war'

---

[63] Gristwood, *The Somme*, 25.

[64] Henry Williamson, *The Flax of Dream: A Novel in Four Books* (1921-8; rpt. London: Faber and Faber, 1936), 1216; Graves, *Goodbye to All That*, 198, 61.

[65] Ramage, journal, I: 21; III: 54.

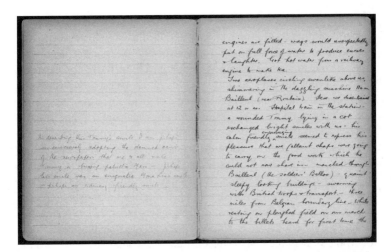

FIG 6 Two pages from George Ramage's journal, including his views of 'damned cant' in the newspapers.

is afforded by the 'balderdash which all over the world was served out to the public by the leaders of every combatant nation from the day war was declared'. Yet he also acknowledges his own part in it—in the distribution to the troops in Gallipoli of 'lamentable...drivel' on multigraphed newssheets. He may speak for many authors mentioned above when he recalls that he 'honestly believed he was being useful'.[66] Similar regrets about propaganda appear throughout war writing during the 1920s. The scale and pervasiveness of 'damned cant' continued simply to seem amazing to Richard Aldington in his novel *Death of a Hero* (1929), which suggests that 'one human brain cannot hold, one memory retain, one pen portray the limitless Cant, Delusion and Delirium let loose on the world during those four years. It surpasses the most fantastic imagination. It was incredible.'[67] For C. E. Montague, disgust was occasionally tempered by fascination about the lengths to which credulity and imagination could be stretched. The astonishment he expressed at newspaper

---

[66] Compton Mackenzie, *Gallipoli Memories* (London: Cassell, 1929), 203.
[67] Richard Aldington, *Death of a Hero* (1929; rpt. London: Hogarth Press, 1984), 223.

reporting of the Somme, quoted earlier, extends in *Disenchantment* into deeper resentments of propaganda generally. But Montague worked for the *Guardian* in civilian life, and was involved, like Mackenzie, in wartime journalism and propaganda work himself, including on occasion the job of looking after authors, such as H. G. Wells, who visited the Front. Perhaps in consequence, elements of grudging admiration, even half-seduction, figure in his assessment of propaganda's potentials. He even criticizes British failures to exploit *more* fully what seemed a new and powerful weapon. He also anticipates ways it might be used in future wars, prophesying that 'the most disreputable of successful journalists and "publicity experts" would naturally man the upper grades of the war staff'. As a result, arguments based on fact might wholly cease, replaced by mere 'trials of skill in fantastic false pretences, and of expertness in the morbid psychology of credulity'. He speculates that 'if we really went the whole serpent the first day of any new war would see a wide, opaque veil of false news drawn over the whole face of our country'.[68]

The opaque veil Montague anticipates grew more familiar as the twentieth century went on. Clear lines connect his concerns with those of later thinkers, confirming Paul Fussell's conclusions about the long-term effects of the Great War on language and media. Views of newspapers making 'black . . . only an aspect of white' anticipate George Orwell's fears about propaganda and the distortions of 'Newspeak', figured in his appendix to *Nineteen Eighty-Four* (1949) as the likely medium for future 'leading articles in *The Times*'.[69] Montague's 'veil' might also be connected with Jean Baudrillard's conclusion that by the 1980s the 'territory' of the real had vanished behind 'maps' or images scarcely any longer even pretending to represent it. Baudrillard's analyses of the image-saturated late twentieth century suggest a kind of final horizon in the modern age's growing scepticism of the media. As the Preface suggested, the Great War, defining crisis of the modern age, also inaugurated many of the deeper scepticisms characteristic of a postmodern one. Montague confirms the origins of some of this era's mistrusts in the extraordinary powers press and propaganda exercised after 1914.

Later commentators have ably analysed these powers and the ways— described in Peter Buitenhuis's *The Great War of Words* (1987)—their

---

[68] Montague, *Disenchantment*, 117, 119, 112.

[69] George Orwell, *Nineteen Eighty-Four* (1949; rpt. Harmondsworth: Penguin, 1969), 241.

creation of an 'illusion of present glory and coming victory...drew a paper curtain across the Western Front and the other campaigns'.[70] In *Keep the Home Fires Burning* (1977), Cate Haste outlines some of the consequences in political and historical terms, highlighting the responsibilities of propaganda for the perpetuation of the war and the mismanagement of its conclusion. Peace initiatives tentatively advanced by Germany late in 1916, and by the United States early the following year, had little appeal to a British public convinced of the gloriousness of the struggle, the certainty of victory, and the monstrosity of the enemy. Lloyd George recognized the effect of these misconceptions at the time, anticipating views later stated publicly in his *War Memoirs*. Late in 1917, he remarked— privately—that 'if people really knew, the war would be stopped tomorrow, but of course they don't—and can't know. The correspondents don't write and the censorship wouldn't pass the truth. The thing is horrible, and beyond human nature to bear'.[71] Similarly, shortly after the war did finally stop, in the General Election of December 1918, though the British public was more widely enfranchised than ever before, it was less than ever able to make an informed, knowing decision. The popular press's baying for the Kaiser's blood and Germany's money, at that time, made it difficult later for Lloyd George and other statesmen, shackled by electoral promises, to do other than impose a punitive settlement at the Treaty of Versailles. Disastrous consequences followed for the internal politics of Germany and, before long, once again, for the peace of Europe. Consequences for Britain's domestic politics were likewise severe, following the press's distraction of the election campaign from the social reforms soldiers had been promised—and believed—they were fighting for.

Veils and Paper Curtains

For the present study, principally concerned with literary consequences of the Great War, images of a 'paper curtain' or 'opaque veil' highlight the stresses it imposed on the imagination, language, and expression of the age. Many commentators have pointed to ways these stresses were

---

[70] Peter Buitenhuis, *The Great War of Words: British, American and Canadian Propaganda and Fiction, 1914–1933* (Vancouver: University of British Columbia Press, 1987), 79.

[71] Quoted in Leon Wolff, *In Flanders Field: The 1917 Campaign* (London: Longmans, Green, 1959), 272.

heightened, throughout the war, by the diverging outlooks of civilians and soldiers and by chasms opening up between life at home and at the Front. Even when seeking to present the war as reassuringly and affirmatively as possible, Ian Hay acknowledges that 'you who live at home in ease have no conception of what it is like to live in a town which is under intermittent shell fire'.[72] One of the difficulties, or ironies, of this chasm in communication was that 'home and ease' seemed astonishingly, tormentingly, close to the Front geographically—in some cases, as little as seventy miles, or a few hours' journey away. In André Maurois's novel *The Silence of Colonel Bramble* (*Les Silences du Colonel Bramble*, 1918), an English officer remarks of returning to the Front that:

> it's such a horrible change…yesterday morning I was still in my garden in a real English valley, with hedges and trees. Everything was clean and fresh and cared-for and happy. My pretty sisters-in-law were playing tennis. We were all dressed in white, and here I am suddenly transposed into this dreadful mangled wood.

On the German side, Ernst Jünger recalls of a return journey to the Front that 'on the way to the station, three girls in light dresses swayed past me, clutching tennis racquets—a shining last image of that sort of life, which was to stay with me for a long time'. Of journeys in the opposite direction, towards home, another ex-combatant's memoir remarks:

> Fancy going on leave from the Ypres Salient to England! It seemed unreal all the way; at Poperinghe rail-head, at Boulogne rest camp. Even when Grisnez at last faded into the sea and Folkestone rose nearer, one could hardly believe it—until the barrier at Victoria.
>
> It *must* have been in a different world.[73]

Life in the world on the other side of the barrier was no less strange. Graves's *Goodbye to All That* records that even in 1915, before much warweariness had set in, 'London seemed unreally itself', immured in 'general indifference to, and ignorance about, the war'. Reasons for this ignorance were only too apparent to servicemen, yet impossible to amend. 'Civilians talked a foreign language', Graves recalled, 'and it was newspaper language'. Because 'civvies…|…read the war-news', George Willis complains in his poem 'To my Mate', 'they think you daft, or shell-shocked, if you speak what ain't a lie'.[74] Throughout the war volumes of *A Chronicle of Ancient Sunlight*, Williamson's central character finds that even when he can bear to describe trench experiences, while in London on leave, these count for nothing, as his father simply accuses him, incredulously, of pretending to know better than the daily press. 'I wished that the daily papers would not reach us', Ford Madox Ford's central figure recalls of life at the Front, in *No Enemy: A Tale of Reconstruction* (1929), since they only added to a 'queer uneasiness' and 'curious dislike' attaching itself to thoughts about civilians. Similar uneasiness is the theme of Owen's 'Smile, Smile, Smile'. Its wounded soldiers smile wryly over their shared, unspoken knowledge that the 'integrity' newspapers claim for the nation as a whole no longer exists, but has steadily 'fled to France' with the army, and can be found nowhere else 'save under France'.[75] This was a prevalent feeling by the end of the war. For many soldiers, Sassoon and Owen included, life with their unit at the Front seemed preferable, despite its dangers, as it offered honesty and community of outlook scarcely discoverable at home. 'Millions of men, suspended on a raft, in limitless space' was Ford's image for the separateness of this community—one which, like Owen, J. B. Priestley considered sometimes as allegiant to the dead, 'under France' as to the life they had left behind at home. 'Combatants', Priestley recalls, 'returned to the civilian world like strangers from another life. They knew too many dead men too early; they were closer to them than to the living.'[76]

The Times of 3 July 1916 provides further evidence of this dis-integrity in wartime lives and worlds. Most of page 10 delivers news of the Somme, but a good deal of it is taken up by advertisements—for Wallis's 'Great Summer Sale', for Mappin and Webbs' jewellery, priced from £15 to £50, and, occupying a quarter of the page, for Kodak cameras (Fig. 7). Three columns to the right of that report of 'fighting…of the most desperate character…fierce beyond description', readers are reminded that 'there's

[74] Graves, *Goodbye to All That*, 120, 188; Vivien Noakes (ed.), *Voices of Silence: The Alternative Book of First World War Poetry* (Stroud: Sutton, 2006), 362.

[75] Ford Madox Ford, *No Enemy: A Tale of Reconstruction* (1929; rpt. Manchester: Carcanet, 2002), 94, 104; Owen, *Complete Poems*, I: 190.

[76] Ford, *No Enemy*, 104; J. B. Priestley, *Literature and Western Man* (London: Heinemann, 1960), 322.

FIG 7   Page 10 of *The Times*, 3 July 1916.

Reproduced with the permission of Edinburgh University Press.

nothing to show for a holiday without a Kodak'. 'Take a Kodak', the advertisement urges, 'and bring home dozens of Kodak snapshots telling the picture-story of every sunny hour'. Appearing two pages after that advert for the Scala's films, Kodak's message seems a further omen of the fate of print in the modern age, with 'picture-story' steadily supplanting textual forms. The new potential of the pictorial was increasingly exploited by newspapers—which were beginning to generate more revenue from advertising than from sales—with arresting line drawings or, eventually, photographs incorporated into advertisements. Along with the growing readership of newspapers, this added to the impact advertising could make on the general public, probably helping to convince the government of what could be achieved through persuasion and propaganda. In *Lord Raingo* (1926), based on Arnold Bennett's own wartime experiences in the Ministry of Information, the central character resembles the 'publicity expert' whom C. E. Montague anticipated being put in charge of future wars. Raingo is promoted to control of the 'Ministry of Records' less for his skills as a business director than as a publicist, expert in buying and controlling newspaper opinion.

Powerful and still fairly new, the influence of advertising interested several other novelists in the early decades of the century—Wells, in *Tono-Bungay* (1909), and James Joyce, whose central figure in *Ulysses* (1922) finds work in advertising and often ponders its powers. The novelty of advertisements and their risibly extravagant claims made them a regular target for parody in the *Wipers Times*, cheerfully ready to extol—sometimes with appropriate pictures—new 'toys' such as the Flammenwerfer (flamethrower), the great advantages of gas, or the attractiveness of tours of 'lovely Belgium'. Kodak's message was relatively modest—perhaps inadvertently so, in revealing the limits of contemporary technology through its stress on 'sunny hours'. In *Mr. Britling Sees It Through*, also dating from 1916, Wells notes that snapshots are mostly 'bright with sunshine' because 'it is the happy instinct of the Kodak to refuse those days that are overcast'.[77]

The real irony of the advertisement, of course—worthy of the *Wipers Times* rather than the London *Times*—is not in its claims, but simply in its juxtaposing sunny hours so closely with reports of the 'devil's cauldron' on the Somme. Much the same irony appears two pages earlier in

---

[77] Wells, *Mr. Britling Sees it Through*, 417.

that juxtaposition, described above, of reporting from 'theatres' of war alongside advertising for the generally lightweight productions currently offered on the London stage. Such ironies are typical of jolting disjunctures within experience in general, during the Great War. Even those mostly enjoying 'home and ease' could encounter sudden death on the streets of London, or other towns throughout Britain, in one of the Zeppelin raids which began in 1915. For soldiers, only a few hours' journey, or a few column inches in a newspaper, separated sunny hours from the trenches, yet with little means of traversing the gulfs of imagination and vision involved. Like other means of directly communicating trench experience, cameras were forbidden to soldiers at the Front—though many were used covertly—and censorship ensured that no pictures of the dead were published at home. Along with propagandist reporting in newspapers, such as *The Times* on 3 July, and the carefully constructed film of the battle, such rules might have allowed the many thousands who died on that first morning of the Somme to vanish almost as completely from public visibility as they did from life itself.

Loss of vision and communication on this scale confirms a conclusion steadily emergent from the material discussed so far. British society encountered between 1914 and 1918 not only a unique historical crisis. It also confronted immense obstacles in comprehending that crisis—in seeing accurately, through 'opaque veils' or 'paper curtains', how events were unfolding, and in maintaining dialogue between civilian and military communities driven apart by the experiences involved. Divisive in contemporary society, disparities of knowledge and vision of this kind also deeply divided the literary world. Where the war was concerned, writers belonging to an older, home-based generation did not fully know what they were talking about, but went on talking and writing about it anyway, with much support and encouragement from the state. A younger generation, meanwhile, often knew only too well what they might have talked or written about, but initially, during the war years, had few channels and little encouragement available for doing so. Instead, they were confronted by all the barriers to expression outlined above—their own reticence; censorship; ignorance or indifference among civilians; the code-like obscurities of wartime usage; mendacious rhetorics dominating publishing about the war; the risk that unprecedented violence might overwhelm literary genres and tactics, or even language itself. A. D. Gristwood sums up an inevitable and widely shared concern—also recorded in Barbusse's remarks, quoted earlier—when he notes that 'journalists will never bring home to the civilian a tithe of what War is', but adds that the task might also be beyond combatants themselves.[78]

A further frustration was the sense that some of these barriers might have been avoidable had civilians not more or less chosen to keep them in place. Ignorance of conditions at the Front was not as universal among the home population as newspapers and propagandists might have wished, or as Lloyd George assumed. Not all war reporting was blandly affirmative. Even some of Donald Hankey's generally optimistic articles for the *Spectator*, for example, written as 'A Student in Arms', offer some disturbing accounts of the fighting. Not all soldiers returning on leave chose to lie, like Bartlettt's protagonist, or to maintain Sassoon's honourable reticence. As Philip Gibbs acknowledged in looking back on work as a war correspondent, despite 'deliberate falsification of news', it remained possible to learn 'the truth...from private channels'.[79] Rose Macaulay's novel *Non-Combatants and Others*, published in 1916, indicates some of these channels, showing the directness with which returning soldiers sometimes revealed conditions at the Front, or the conclusions that could be drawn from their shattered states of mind or body. Unusually frank in her own descriptions of the trenches, Macaulay suggests a population sometimes well aware of 'unwritten facts behind and so different from the printed words'.[80] As well as eventually contributing to new forms of writing, the war taught civilians newly sceptical or deductive forms of reading, of newspapers and official communications particularly. Even if the scale of losses on the Somme was unavailable from reports in *The Times*, it was soon readily apparent—though necessarily 'printed small', in the way Owen mentions—from the casualty lists, especially in the communities from which battalions devastated in the battle had been recruited.

These and other channels ensured that civilian and soldier were not necessarily altogether differently informed about the war. They were nevertheless separated by the extent to which they were able—or

[78] Gristwood, *The Somme*, 146.

[79] Gibbs, *Realities of War*, 436.

[80] Rose Macaulay, *Non-Combatants and Others* (1916; rpt. London: Hodder and Stoughton, 1986), 89.

chose—to suppress what they knew. Sassoon regretfully concludes of an older generation at home that 'they weren't capable of wanting to know the truth', preferring 'patriotic suppression of those aspects of war which never got into the newspapers'. Wondering in his memoir of the Western Front 'why people endured such cheap journalism', Bernard Adams considers that 'it was as though they dared not think things out, lest what they held most dear should be an image shattered by another point of view'. In his novel *All Our Yesterdays* (1930), another former war correspondent, H. M. Tomlinson, likewise concludes that 'facts... do not always accord with a likeable story' and that it would be foolish to 'suppose that what the people round the home fires prefer to hear is what veritably is extant'.[81] Wartime wish-fulfilment kept the Angels of Mons aloft in many civilian imaginations, or warmed at their fireside couples such as Williamson portrays in *The Patriot's Progress*, cheered by their newspaper's heroic view of Ypres. But it left a particular set of problems for combatants, scarred by the war, in reaching a population often apparently inclined, during and after the hostilities, to keep romantic images intact, or to look away from the scars and their causes. Often thought to have split Britain almost into two nations, civilian and military, the war certainly left the population in two minds, two phases of awareness and understanding. 'Your secret thought... we do not know', Margaret Sackville remarks in her poem 'The Women to the Men Returned', adding that 'never such gulf divorced you from the foe | As now divides us, for how may you tell | What Hell is to us who only read of Hell?'[82] How could this 'gulf' be bridged? How could combatants teach civilians the 'different language where men die' that Sackville mentions? How could private knowledge of the war be made into public discourse about it? What were the consequences of these challenges for writing about the war, and for later literature generally? These are questions discussed further, in relation to prose and poetry, in Chapters 2 and 3. Some general issues about wartime language and communication should be clarified first.

[81] Sassoon, *Siegfried's Journey*, 14–15; Bernard Adams *Nothing of Importance: A Record of Eight Months at the Front with a Welsh Battalion: October, 1915, to June, 1916* (London: Methuen, 1917), 297; H. M. Tomlinson, *All Our Yesterdays* (London: William Heinemann, 1930), 344.

[82] Dominic Hibberd and John Onions (eds), *The Winter of the World: Poems of the First World War* (London: Constable, 2008), 276–7.

Words...Cancelled

One of these issues, already clear from work discussed above, is that many authors were naturally aware of the war's effects on language and communication, and regularly made resulting difficulties a theme of their writing. Gaps between combatant experience and civilian awareness are vividly dramatized in Ernest Hemingway's short story 'Soldiers Home' (1926), for example. Delayed in his demobilization from the US Army until the summer of 1919, Hemingway's protagonist, Krebs, returns to his home town too late for a hero's welcome. He nevertheless finds everyone he encounters still 'barred by their patriotism' from interest in his experience:

> no one wanted to hear about it. His town had heard too many atrocity stories to be thrilled by actualities. Krebs found that to be listened to at all he had to lie, and...had a reaction against the war and against talking about it...
>
> Krebs acquired the nausea in regard to experience that is the result of untruth or exaggeration.[83]

Untruths are further examined in Hemingway's *A Farewell to Arms* (1929). Of experience on the Italian front, Hemingway's narrator explains that he was

> always embarrassed by the words sacred, glorious, and sacrifice and the expression in vain. We had heard them, sometimes standing in the rain almost out of earshot, so that only the shouted words came through, and had read them, on proclamations that were slapped up by bill posters over other proclamations, now for a long time, and I had seen nothing sacred, and the things that were glorious had no glory and the sacrifices were like the stockyards at Chicago if nothing was done with the meat except to bury it. There were many words that you could not stand to hear and finally only the names of places had dignity. Certain numbers were the same way and certain dates and these with the names of the places were all you could say and have them mean anything. Abstract words such as glory, honour, courage, or hallow were obscene beside the concrete names of villages, the numbers of roads, the names of rivers, the numbers of regiments and the dates.[84]

---

[83] Ernest Hemingway, 'Soldier's Home' (1926), in *The Essential Hemingway* (London: Panther, 1977), 303.

[84] Ernest Hemingway, *A Farewell to Arms* (1929; rpt. London: Vintage, 2005), 165.

In *The Good Soldier* (1915), completed mostly before the outbreak of war, Ford Madox Ford's narrator still considers that 'for all good soldiers... their profession... is full of the big words, courage, loyalty, honour, constancy'.[85] Hemingway's narrator reverses that conclusion. The passage above also reverses constraints imposed by officialdom on soldiers' discourse during the war. Hemingway favours just those concrete identities of place, name, regimental number, and date which censorship excised from soldiers' communications, while deploring the empty, inflated abstractions official rhetoric offered instead.

Suspicion of grand abstractions and 'big words' spread widely through post-war writing in the work of non-combatants as well as those directly involved in the war. 'I fear those big words... which make us so unhappy', Stephen Dedalus remarks in Joyce's *Ulysses*, taking 'glorious' as one of his examples. A character in Edith Wharton's *A Son at the Front* (1923) considers that 'the meaning had evaporated out of lots of our old words'. In *Lady Chatterley's Lover* (1928), D. H. Lawrence envisages a 'tragic age' following the 'cataclysm' of the war, summing up one of its sadder aspects in his heroine's conclusion that 'all the great words... were cancelled for her generation'. She considers that 'love, joy, happiness, home, mother, father, husband, all these great, dynamic words were half dead now', and finds them 'always coming between her and life', occluding experiences they were once supposed to represent. Looking back in a later poem, 'Talking with Five Thousand People in Edinburgh', Hugh MacDiarmid likewise discusses 'big words that died', concluding that 'most of the important words were killed in the First World War'.[86] Henry James seems to have reached a similar conclusion as early as March 1915, in a rare interview—one which Hemingway may later have read. Asked about the charity he supported, the American Volunteer Motor Ambulance Corps, James talks fluently, and with a complexity rivalling the intricate syntax of his fiction, until he reflects on 'casualties... occurring at the rate, say, of 5,000 in twenty minutes'. The interviewer records that

[85] Ford Madox Ford, *The Good Soldier: A Tale of Passion* (1915; rpt. Harmondsworth: Penguin, 1977), 31.

[86] James Joyce, *Ulysses* (1922; rpt. Harmondsworth: Penguin, 1992), 38; Edith Wharton, *A Son at the Front* (1923; rpt. DeKalb: Northern Illinois University Press, 1995), 101; D. H. Lawrence, *Lady Chatterley's Lover* (1928; rpt. Harmondsworth: Penguin, 1960), 5, 64, 96; Hugh MacDiarmid, *Complete Poems*, ed. Michael Grieve and W. R. Aitken (Manchester: Carcanet, 1994), II: 1156.

at this point 'Mr James broke off as if these facts were, in their horror, too many and too much for him'. Resuming, James explains that he finds it

> as hard to apply one's words as to endure one's thoughts. The war has used up words; they have weakened, they have deteriorated like motor car tires; they have, like millions of other things, been more over-strained and knocked about and voided of the happy semblance during the last six months than in all the long ages before, and we are now confronted with a depreciation of all our terms.

James's silence may suggest as much as the comments made when he resumes. Faced with what he calls 'such enormous facts of destruction', silence may be a more natural reaction than continued use of weakened words.[87]

It was a reaction regularly shared by those who—like Owen's soldiers in 'Smile, Smile, Smile'—had witnessed 'enormous destruction' for them-selves, close at hand. As Walter Benjamin pointed out, 'men returned from the battlefield grown silent—not richer, but poorer in communica-ble experience'.[88] In addition to deliberate reticence, when describing military experience to civilians, or when encountering newspapers' attempts to describe it, many forms of involuntary or pathological silence resulted from the war. Psychoanalysis developed rapidly at the time, in response to the need to treat nervous disorders usually described during the war as 'shell shock'. Published by Sigmund Freud, Ernest Jones, and others in 1921, *Psychoanalysis and the War Neuroses* describes how fre-quently 'attacks...associated with mutism' figured among ailments con-cerned.[89] These are explained as the result of instinctive reactions—fear, primarily—which military discipline made it impossible to act upon or even express. For several writers, at the time and later, such mutism high-lights literally unspeakable aspects in the Great War—experiences before which mind and articulacy inevitably renege. Pat Barker's Great War novel *Regeneration* (1991) shows the pioneer psychotherapist W. H. R.

---

[87] 'Henry James's First Interview', in Pierre A. Walker (ed.), *Henry James on Culture: Collected Essays on Politics and the American Social Scene* (Lincoln/London: University of Nebraska Press, 1999), 144.

[88] Walter Benjamin, *Illuminations*, ed. Hannah Arendt, trans. Harry Zohn (New York: Schocken Books, 1969), 84

[89] S. Ferenczi, Karl Abraham, Ernst Simmel, and Ernest Jones, *Psychoanalysis and the War Neuroses*, Introduction by Professor Sigmund Freud (London/Vienna/New York: International Psycho-Analytical Press, 1921), 39.

Rivers treating a central figure traumatized into temporary dumbness. Sebastian Faulks's protagonist in *Birdsong* (1993) is similarly afflicted, unable to speak for two years after the war. A character in Ford Madox Ford's *Parade's End* tetralogy (1924–8) is condemned to still longer silence after the armistice. His speechlessness is in a way indicative of tactics followed more widely by 1920s fiction in representing the war. The central figure in Virginia Woolf's *Jacob's Room* (1922), Jacob Flanders, exists mostly as silence and vacancy—as an emptied space, sharing the name of the battlefields, towards which desires and memories are hopelessly directed. Similar silence pervades the empty holiday home Woolf describes in *To the Lighthouse* (1927), abandoned by human inhabitants for most of the duration of the war. Its silence is broken only by creaking decay and 'the prying of the wind': by rampant entropy the war extends even through the once-pristine seas and breezes of the Hebrides.[90] Silence in all these novels might be read as symptomatic—of an immense burden of experience and memory made more intractable because its nature, along with constraints on contemporary communication, made its expression so profoundly difficult. Authors who did manage to articulate some of this experience deserve to be read with exceptional care. Like relics or artefacts surviving from some vanished world, their work should be valued not only for itself, but for its indications of far wider loss and pain, so often silenced or invisible at the time, now further buried in history and the past.

Silence is also the eventual response to 'enormous facts of destruction' in Wells's partly autobiographical *Mr. Britling Sees It Through*, published the year after James's interview. It appeared the following year in French, under the more appropriate title *M. Britling commence à voir clair* (Mr. Britling starts seeing clearly). An equally viable English title might have been *Mr. Britling Sees Through It*—if 'it' could represent the progressive, reasonable outlook shared by Wells himself, by much of the British population, and, supposedly, by the Liberal government in power in 1914. 'Liberal Governments can't go to war. That would not be liberal', Wyndham Lewis recalled believing at the time. But this one did go to war, even though Lloyd George admitted that 'war has always been fatal to Liberalism'.[91] In his study *The Great War and the Language of Modernism* (2003), Vincent Sherry charts

---

90   Virginia Woolf, *To the Lighthouse* (1927; rpt. Harmondsworth: Penguin, 1973), 148.
91   Lewis, *Blasting and Bombardiering*, 58; Lloyd George, *War Memoirs*, I: 448.

the subsequent breakdown of faiths in liberalism, and in the reasoned discourses that supported it, undermined by contortions required of a Liberal government engaged in a war. *Mr. Britling Sees It Through* shows the consequences within one individual. Like Wells's own essays in *The War That Will End War*, Britling's newspaper articles seek progressive, affirmative rationales for the war, in terms of enhanced civilization, defeated militarism, securer peace, and 'opportunity for liberalism' in general. But as the early weeks of war wear on into slaughter and stagnation, and especially after the death of his son, shot through the eye in the trenches, Britling's attempted affirmations begin to wear out. He is forced 'to think and rethink the war…until all his writing seemed painfully shallow to him'. This 'quarrel with his style' leaves him in 'incomplete control of…rebel words and phrases', further encumbered by his penchant for inappropriate metaphor. Britling tries, for example, to develop the idea that '*war is a curtain of dense black fabric across all the hopes and kindliness of mankind. Yet always it has let through some gleams of light*'. But by this stage of his writing, it is his own language and imagination's grasp of reality which is beginning to shred or seem easily seen-through. This process is graphically extended in the last pages of the novel. One of them simply reproduces, as if in facsimile, Britling's doodling, of his son's name, amid much blank space, and of random words including 'blood' and 'honesty'.[92]

This is a striking conclusion, suggesting that means of communicating experiences threatening to overwhelm ordinary language might have been found in extraordinary, incoherent forms of writing, mixing silence and disorder. Edmund Blunden toys with this idea. In his memoir *Undertones of War* (1928), he envisages survivors of war experience so appalling that they either 'will never open their mouths' or will be able only at the end of their lives to produce phrases sounding 'like "the drums and tramplings" of a mad dream'.[93] War fiction sometimes does employ 'mad dream' in this way. In *The Middle Parts of Fortune*, disconnected phrases Manning's hero overhears, and gibberish he doodles into his typewriter, indicate his distress after a particularly shocking experience. Chaotic, fragmented language also figures occasionally in Patrick Miller's *The Natural Man* (1924), and likewise communicates wounding and loss of consciousness in Henry Williamson's *The Patriot's Progress*.

---

[92] Wells, *Mr. Britling Sees It Through*, 259, 419, 431.
[93] Edmund Blunden, *Undertones of War* (1928; rpt. Harmondsworth: Penguin, 1986), 34.

Yet incoherence and the language of 'mad dream' do not appear widely in literature, and sometimes seem as much a feature of official or factual discourse about the war, in ways Vincent Sherry discusses, as of imaginative representations. In one of its reports of the Somme, for example, *The Times* of 3 July 1916 mentions that in the battle

> many interesting novelties have been introduced, such as the massacre of Drachen observation balloons, by which the Germans are deprived of some of their eyes...the Flying Corps has been as active as ever, while the cavalry in this country have more chance of bearing a hand, and in short, all the means of modern war can be profitably employed.[94]

Mention of the cavalry still taking part in 'modern war', along with the Flying Corps, incidentally highlights incongruities and anachronisms that the war often produced, on the edge of a fully modern age. French mounted troops in 1914 still wore cuirasses—armoured breastplates—almost as if expecting a joust. On the British side, though seldom used effectively, mounted troops were present in large numbers alongside the infantry of the BEF, much of which was commanded—also ineffectively, in the view of many commentators—by cavalry-trained officers. Incongruities in the passage quoted, though, derive more from word choice than anachronism. In describing the cavalry 'bearing a hand', and the aim of depriving the Germans of 'some of their eyes', the glib metonymies of *The Times* seem inadvertently complicit with the mutilation and dismemberment of the battlefield itself. Talking of a massacre as an interesting novelty, and one to be 'profitably employed', might seem similarly callous if it was not also—in the intention to 'massacre... balloons'—vaguely surreal. At such moments, the language of official reporting almost outdoes the parodies produced in the *Wipers Times*. No wonder authors such as R. C. Sherriff and James Bridie considered Lewis Carroll's *Alice's Adventures in Wonderland* (1865) peculiarly appropriate reading matter in wartime.[95] Analogies could even be drawn with the radical artistic experiments begun around this time by the Dadaists, one of whose first major performances took place later in July 1916 at the

---

[94] 'New Tactics', *The Times*, 3 July 1916, 8.
[95] See James Bridie, 'Under Fire on the Western Front', in Trevor Royle (ed.), *In Flanders Fields: Scottish Poetry and Prose of the First World War* (Edinburgh: Mainstream, 1990), 140, and R. C. Sherriff, *Journey's End*, 62–3.

Cabaret Voltaire in Zürich. For the Dadaists, the 'mad dream' of the Great War rendered Western rationality, institutions, and language comprehensively absurd and dysfunctional. An appropriate response could be found only in empty syllables such as 'Dada', drained of meaning, and in anti-aesthetic styles of art and performance, altogether denying conventional artistic aims of form and coherence.

Dada extended to a logical conclusion, in this way, an illogic or incoherence in the Great War, helping to initiate radical, reductive forms of art which continued to evolve throughout the twentieth century, gathering further force after the Second World War and in later, postmodernist writing. Illogic and incoherence in the Great War may also have silenced many potential authors altogether—ones unsure, like Hemingway's Krebs, of ever reaching a worthwhile audience, or of finding a form to contain the chaos of recent experience. But for the many authors who *did* write about the war, much as silence or incoherence might have seemed natural responses, obviously neither could be of more than limited usefulness, and other tactics were required. Typically, when Private Smith's journal mentions that a bombardment is 'beyond description' or a landscape indescribable even by 'clever writing', this interrupts neither his writing nor his descriptions—often very vivid ones. His journal demonstrates instead what could be achieved by avoiding 'clever writing' in favour of a style he hopes will be 'easy to read and understand' and that likely 'rings true...as a faithful portrayal'.[96] Smith, in other words, is one of many combatants or ex-combatants who sought alternatives to official, conventional, or 'clever' rhetoric through creating counter-rhetorics of their own, purged of the inflated vision or shining spires prominent in propaganda produced by Buchan and others.

Living Voice and Speaking Silence

Alternative stylistic and rhetorical possibilities were in view even by 1916, in Barbusse's *Under Fire*. Barbusse follows one obvious means of resisting official or inflated discourse and compromised print culture— by favouring the spoken word, as far as this is possible in a novel, and by

---

[96] Smith, *Drawing Fire*.

representing it in highly characterized dialectal forms. Diversities of dialect so often encountered in military life may sometimes have obstructed soldiers' communications with each other, but they provided writers with new voices, and by extension visions, vividly alternative to official versions of events. This potential is developed throughout *Under Fire*, much of which is in the form of dialogue exchanges between ordinary soldiers. Barbusse's tactics are difficult to sustain in translation, but by the 1920s several writers had adopted or reinvented them for use in English. Montague's *Rough Justice*, for example, reproduces six different dialects in a couple of pages, continuing to use them to differentiate characters and their views throughout. John Dos Passos is equally adept in reproducing the diverse dialects of US infantrymen in *Three Soldiers* (1921), a tactic strongly developed in his later fiction and summed up in his view that 'U.S.A. is the speech of the people'.[97] Dialect also began to figure more widely in the period's poetry—in writing by Owen, Wilfrid Wilson Gibson, Robert Service, and many others. In Hugh MacDiarmid's work in the 1920s, the rediscovery, or reinvention, of forms of Scots language—often colloquial ones—might also be seen as an alternative to English words 'killed' or compromised in the official discourses of the war.

Many writers also followed, or approved, a further emphasis in *Under Fire*. In its chapter on 'Swearwords' ('Les Gros Mots'), Barbusse's narrator is asked by a soldier 'if you get the squaddies in your book to speak, will you make them speak like they really do, or will you tidy it up and make it proper?' He reassures him that speech will be faithfully reproduced, swear words included, 'because it's the truth'.[98] George Coppard was one of several war authors for whom swearing had an even greater significance, figuring not only as the true or 'proper way to talk', but as 'an unconscious protective shield to keep us from becoming crazy'. Wilfred Owen's 'Apologia Pro Poemate Meo' similarly finds 'much beauty | In the hoarse oaths that kept our courage straight'. This function is recognized even in Ernest Raymond's popular, patriotic novel *Tell England* (1922), in which the padre decides to give up his assault on bad language. He concludes instead that swearing corresponds to 'the rock-bottom level on which we are fighting this war' and should not be condemned by

---

[97] John Dos Passos, *U.S.A.* (1932–6; rpt. Harmondsworth: Penguin, 1973), 7.
[98] Barbusse, *Under Fire*, 155.

anyone 'who hasn't floundered in mud under shell-fire'. David Jones goes further in the Preface to his epic account of the war, *In Parenthesis* (1937), finding an almost religious or artistic function for swearing. Words concerned, he explains, were repeated frequently enough to become largely innocent or even 'liturgical', adding dignity, significance, and sometimes 'real poetry' to the discourse concerned.[99]

Jones regrets that constraints on publishing excluded supposedly 'impious and impolite words'—a huge loss, as these conditioned 'the whole shape of...discourse' at the Front. This was a problem for many authors at the time. Dos Passos recalled that 'the printer refused to print the swearwords' he had intended to appear in *One Man's Initiation* (1920).[100] Hemingway deeply resented the emasculation of the language of *A Farewell to Arms*, forced on him by editors far from sharing the novel's view that it was 'abstract words' which were the most obscene. Frederick Manning managed partly to avoid such constraints by issuing a limited, private, edition of *The Middle Parts of Fortune*, then an expurgated one—*Her Privates We*—when publishing his novel at the end of the 1920s. Like *Under Fire*, much of it is in the form of dialogue—strongly dialectal, and, in unexpurgated versions, freely deploying 'all the fuckin' patter', as one character describes the (bad) language of the army. Unlike Barbusse, Manning does not discuss swearing directly. But his central character indicates the importance of slang, swearing, and 'patter' generally to the novel, and to war fiction more widely, when he reflects that 'dead words there on the paper...graven and rigid symbols, could never again kindle with the movement and persuasion of...living voice'.[101]

Contemporary critics and commentators also emphasize the importance of voice, vernacular, and colloquialism in communicating war experience and in extending the 'protective shield' Owen and Coppard recognized in swearing. Writing in *John O'London's Weekly* shortly after the war, Wilfred Whitten suggests that soldiers' verbal inventiveness demonstrated 'an instinct of self-protection against the terrible assaults of reality', and 'the amazing powers of adaptation which the human mind

---

[99] George Coppard, *With a Machine Gun to Cambrai* (1980; rpt. London: Macmillan, 1986), 47; Owen, *Complete Poems*, I: 124; Ernest Raymond, *Tell England: A Study in a Generation* (1922; rpt. London: Cassell, 1929), 190–1; Jones, *In Parenthesis*, xii.

[100] Jones, *In Parenthesis*, xii; John Dos Passos, *One Man's Initiation: 1917: A Novel* (1920; rpt. Ithaca, NY: Cornell University Press, 1969), 34.

[101] Manning, *Middle Parts of Fortune*, 38, 117.

can summon to the breach of all ordinary habit, outlook and experience'. Referring to soldiers' inclination to give friendly, familiar names even to enemy shells, Whitten adds of these terms that 'under all their humour is to be found the sense of the unutterable'. Edmund Blunden's account of slang—of 'Trench Nomenclature', as he calls it in the title of the poem concerned—likewise celebrates the 'genius' demonstrated in compressing into single words 'what man's humour said to man's supreme distress'.[102] In this view, unprintable or 'unutterable' experience need not lead only to silence or incoherence. It can contribute instead—almost necessarily—to invention and adaptation, and to language-use reshaped by the very threat of its ruin. In their invented, ingenious, extra-official forms of language, soldiers maintained a second life, remote from the reaches of public discourse, and often endowed with a humour further protecting them from the 'assaults of reality'. For writers troubled by propaganda's precarious relation to the truth, and by the precariousness of life itself during the war, there was a natural appeal in the direct, declarative immediacy of speech, and the inventive, idiosyncratic mobility of 'living voice'. Further considered in Chapters 2 and 3, this appeal extended into and beyond the 1920s, and is one of the Great War's lasting influences on later literature and imagination.

Barbusse indicates another alternative to conventional or official discourse, one which also begins to address his worry, quoted earlier, that 'the war is unimaginable'. Of war experience, one of his soldiers remarks that 'it all gets worn away inside you and goes, you can't tell how or where, leaving you only with the names, the words for things, like in a dispatch'. His comment offers in one way an early version of the preferences Hemingway expresses in *A Farewell to Arms*: for 'words for things', and for the concrete details of name and place soldiers were generally forbidden to communicate from the Front. But Barbusse offers further reasons for these preferences, arising less from a need to avoid censorship, or the abstractions of propaganda, than from a sense of emptiness in dimensions 'inside'. The focus of *Under Fire* is correspondingly much less on feeling or inner reflection than on the physical: for example, on

---

[102] Wilfred Whitten, '"What the Soldier Said": Collecting the Slang of the Great War', *John O'London's Weekly*, 6(145) (14 Jan. 1922), 480; Edmund Blunden, *The Poems of Edmund Blunden* (London: Cobden-Sanderson, 1930), 173.

marching which tramples the earth backwards and forwards, bruises the feet and wears the bones under the weight of the load that seems to get bigger in the sky, under the unspeakable exhaustion, the moving about and the standing still that crushes you, the work that is beyond your strength, the endless nights without sleep.[103]

Not all writing about the war is as earthy as Barbusse's, nor as focused on the external, but much of it does concentrate on immediate physical presences and pressures, rather than emotions these induced. In journals kept during the war, and in novels about it published later, words for things often predominate over words for thoughts, with several effects on the writing involved.

The first of these concerns the struggle to describe the indescribable—events and landscapes breaching 'all ordinary habit, outlook and experience', in Whitten's view, and potentially beyond the reach of conventional imaginative devices. George Ramage's journal exemplifies this struggle. While he is still some distance from the front line, it relies heavily on simile, finding comparisons for new and unfamiliar experience within the domestic and everyday. Eight instances appear on a single page, comparing rifle fire to 'the noise of rivetting in a ship building yard', the continual crash of distant big guns to 'breakers on the shore or the rumbling of a storm in the chimney', and so on. In the front-line trenches, on the other hand, nothing any longer seems much like anything else, or familiar at all, and Ramage moves from simile to a kind of synecdoche. A succession of 'words for things' or individual objects allows a view of the wider scene to be assembled from an account of its components, with the help of readers' imaginations. Private Smith's journal likewise encourages readers to reconstruct for themselves a whole landscape through a succession of brief, local descriptions of objects in it. He records of one section of the Front, for example, that 'from one shell hole to another, the place was strewn with all sorts of ghastly witnesses to past bad days—huddled up heaps of dead, burst bespattered sandbags, parts of dug-out structures, pieces of men—and now a rising mist hung about'. 'Ghastly witnesses' and 'parts of structures' operate similarly in A. D. Gristwood's account of the Somme—in lists of

the miscellaneous débris of war—men living, dying and dead, friend and foe broken and shattered beyond imagination, rifles, clothing, cartridges, fragments of men, photographs of Amy and Gretchen, letters, rations and the last parcel from home…bodies buried a week ago and now suffering untimely resurrection, the chatter of machine-guns, and the shouts and groans of men—such were the woods of the Somme, where once primroses bloomed.[104]

Another advantage of concentrating on 'words for things' is that, rather than eliminating inner feelings, it may communicate them as effectively, through implication, as any direct statement could. Rapidly alternating attention to diverse battlefield objects can suggest some of the restless, wide-eyed stress with which they were first apprehended. Concentration on an external, object world can also create a still more loquacious silence, suggestive of pressures wearing away the inner one. The war widely imposed this kind of silence—sometimes, as discussed earlier, as an extreme reaction to experience of the unutterable. Even when suppression of inner feelings did not extend into pathologic forms, some reticence was often essential just to ensure the survival of sanity. The view Lieutenant-Colonel Hermon mentions in a letter—'one couldn't carry on, I don't think, if one lets oneself think too much'—was often expressed. At the other end of the military hierarchy, Smith's journal records that after witnessing a dozen close comrades killed or wounded by a shell, he 'had to just go on sitting tight on [the] fire-step—"saying nuffin" but thinking "some"'. Another private's journal records the opinion that 'the man who thinks is done. He'll never know a moment's peace. Don't look too deep and above all don't think too deeply'. Many wartime narratives follow comparable priorities. Wyndham Lewis, for example, declares a preference for 'keeping out the pale cast of thought as far as possible' in favour of 'a plain tale of mere surface events'.[105] The very plainness of such tales nevertheless allows, even encourages, thoughts and feelings to be reconstructed by readers even—perhaps especially—when 'nuffin' is said.

This implicative form of writing—minimal, unsentimental, and distant from abstraction—came to be widely practised in later years, perhaps marking a lasting reconsideration of the balance between silence

[104] Ramage, journal, II: 39; Smith, *Drawing Fire*; Gristwood, *The Somme*, 23.
[105] Hermon, *For Love and Courage*, 109; Smith, *Drawing Fire*; E. P. F. Lynch, *Somme Mud: The Experiences of an Infantryman in France, 1916–1919* (London: Bantam Books, 2006), 58; Lewis, *Blasting and Bombardiering*, 188.

and statement in literature. At any rate, it soon extended into writing not directly connected with the war. In the 1920s, Hemingway was the most celebrated exponent of the implicative style, developing a restrained, understated vision of the war in *A Farewell to Arms* and some of the short stories of *In Our Time* (1926). This also extends into fictions about restless, hedonistic postwar life, such as *The Sun Also Rises* (1927). In his short story 'Hills Like White Elephants' (1928), almost nothing is mentioned explicitly about the covert struggle, literally about life and death, preoccupying the two main characters. Legacies of this style continue to appear in a range of Anglophone writing later in the century. Much of the 'hard-boiled' genre fiction which began to appear in the 1930s features characters whose inner, emotional lives are at most implied rather than directly described. Another, more specific indebtedness appears in the early work of Hemingway's admirer Harold Pinter. An influence extends from the mendacities of Great War reporting to the character in *The Dumb Waiter* (1957) who is obsessed by facts 'down here in black and white' in his newspaper, yet unable to believe that events could ever have occurred in the way its reporting describes. Much of Pinter's dialogue, too, in *The Dumb Waiter* and other plays, reveals characters engaged—like Hemingway's in 'Hills Like White Elephants' or 'The Killers' (1928)—in covert struggles scarcely mentioned in their actual conversation. In summing up his own interest in 'a language...where underneath what is said another thing is being said', Pinter further indicates legacies in later writing of the stresses imposed on language during the Great War. He also suggests the continuing usefulness of skills in decipherment—in seeking 'below the word spoken...the thing known and unspoken', a tactic many readers learned to apply to their newspapers at the time.[106]

As these examples suggest, some literary advantage can be seen to have resulted from the Great War's stresses on language—from 'powers of adaptation' demanded by experience potentially unspeakable or beyond description. Yet this should not obscure the lasting difficulties imposed on writing by what Henry James saw as the weakening and wearying of words in the war. A summary, or analogy, for the effect on writers in the 1920s might be provided by a brisk exchange in Ford's

---

[106] Harold Pinter, 'Introduction' and *The Dumb Waiter* in *Plays: One* (London: Eyre Methuen, 1976), 13–14, 163.

Parade's End. In response to General Campion's request—'say what you want to say. What the devil do you mean?... What's this all about?'— Ford's long-suffering central figure, Tietjens, acknowledges that 'it's difficult to make myself plain'. This only provokes the General to demand 'What is language for? What the *hell* is language for?'[107] As the exchange suggests, after the mendacities and failures of communication in the Great War, plain speaking was more than ever essential, but harder than ever to provide, or to liberate from doubts about the function and reliability of language. These doubts were strengthened by comparable ones extending through British public life at the time, and through systems and structures on which it had once more confidently been based. An analogy with the position of language might even be found in the fate of the currency during the war. Stresses on the wartime economy forced Britain largely to move away from the gold standard, and from a currency backed by gold reserves—increasingly, from 1915, replacing gold sovereign coins with paper pound notes. Their promise to 'pay the bearer on demand the sum of...' risked seeming hollow—very different from values supported by the worth of metal in the coins on which they were stamped. Detached in this way from a fixed, tangible referent, money began to seem just another 'paper curtain' or abstraction. In the view of a later analyst, this 'double crisis of money and language' suggested a general 'collapse of guarantees and frames of reference, a rupture between sign and thing, undermining representation'.[108]

The same rupture or devaluation continued to afflict the currency of language after 1918. 'The meaning of words had no longer the same relation to things', C. E. Montague concluded of a 'new world' after the war, indicating a continuing loss of the 'happy semblance' whose dwindling James deplored in 1915.[109] Words—journalists' words especially—had probably never related to the world with the easy transparency Wells suggests when describing newspaper columns as a 'window' on reality. Yet the change of image, from Wells's window to Montague's 'opaque veil'—or to Lawrence's idea of words coming *between* the individual and life—summarizes a genuine change in ways words seemed to relate to

[107] Ford Madox Ford, *Parade's End* (1924–8; rpt. Harmondsworth: Penguin, 1982), 491–2.

[108] Jean-Joseph Goux, *The Coiners of Language,* trans. Jennifer Curtiss Gage (Oklahoma City/London: Oklahoma University Press, 1994), 3.

[109] Montague, *Disenchantment*, 121–2.

the world at the time. Something of this change might have occurred in any case, even without the Great War's intervention. But it would not have happened as rapidly, nor on the same scale. The war ensured that changed communicative practices and promises—or the absence of the latter—were encountered by all sections of the population, even if not all equally. By the 1920s, Nietzsche's ideas of language as 'tremendous error', and as 'a separate world beside the other world' were potentially every-day conclusions as much as philosophic ones, with profound conse-quences for the writing of the period. General Campion concludes his tirade by remarking 'What the *hell* is language for? We go round and round... *That's* modernism.' He does not have literary modernism in mind, but rather the mendacities of modern manners and lifestyles gen-erally. Yet the literary modernism of the 1920s, and to an extent the writ-ing about the war which developed alongside it, did continue to go round and round issues of 'semblance'—happy or otherwise—along with ques-tions about the kind of windows words could open on the world. Along with other developments the Great War forced upon literary forms and genres, these gyrations are assessed in the next chapters.

| 2 |

Unaccountable War

I wasnt about 6 yds away from him when he was shot. It was on Monday the 12th of Oct [1914] we was ordered to take the bridge over the canal which was held by the Germans and we formed up about 2 p.m. and advanced towards the bridge under very heavy fire and we had advanced about ¾ of a mile when your Son was shot...all the men was sorry to loose him as he seemed to have no fear and was a good leader of men and Died like an hero.

Bereaved families naturally wanted to know how loved ones had died, and how their death might have contributed to winning the war. In *Testament of Youth* (1933), Vera Brittain records piecing together information about her fiancé's fatal wounding in France, late in 1915, from letters of condolence received from his fellow officers. She was equally determined later, in accumulating details of her brother's death in the Italian campaign. The letter quoted above was written in similar circumstances—by a private in the Royal Scots, H. E. Beaven, in response to a request for information from a bereaved family. Nigel Trotter had been promoted to lieutenant at the outbreak of the war, and was killed ten weeks later, while the Royal Scots—according to a letter from his commanding officer, Capt. C. Tanner—were 'fighting sixteen hours a day' around Béthune.[1] Volume 2 of the official *History of the Great War* suggests that these operations shared in 'the attempt of the II. corps to turn the German northern flank'. This was part of a 'Race to the Sea' undertaken by both armies early in the war, with the eventual effect only of extending defensive positions all the way to the Channel.

The official *History* finds it difficult to sum up these operations, which it records involving a 'large number of troops scattered over seventy miles of front' and a series of actions developing confusedly, throughout October 1914, towards the First Battle of Ypres.[2] A contemporary newspaper report—deposited among papers Lieutenant Trotter's family left in the National Library of Scotland—fares little better, and scarcely mentions the action in which he died. Even the immediate participants in this action, Captain Tanner and Private Beaven, differ in the details they record in their letters. All these varying accounts demonstrate how difficult it was to create coherent narratives of the war, or to locate individual experience within its wider movements. Vera Brittain struggled to find 'coherence in [her] mind', or any 'military purpose', regarding her fiancé's death, even once she had learned more or less how it occurred.[3] For combatants, the significance of actions often seemed equally elusive. Marc Bloch later became one of France's most influential historians, and his *Memoirs of War 1914–15* (*Souvenirs de Guerre, 1914–15*, 1969) vividly describes fighting on the Marne. Yet he acknowledges that he had 'little comprehension of the battle' as a coherent action. 'It was the victory of the Marne', he explains, 'but I would not have known what to call it'. Writing about another of the French army's huge battles, Verdun, Jules Romains comments that 'there was no lack of eyewitnesses, but none of them could get far enough away from the drama to see it as a whole'. The distancing required, he reflects, might be impossible for any individual. 'What hope was there of finding a single brain capable of envisaging the

---

[1] Letters, 1912–14, of Nigel Trotter to his family, National Library of Scotland, Acc. 6614.

[2] Brigadier-General Sir James E. Edmonds, *History of the Great War: Based on Official Documents: By Direction of the Historical Section of the Committee of Imperial Defence: Military Operations: France and Belgium* (London: Macmillan/Shearer, 1922–47), II: 77, 69, 76.

[3] Vera Brittain, *Testament of Youth: An Autobiographical Study of the Years 1900–1925* (1933; rpt. London: Virago, 2004), 215, 217.

war as a whole, of seeing it steadily through all its endless ramifications', he asks in *Verdun* (*Les Hommes de Bonne Volonté*, 1938), adding that 'the connexion between…partial visions…could be seen only by some watcher far removed from humanity'. Siegfried Sassoon hints at how distant any human observer might have needed to be. In *Memoirs of an Infantry Officer* (1930), he recalls contemplating, during the Somme offensive of 1916, 'the War as it might be envisioned by the mind of some epic poet a hundred years hence'.[4]

Mere Automatons

The war's scarcely imaginable violence and chaos, Chapter 1 suggested, generally resisted effective description. This chapter outlines particular challenges to narrative, beginning with the problems of scale and complexity suggested in the comments above. The difficulties concerned inevitably affected the writing of histories, obliged somehow to assimilate eyewitness testimony, 'partial vision', and scattered actions into a coherent account of battles and campaigns. One of the first volumes of the official *History* opens with a Preface acknowledging that 'on a modern battlefield…knowledge of events is extraordinarily local', and warning of the limitations of individual testimony.[5] Its own account of actions preceding the First Battle of Ypres demonstrates how difficult these problems were to resolve for historians. For the literary genres of autobiography and the novel—the main concerns of this chapter—difficulties with individual testimony were compounded by the war's assault on individuality itself. Autobiography and the novel each depend on, and assert, a sense of significance in individual life and in the experiences and decisions shaping it. Yet individuals risked being overwhelmed by the war's scale, its destructiveness of so many lives, and the nature of its military organization. 'The whole affair was so huge', R. H. Mottram reflects in *The Spanish Farm* sequence (1924–7), 'that the individual man was reduced and reduced in importance until he went clean out of sight.'

---

[4] Marc Bloch, *Memoirs of War, 1914–15*, trans. Carole Fink (1969; rpt. Ithaca, NY: Cornell University Press, 1988), 94–6; Jules Romains, *Verdun: The Prelude to Battle*, trans. Gerard Hopkins (New York: Alfred A. Knopf, 1939), 36–7, 35; Siegfried Sassoon, *The Complete Memoirs of George Sherston* (1937; rpt. London: Faber and Faber, 1972), 362.

[5] Edmonds, *History of the Great War: Based on Official Documents*, I: viii.

Mottram records that the Somme, once again, marked a key stage in this disappearance:

> at the beginning, there had been the personal appeal to enlist, the attraction of units whose names or deeds called…upon local patriotism or historical glory, or whose terms of enlistment or the personality of whose commanders were well known and appreciated. All this was lost to men's minds during the Somme.

This loss was followed, Mottram re-iterates, by 'the disappearance from the War of the last shred of individuality'.[6]

During the war, popular fiction owed some of its appeal to imaginative reversals of this process. Popular narratives generally continue to emphasize opportunities for glorious adventure on the battlefields, sustaining faiths in living or dying like a hero still widely shared in 1914. Capt F. S. Brereton's patriotic boys' stories, for example, maintain conventions of imperial or military romance established in the later nineteenth century by the novels of G. A. Henty. *Under French's Command: A Story of the Western Front from Neuve Chapelle to Loos* (1915) offers a resounding encouragement to enlistment. Brereton suggests that a determined seventeen year old might have little difficulty in joining the army—under age—and in becoming an accomplished pilot and despatch-rider within a few weeks. Rapid promotion naturally follows for his hero, further assured by his easy mastery of dastardly German spies. Some of the same patriotic spirit informs the popular short stories of 'Sapper' (H. C. McNeile), published in the *Daily Mail* and other journals throughout the war. 'Jim Brent's V.C.' and many other stories share the immense confidence in individual enterprise of *Under French's Command*.

Yet McNeile used his experience of the war—as an officer in the Royal Engineers, hence his pseudonym—to ensure that his stories offered, alongside their idealism, details realistic enough to persuade an adult audience of the authenticity of what they read. In an 'Introductory' section to his collection *Men, Women and Guns* (1916)—which sold 100,000 copies by the end of the war—Sapper replies convincingly to a hypothetical aunt who asks, 'What does it feel like to be shelled?' His answer is candid about the sodden and muddy landscape of the war in

---

[6] R. H. Mottram, *The Spanish Farm Trilogy* (New York: Dial Press, 1927), 455, 302.

general. It also emphasizes the helplessness of soldiers during a barrage, their life or death decreed by the unpredictable flight of the shells. 'Nothing in this war has so struck those who have fought in it as its impersonal nature', Sapper continues in the collection's first story, 'The Motor Gun'. The story adds that 'from the day the British Army moved north, and the first battle of Ypres commenced—and with it trench warfare as we know it now—it has been, save for a few interludes, a contest between automatons, backed by every known scientific device'.[7] Emphasis on such 'interludes' nevertheless allowed wartime popular writing to continue celebrating individual agency, even when acknowledging, like Sapper, the scarcity of opportunities for its exercise. The war's impersonal nature was more firmly focused in later writing, which generally shows individual fate determined quite independently of individual will—by 'scientific device', the random flight of shells, and the vagaries of military organization. 'What chance was there for anyone in that war of guns and mathematics', one former soldier wondered. Another—George Coppard, in *With a Machine Gun to Cambrai* (1968)—simply describes war as a lottery, with death awaiting, almost inevitably, 'those with ill-fated regimental numbers'.[8]

Even before facing the guns, soldiers were often struck by another malignancy in numbers. Almost without exception, novels, journals, and memoirs describing arrival in France mention soldiers' surprise on discovering they were to be transported in railway trucks whose designated capacity was 'Hommes 40, Chevaux 8' (40 men, 8 horses). As soldiers moved closer to the Front, equations of man and beast often extended into equivalences of man and machine. These appear very widely in writing about the war. Liam O'Flaherty's soldiers in his novel *Return of the Brute* (1929) consider army authority a 'great machine that stretched, covering the whole battle front'. Frederic Manning's novel *The Middle Parts of Fortune* (1929) likewise describes military organization as 'an inflexible and inhuman machine'—an 'inscrutable power ... utterly indifferent to ... individuals', who are moved around France as if 'mere automatons'. For John Dos Passos, US infantry are likewise 'automatons

---

[7] 'Sapper', *Men, Women and Guns* (London: Hodder and Stoughton, 1916), 15, 27.

[8] E. N. Gladden, 'At Messines Ridge in 1917', in C. B. Purdom (ed.), *True World War I Stories: Sixty Personal Narratives of the War* (1930; rpt. London: Robinson, 1999), 121; George Coppard, *With a Machine Gun to Cambrai* (1980; rpt. London: Macmillan, 1986), 49.

in uniforms', products of a process of 'making men into machines' emphasized by the titles of individual books in his novel *Three Soldiers* (1921)—'Making the Mould', 'The Metal Cools', 'Machines', 'Rust', 'Under the Wheels'. 'The war machine...needed so much flesh and blood to keep it working', Siegfried Sassoon reflects in *Sherston's Progress* (1936), acknowledging that he had come to be moved about by it 'automatically'. Like Mottram, Sassoon considered the period of the Battle of the Somme a turning point. Thinking about the effects of conscription, fully enforced a few weeks before it began, he records in *Memoirs of an Infantry Officer* that 'the War had become undisguisedly mechanical and inhuman. What in earlier days had been drafts of volunteers were now droves of victims'.[9]

D. H. Lawrence describes the conscription process in his novel *Kangaroo* (1923). Experience of it helped persuade him that even on the Home Front 'every man was turned into an automaton...turned into a mere thing'.[10] The same transformation threatened women at the time, drawn in large numbers into work in munitions factories, the Army Service Corps, or the Voluntary Aid Detachment (VAD). Soulless, exhausting routines and 'tutelage to horror and death as a V.A.D nurse', described in *Testament of Youth*, left Vera Brittain feeling 'at last, the complete automaton'.[11] Military or industrial routines suppressed individual will and selfhood: hospital work further questioned the physical constitution of the self, threatened by innumerable intrusions, mutilations, and amputations. This questioning extends throughout a subgenre of war writing, detailing what the French army surgeon Georges Duhamel describes as the 'savage dispersal of human bodies' resulting from 'noisy, complicated mechanism...the stupid machine of war'.[12] The fragmentation and disintegration of the body is a central concern of hospital memoirs such as Duhamel's *New Book of Martyrs* (*Vie des*

---

[9] Liam O'Flaherty, *Return of the Brute* (1929: rpt. Dublin: Wolfhound Press, 1998), 56; Frederic Manning, *The Middle Parts of Fortune: Somme and Ancre, 1916* (1929; rpt. London: Peter Davies, 1977), 92, 181–22, 54; John Dos Passos, *Three Soldiers* (1921; rpt. New York: Sun Dial Press, 1937), 331; Sassoon, *Complete Memoirs of George Sherston*, 653, 382.

[10] D. H. Lawrence ['Lawrence H. Davison'], *Movements in European History* (1921; rpt. Oxford: Oxford University Press, 1971), 312–13.

[11] Brittain, *Testament*, 419.

[12] Georges Duhamel, *The New Book of Martyrs*, trans. Florence Simmonds (London: William Heinemann, 1918), 108, 192.

Martyrs, 1917), the US field-hospital director Mary Borden's *The Forbidden Zone* (1929), and the VAD nurse Enid Bagnold's *Diary Without Dates* (1918). It also figures in the novelist May Sinclair's *Journal of Impressions in Belgium* (1915), which records work with an ambulance unit and with hospital patients described as 'repeated units of torture... ruled by some inhuman mathematics and given over to pure transcendent pain'.[13]

Manning's soldiers recognize that 'they had nothing; not even their own bodies, which had become mere implements of warfare'.[14] Threatened in body and spirit, reduced to implement or automaton, the individual in wartime scarcely offered its conventional potential to narrative imagination. Outside the pages of popular fiction, empowered individuality might have seemed buried in the muddy earth of the trenches, remaining visible only in the air above them. In his memoir *Sagittarius Rising* (1936), Cecil Lewis suggests that pilots continued to enjoy, almost uniquely, 'a sense of mastery over mechanism', and an opportunity 'to have your life in your own hands, to use your own skill, single-handed, against the enemy'. Pilot-poets such as Paul Bewsher shared Lewis's conviction that this single-handed combat even sustained some sense of chivalry or knightly honour. In 'Towards Lillers', looking from the trenches 'up to the high above aeroplanes', the solider-poet Ivor Gurney likewise suggests of pilots that 'honour rides on the frame with them... | As the heroes of Marathon'. For Lewis, one-to-one combat in the air was at any rate infinitely preferable to sitting 'in a muddy trench while some one who had no personal enmity against you loosed off a gun, five miles away, and blew you to smithereens—and did not know he had done it'.[15]

Flying even offered a version of the distanced, godlike perspective Jules Romains considered so difficult to imagine during the war. *Sagittarius Rising* regularly records looking down 'with detachment, dispassionately' toward massed armies struggling beneath, while also being able to look 'fifty, sixty, seventy miles beyond... so much beyond'. In Barbusse's *Under Fire* (1916), an aviator recalls similar detachment from the armies while hearing murmurous, mingling prayers from two 'exactly

[13] May Sinclair, *A Journal of Impressions in Belgium* (London: Hutchinson, 1915), 47.

[14] Manning, *Middle Parts of Fortune*, 205.

[15] Cecil Lewis, *Sagittarius Rising* (1936; London: Warner, 1998), 160, 45; Ivor Gurney, *Collected Poems of Ivor Gurney*, ed. P. J. Kavanagh (Oxford: Oxford University Press, 1982), 112.

similar' Sunday morning services, one on either side of No Man's Land, 'unified in the heights of the sky where [he] was suspended'.[16] Flying also allowed Cecil Lewis, gifted with an aureate lyricism, the opportunity for many colourful descriptions of earth and sky. Similar tactics contribute a surviving sense of romance and heroism to other accounts of life in the Royal Flying Corps, such as the wartime flying ace Billy Bishop's memoir *Winged Warfare* (1918), V. M. Yeates's autobiographical novel *Winged Victory* (1934), and Capt. W. E. Johns's 'Biggles' stories for children. Description in 'The Bomber' (1932) of flying in 'the first gleam of dawn', above 'a vast basin of indigo and deep purple shadows, stretching, it seemed, to eternity' is typical of vivid accounts of life as a pioneer pilot, some based on Johns's own service on the Western Front.[17]

War Time

Even the airmen, though, were not immune to other challenges the Great War imposed on narrative convention. Novel and autobiography conventionally show the shaping of personal destiny by experience, and its evolution, through time, towards a point of fulfilment and fixity sufficient for a satisfactory sense of closure. But opportunities for an individual life to evolve fully and meaningfully—or to reach a coherent conclusion—were greatly reduced by the war, in a whole range of ways. For front-line soldiers, trapped in the stalemate of trench warfare, time scarcely seemed to flow as once it had, but to be immobilized in dreary, immeasurable extension. 'Time went by, but no one felt the passage of it, for the shadow of death lay over the dial', Edmund Blunden records in his memoir *Undertones of War* (1928), while Mottram suggests that 'the great art of war lay not in killing Germans but in killing time'. Ford Madox Ford's central figure in his *Parade's End* novel sequence (1924–8) worries over 'eternal hours when Time itself stayed still as the true image of bloody War'.[18] Yet 'months of boredom' of the kind Sapper mentions

[16] Lewis, *Sagittarius Rising*, 57, 93; Henri Barbusse, *Under Fire* (1916), trans. Robin Buss (Harmondsworth: Penguin, 2003), 260.

[17] Capt. W. E. Johns, *Biggles: Pioneer Air Fighter* (London: Dean and Sons, 1961), 125.

[18] Edmund Blunden, *Undertones of War* (1928; rpt. Harmondsworth: Penguin, 1986), 169; Mottram, *Spanish Farm*, 432; Ford Madox Ford, *Parade's End* (1924–8; rpt. Harmondsworth: Penguin, 1982), 569.

were also, he remarks, 'punctuated by moments of intense fright'—
sometimes intense enough further to suppress a conventional sense of
chronology. David Jones's *In Parenthesis* (1937) describes the last minute
before an attack is launched at zero hour as a 'taut millennium'. In *A Subaltern on the Somme* (1928), Max Plowman records tensions disrupting
not only the ordinary sense of time, but even the tense systems of ordinary language. To employ the phrase 'in an hour's time', he remarks, was
a way of inadvertently 'challenging Fate'. Instead, it was better 'to forget
"I shall"…"if" stands before every prospect, and it is no small "if" in
this war'.[19]

Manning's central figure in *The Middle Parts of Fortune* experiences
'the shock and violence of [an] attack' with similar intensity, as a 'peril-
ous instant' or 'timeless interval', somehow 'lived instantaneously'.
Richard Aldington's main character in *Death of a Hero* (1929) also recalls
battle as 'a timeless confusion…he did not know how many days and
nights it lasted, lost completely the sequence of events, found great gaps
in his conscious memory'. An Austrian soldier, Fritz Kreisler, likewise
identifies a 'curious indifference of the memory to values of time and
space'. He recalls of the experience of battle that 'two or three events
which took place in different localities seem merged into one, while in
other instances recollection of the chronological order of things is missing'. Marc Bloch struggles similarly with chronology in describing the
Battle of the Marne. He acknowledges that 'my recollections of that day
are not altogether precise…poorly articulated, a discontinuous series of
images, vivid in themselves but badly arranged like a reel of movie film
that showed here and there large gaps and the unintended reversal of
certain scenes'.[20] Forms of apparent reversal on the battlefield were not
necessarily the result only of confused memory. In his propaganda travelogue *Over There: Scenes on the Western Front* (1915), Arnold Bennett
mentions an experience familiar to most soldiers—that shells, travelling
faster than sound, exploded before their firing could be heard. 'The
sounds reach your ears in inverse order—if you are alive', Bennett records

[19] 'Sapper', *Men. Women and Guns*, 282; David Jones, *In Parenthesis* (1937; rpt. London:
Faber and Faber, 1963), 159; Max Plowman ['Mark VII'], *A Subaltern on the Somme: in 1916*
(1927; rpt. New York: E. P. Dutton, 1928), 54.
[20] Manning, *Middle Parts of Fortune*, 3; Richard Aldington, *Death of a Hero* (1929; rpt.
London: Hogarth Press, 1984), 323; Fritz Kreisler, *Four Weeks in the Trenches: The War Story
of a Violinist* (Boston/New York: Houghton Mifflin, 1915), 2; Bloch, *Memoirs of War*, 89.

an officer explaining.[21] Erich Maria Remarque's soldiers in *All Quiet on the Western Front* (1929) encounter an equally disturbing reversal, noticing as they march towards a battle that many coffins have already been prepared in anticipation of its results.

Prior to the war, one of Robert Graves's characters suggests in his play *But it Still Goes On* (1930), 'afterwards always came after before. Now it doesn't, necessarily, at all'. Distortions in the usual order of life and death, and in the flow of time generally, could be encountered even on the Home Front. As Vera Brittain records, letters from soldiers serving in France generally took at least four days to be delivered in Britain, so 'the writer since sending them had had time to die over and over again'. Letters could easily arrive at home—and did arrive, in Brittain's experience—some time after families had received news of the author's death from the War Office. Her account of anguished waiting for news resembles descriptions of alternating stasis and crisis at the Front. 'The clock', she recalls, 'marking off each hour of dread, struck into the immobility of tension with the shattering effect of a thunderclap'.[22] For the home population generally, there were other ways in which the clock struck with renewed vigour during the war years. Legislation introduced under the Defence of the Realm Act had by 1915 curtailed pub opening hours in areas of the country deemed to be closely involved in the war effort. In 1921, these restrictions were extended nationwide. The pub-closing call, 'HURRY UP PLEASE IT'S TIME', punctuating the second section of T. S. Eliot's *The Waste Land*, seemed not only vaguely menacing but topical and newly familiar when the poem was first published in 1922. The metaphor employed by a psychoanalyst in Rebecca West's novel *The Return of the Soldier* (1918)—of the superego as 'a sort of barmaid of the soul that says, "Time's up, gentlemen"'—would likewise have been less intelligible three or four years previously.[23]

Another government measure obliged even teetotallers—indeed, the whole British population, including most of those serving abroad—to reconsider the nature of time and its passage. The wartime

[21] Arnold Bennett, *Over There: War Scenes on the Western Front* (London: Methuen, 1915), 66.

[22] Robert Graves, *But It Still Goes On* (London: Jonathan Cape, 1930), 295; Brittain, *Testament*, 121.

[23] Rebecca West, *The Return of the Soldier* (1918; rpt. London: Virago, 2004), 163.

need to conserve energy encouraged the acceptance in 1916 of the Summer Time Act—a measure first recommended by William Willett in 1907—decreeing that all clocks should be moved an hour forward in Britain on 21 May. The change was followed by the British Expeditionary Force in France on 14 June. As Germany had already adopted Summer Time on 30 April, its soldiers remained free to boast, as Henry Williamson recalls, that their 'proper place in the sun' was an hour ahead of Britain—a difference which occasionally caused confusion.[24] It had previously raised doubts about the timing of any impromptu Christmas truces, and even about the exact moment at which the war began on 4 August 1914, as C. E. Montague mentions in his novel *Rough Justice* (1924)—actually at 11pm, British time; midnight in Germany.

Within Britain, Summer Time was hotly debated in the newspapers, and made a strong impression on the public when finally introduced—children even asking to be allowed to stay up to see the clocks adjusted. Set in London in 1916, Arnold Bennett's *The Pretty Lady* (1918) mentions early impressions of 'the ingenious process of lengthening the summer days by altering clocks'. Bennett records that 'long after ten o'clock… an exquisite faint light lingering in the sky still revealed the features of the people in the streets'. Seven years later, the change still seemed topical enough to Virginia Woolf to mention in *Mrs Dalloway* (1925), set in 1923. Like Bennett, Woolf records how slowly the summer sky 'paled and faded' above the city streets, in consequence of 'the great revolution of Mr Willett's summer time'.[25] In the streets of Britain, as in the trenches in France, the war's 'revolution' in the hours seemed to be changing the experience of time itself, adding a further significance to posters distributed in May 1916 to warn the public of an 'Alteration of Time' (Fig. 8). After serving as an infantryman throughout the conflict, J. B. Priestley even wondered whether 'the very hours began shrinking during the murderous imbecility of the First World War. I will swear that afternoons were never the same again'. Siegfried Sassoon reflects more strangely that

[24] Henry Williamson, *A Fox under My Cloak* (1955; rpt. Stroud: Alan Sutton, 1996), 49.

[25] Arnold Bennett, *The Pretty Lady* (1918; rpt. Leek, Staffordshire: Churnet Valley Books, 2009), 277; Virginia Woolf, *Mrs Dalloway* (1925; rpt. Harmondsworth: Penguin, 1975), 178–9.

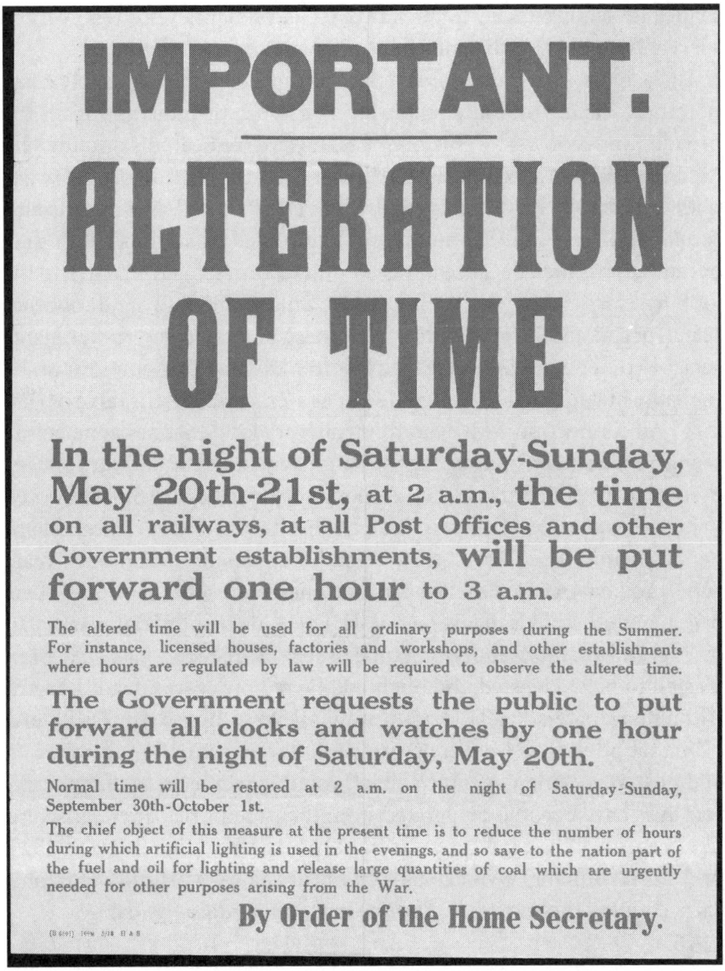

FIG 8 A Home Office poster informing the public of the first-ever introduction of Summer Time, in May 1916.

© Imperial War Museums (Art. IWM PST 5879)

a clock he acquired early in the war years had a manner noticeably more 'alert and inquisitive' than any of its predecessors in his home.[26]

Uneasiness with the altered passage of the hours was inevitably compounded, during and after the war, by a sense of interruption in the broader movements of history. Feelings of radical disjuncture are described in many accounts of the times. Thinking back across the twentieth century in his autobiography *Margin Released* (1962), Priestley recalls that 'the First War cut deeper and played more tricks with time because it *was* first, because it was bloodier…a great jagged crack in the looking-glass'. One world, he adds 'ended in 1914 and another one…began about 1919, with a wilderness of smoke and fury, outside sensible time, lying between them'. Ford's *Parade's End* employs much the same metaphor, describing the war as a 'crack across the table of History'. 'All connection with everything of every kind that has gone before seems to have been broken', Henry James concluded of the war's effects, even a few weeks after it began. A month or so later, May Sinclair noted in her *Journal of Impressions in Belgium* that 'things that existed and happened before the War…existed and happened a hundred years ago…You have ceased to have any personal interest in them.' In a novel begun in 1918, *Bid Me to Live* (1960), H. D. (Hilda Doolittle) remarks that by the end of the war it sometimes seemed that 'the past had been blasted to hell…blasted and blighted, the old order was dead'. Richard Aldington, married to H.D. until 1919, likewise suggests in *Death of a Hero* that 'adult lives were cut sharply into three sections—pre-war, war, and post-war…many people will tell you that whole areas of their pre-war lives have become obliterated from their memories. Pre-war seems like prehistory'. 'We say "pre-war" and "post-war", rather as we say B.C. or A.D.', Wyndham Lewis explains on the first page of his autobiographical account of the war years, *Blasting and Bombardiering* (1937).[27]

[26] J. B. Priestley, *Margin Released: A Writer's Reminiscences and Reflections* (London: Heinemann, 1962), 29; Siegfried Sassoon, *Siegfried's Journey: 1916–1920* (London: Faber and Faber, 1945), 121.

[27] Priestley, *Margin Released*, 88; Ford, *Parade's End*, 510; Henry James, Letter of 2 Sept. 1914 to Mrs Richard Watson Gilder, *The Letters of Henry James*, ed. Percy Lubbock (London: Macmillan, 1920), II: 416–17; Sinclair, *Journal*, 134; H.D., *Bid Me to Live* (1960; rpt. London: Virago, 1984), 24; Aldington, *Death of a Hero*, 199; Wyndham Lewis, *Blasting and Bombardiering* (1937; rpt. London: John Calder, 1982), 1.

Redundant Genres and Mythical Realms

Fracture and disjuncture in history, and even in the passing of the hours, offered particular opportunities for the short story, widely exploited during the war. Convenient for newspapers and magazines seeking succinct, war-related material, short stories were also well suited to describing 'interludes', 'timeless intervals', or hectic passages of action Sapper and other authors identified as characteristic of war experience. But experience of this kind generally denied the meaningful development of life through time conventionally required by extended narrative forms, and particularly resisted some of the ways these had developed in the Victorian period and the earlier twentieth century. Enlightenment ideals of progress and improvement had encountered few major historical obstacles during this period. Faith in these ideals continued to underwrite forms of fiction—in particular, *bildungsromane* such as Charles Dickens's *David Copperfield* (1849–50), or Compton Mackenzie's *Sinister Street* (1913–14)—which trace the gradual education and advancement of individuals towards maturity, self-understanding, and a satisfactory position within society. Mackenzie suggests a kind of epitaph for this genre when he recalls almost unconsciously doodling 'names like Louvain and Ypres' over the manuscript of *Sinister Street* as he completed its second volume later in 1914.[28] A violent and changeful world, 'jagged cracks' separating phases of personal experience, social instabilities imposed by the war, and the uncertainty even of personal survival, scarcely encouraged the *bildungsroman* form, even inverting its usual patterns. Many Great War narratives follow a kind of *unbildungs*—an education leading not to satisfactory stability, but towards disillusion and disaster. This pattern shapes novels such as C. E. Montague's *Rough Justice*, J. L. Hodson's *Grey Dawn—Red Night* (1929), and Henry Williamson's ironically entitled *The Patriot's Progress* (1930), as well as *How Dear is Life* (1954) in his *Chronicle of Ancient Sunlight* sequence (1951–69). In each, the idealism of recruits is worn down by wearisome military training, then overwhelmed by the murderous experience of the trenches. Much the same pattern is followed in David Jones's epic account, in the intermingled prose and verse of *In Parenthesis*, of experience leading up to the Battle of the Somme. A variant

---

[28] Compton Mackenzie, *Gallipoli Memories* (London: Cassell, 1929), 2.

appears in Ernest Raymond's *Tell England* (1922). Raymond's main character narrowly escapes complete 'discouragement and debasement' at Gallipoli, avoided through religious faith and through recollection of the sporting ideals which the first half of the novel shows him learning at an English public school.[29] More muted optimism, and a similar division between public-school novel and war novel, figure in Stephen McKenna's equally popular *Sonia* (1917), which had gone through more than twenty editions by 1921.

The pattern also shapes many autobiographical accounts of the war— Montague's *Disenchantment* (1922), for example, or Bernard Adams's *Nothing of Importance* (1917). Adams's choice of title employs an irony similar to Remarque's *All Quiet on the Western Front*, his Preface anticipating that the period he covers, between October 1915 and July 1916, will be dismissed in official histories as one in which 'nothing of importance' occurred. Experience of the Front he records is eventful enough, though the most significant development is in his attitude to the war. A classical scholar by training, Adams regularly seeks Homeric analogies for the current conflict, acknowledges its 'deadly fascination and excitement', and finds his initial experience of it 'thrills like the turning up of the footlights'.[30] His enthusiasms and descriptive powers—extending into several maps and diagrams—make *Nothing of Importance* an unusually good introduction to the conditions of trench warfare, at least as these had developed after a year or so of the war. Later sections of *Nothing of Importance* go on to recognize the limitations of his initial innocence and idealism, and to express disillusion with the 'vile instrument' of the war and the 'cheap journalism' and propaganda used to support it. Like so many of the writers quoted above, Adams also comes to recognize the insignificance of individual life, and its frailty—'unutterably weak and powerless'—when faced with 'this irresistible impersonal machine, this war'.[31] Poignancy is added to his views by the publication of *Nothing of Importance*, with a memorial introduction, in 1917—the year he died, of wounds, after leading an attack.

---

[29] Ernest Raymond, *Tell England: A Study in a Generation* (1922; rpt. London: Cassell, 1929), 318.

[30] Bernard Adams, *Nothing of Importance: A Record of Eight Months at the Front with a Welsh Battalion: October, 1915, to June, 1916* (London: Methuen, 1917), xvi, 299, 95.

[31] Ibid. 302, 297, 193.

Conditions war imposed were no more favourable for genres and modes longer established than the *bildungsroman*. Neither tragedy nor comedy could be conventionally employed in narrating the experience of the war years, though there was more potential for the latter genre than might have been expected. Bernard Adams finds a particular appeal, even 'greatness', in laughter 'uttered beneath the canopy of ever-impending death'.[32] Wyndham Lewis, Robert Graves, and many other memoirists likewise recall humour playing a great and indispensable part in soldiers' lives. R. C. Sherriff's play *Journey's End* (1929) develops dark laughter in several forms, some—arising from the eccentricities of the officers' servant—drawing on long-standing comic traditions still at work in the Great War episodes of Rowan Atkinson's *Blackadder* television series, late in the twentieth century. Other conventional components of comedy—romance and relationship—might have seemed in shorter supply in wartime, at any rate in military contexts largely or exclusively male. For many writers, including Remarque, soldiers' comradeship was 'the finest thing that arose out of the war'.[33] It was sometimes seen—fairly explicitly in Patrick Miller's novel *The Natural Man* (1924)—as a sufficient substitute, temporarily at least, for relations with women. Later commentators, and later novelists, such as Susan Hill in *Strange Meeting* (1971), have often explored its homoerotic or homosexual potentials. At the time, constraints on publishing, and in society generally—as well as the outlook of most of the authors concerned—thoroughly prevented development of these potentials. Even reticent treatment of homosexuality in *Despised and Rejected* (1918) by 'A. T. Fitzroy' (Rose Allatini) drew strong condemnation during the novel's prosecution, though this had been instigated, under the Defence of the Realm Act, principally on the grounds of its promotion of pacifism.

Conventional romantic relationships nevertheless play a strong part in Great War fiction, including some of the best of it. They figure centrally in Mottram's *Spanish Farm* sequence, Ford's *Parade's End*, Hugh Walpole's *The Dark Forest* (1916), John Dos Passos's *Three Soldiers*, Enid Bagnold's *The Happy Foreigner* (1920), Ernest Hemingway's *A Farewell*

---

[32] Ibid. 116.
[33] Erich Maria Remarque, *All Quiet on the Western Front* (1929), trans. A. W. Wheen (London: Mayflower, 1963), 23.

to Arms (1929), and Katherine Mansfield's short story 'An Indiscreet Journey' (1924). Yet with the partial exception of Parade's End, romance in these narratives does not lead to any comedic conclusion, but highlights instead the fragile, ephemeral nature of all emotions and relationships in the face of war's ubiquitous destructiveness. Relationships reaffirming the significance of individuals and their emotions in the end confirm only the inevitability of its loss. On the whole, it was only in popular fiction written during the war—in novels such as McKenna's Sonia, or Ruby M. Ayres's Richard Chatterton, V.C. (1915), which had sold nearly 90,000 copies by 1918—that romance continued to play a central and conventionally affirmative role. Inevitably, it was usually shown developing on the Home Front, often during periods when the hero was on leave. It works in this way, though in combination with some detailed descriptions of the trenches, in another popular novel about the war, Gilbert Frankau's Peter Jackson: Cigar Merchant: A Romance of Married Life (1920), which went on to sell nearly 200,000 copies by the early 1930s. Frankau served in the artillery and regularly contributed poetry to the trench journal The Wipers Times. Like Sapper, he was able to combine convincing authenticity in describing the war, which deeply damages the health and equanimity of his protagonist, alongside elements reassuringly resisting the destructiveness of the times. An ex-Etonian, Peter Jackson begins and ends the novel in affluence guaranteed by his enterprising business sense. He is also much restored by the 'romance of married life'. As well as helping him back towards health—with the assistance of her father, knighted for research into shell shock—his adoring wife arranges an idyllic marriage for his war-wounded cousin, gradually persuades Peter to fall thoroughly in love with her again, and soon bears him a son. The novel ends with health restored, family relations improved, a huge dance spreading across London on the day of the armistice, and a strong sense of wishes romantically fulfilled.

Happy or comedic conclusions of this sort are understandably rare in Great War fiction. Given the omnipresence of death at the time, the apparent scarcity of conventionally tragic narratives might seem more surprising, though reasons for it may not be hard to suggest. So unfavourable for the exercise of personal will and agency, military life did not offer an ideal context for exalted or tragic vision of individuals' relations with their destiny. The omnipresence of death likewise tended to diminish the tragic potential of any individual demise. Even on the Home Front, death's meaningfulness was diluted by its multiplicity. Like Vera Brittain, thinking of a loved one having 'time to die over and over again', in *Bid Me to Live* H.D.'s heroine wrestles with the conviction that her husband 'was dead already, already he had died a half dozen times, he was always dying'.[34] At the Front, comrades 'always dying' left most soldiers with a resigned familiarity with death, rather than much sense of awe. 'When a man has seen so many dead', Remarque's narrator reflects, 'he cannot understand any longer why there should be so much anguish over a single individual'. One of Sapper's stories likewise suggests that 'one gets so used to death on a large scale that it almost ceases to affect one'. In *Sagittarius Rising*, Cecil Lewis records regularly eating dinner while 'faced by the empty chairs of men you had laughed and joked with at lunch. They were gone. The next day new men would laugh and joke from those chairs.'[35] Beyond the relative tranquillity of Lewis's Royal Flying Corps mess, the dead often turned out—still more disturbingly—*not* to be gone, but to remain as cadaverous dinner companions, embedded in the walls or floors of trenches. 'Some parts of the parapet had been built up with dead men', Frank Richards records in *Old Soldiers Never Die* (1934), 'their teeth were showing so that they seemed to be grinning horribly down on us.' George Coppard also recalls 'the dead sandwiched so close to us. We took our meals and tried to sleep with them as our neighbours.' They could even be rowdy neighbours. *All Quiet on the Western Front* mentions that the corpses left lying in No Man's Land 'hiss, belch and make movements. The gases in them make noises.' For Georges Duhamel, death had in general become

> closely bound up with the things of life … its daily operations are on a vast scale … it has become a thing so ordinary that it no longer causes us to suspend our usual activities, as it used to do: we eat and drink beside the dead, we sleep amidst the dying, we laugh and sing in the company of corpses.

[34] H.D., *Bid Me to Live*, 32.
[35] Remarque, *All Quiet*, 120; 'Sapper', *Men, Women and Guns*, 300; Lewis, *Sagittarius Rising*, 59.

'Out there, we walked quite friendly up to Death,— | Sat down and ate beside him, cool and bland', Wilfred Owen likewise remarks in his poem 'The Next War'.[36]

Guy Chapman's memoir *A Passionate Prodigality* (1933) recalls reading Thomas Hardy's *Jude the Obscure* (1895) in the trenches and finding the novel's tragedy inadequate to 'the long crucifixion of the men in the front line'. Describing the random, commonplace nature of death at the Front, Ford Madox Ford similarly concludes that 'the idea of tragedy is just incongruous'.[37] Though inappropriate for tragedy, death's omnipresence, ordinariness—even dinner-table familiarity—had distinctive consequences for contemporary imagination. Robert Graves indicates some of these in *Goodbye to All That* (1929) when he recalls—another strange temporal inversion—that while he was recovering from near-fatal wounding on the Somme, both *The Times* and official communications to his family reported him as having died. Letters recently sent to him in France were returned, officially marked 'died of wounds—present location uncertain'.[38] As this verdict suggests, death during the war sometimes came to be considered not a cessation of existence, but merely a shift in its location: not an absolute boundary, but possibly a permeable one. Hodson's protagonist in *Grey Dawn—Red Night* is typical in thinking of dead comrades 'somewhere up there looking down as if from a high grand-stand, as cricketers do who have played a good innings and are now in the pavilion watching'. A character in *Journey's End* similarly reflects of death that 'it can't be very lonely there—with all those fellows. Sometimes I think it's lonelier here.' In a period when many people, in John Buchan's phrase, 'found the world of time strangely empty and eternity strangely thronged', there were obvious encouragements to think of death in some such manner. Or, as Jay Winter suggests in *Sites of*

[36] Frank Richards, *Old Soldiers Never Die* (1933; rpt. London: Faber and Faber, 1964), 199; Coppard, *Machine Gun to Cambrai*, 47; Remarque, *All Quiet*, 86; Duhamel, *New Book of Martyrs*, 210–11; Wilfred Owen, *Wilfred Owen: The Complete Poems and Fragments*, ed. Jon Stallworthy (London: Chatto and Windus, Hogarth Press, and Oxford University Press, 1983), I: 165.

[37] Guy Chapman, *A Passionate Prodigality: Fragments of Autobiography* (1933; rpt. London: Buchan and Enright, 1985), 136; Ford Madox Ford, 'A Day of Battle: Arms and the Mind' (1916), *The Ford Madox Ford Reader*, ed. Sondra J. Stang (London: Paladin, 1987), 460.

[38] Robert Graves, *Goodbye to All That*, rev edn (1957; rpt. Harmondsworth: Penguin, 2000), 188.

Memory, Sites of Mourning (1995), there should be no surprise in finding that 'the magical and mythical realm flared up at a time of mass death and destruction'.[39]

Evidence of this resurgence was especially marked in the expansion of the spiritualist movement. 'The importance of psychical investigation has never been so forcefully demonstrated to us as by the present great World War', Hereward Carrington claims in his study *Psychical Phenomena and the War* (1919). He goes on to insist that, despite appearances, none of the combatants had ' "died" in any real sense'. Instead, their bodies had been borne away by 'hosts of angels'—'not their mangled corpses, but their spirit bodies, unscathed by shot or shell'. By 1916, Graves records, there were 'thousands of mothers' subscribing to such views and 'getting in touch with their dead sons by various spiritualistic means'.[40] There were also fathers. Carrington records his indebtedness to Oliver Lodge, a distinguished scientist who published in 1916 a book-length account of spiritualist contacts with his son Raymond, killed in that year. *Raymond* went through numerous editions during the war, and was republished in 1922. Another, more sceptical father appears in J. M. Barrie's drama *A Well-Remembered Voice* (1918). Despite disdain for séances and spiritualism, he finds himself in conversation with his dead son, returned from the grave strangely convincingly, in Barrie's play, through theatre's potential to grant ghosts palpable presence on the stage. This potential was later put to good use in Noël Coward's play about the legacies of war, *Post-Mortem* (1930). Around the same time, the former war correspondent Philip Gibbs's novel *Darkened Rooms* (1928) indicated spiritualism's continuing hold on the imagination of the late 1920s.

Many other authors were intrigued by possible post-mortem or spiritual 'locations'. Sassoon mentions that it seemed, later in the war, as if long-dead 'companions of the Somme and Arras battles' still remained close to him.[41] In *Testament of Youth*, Vera Brittain describes patients

[39] J. L. Hodson, *Grey Dawn—Red Night* (London: Victor Gollancz, 1929), 206; R. C. Sherriff, *Journey's End* (1929; rpt. Harmondsworth: Penguin, 2000), 58; John Buchan, *The Battle of the Somme: First Phase* (London: Thomas Nelson, 1916), 108; Jay Winter, *Sites of Memory, Sites of Mourning: The Great War in European Cultural History* (1996; rpt. Cambridge: Cambridge University Press, 1998), 76.

[40] Hereward Carrington, *Psychical Phenomena and the War* (New York: Dodd, Mead, 1918), 1, 243, 254; Graves, *Goodbye to All That*, 192.

[41] Sassoon, *Siegfried's Journey*, 53.

convinced that when fighting raged again across the old ground of the Somme, during the retreat of 1918, comrades killed in earlier struggles there were once again fighting at their sides. Though generally dismissive of 'weird experience', Frank Richards acknowledges a similar belief, admitting that 'many of us...saw things on the Retirement'.[42] Brittain is sceptical of her patients' claims, but they were not so different from a pact she describes making herself, with her brother and her fiancé: that 'if a life existed beyond the grave', they 'would somehow come back and make [her] know of it'. She does not record this occurring, though the possibility had obvious imaginative appeal. Several of Rudyard Kipling's short stories are based around it, including 'A Madonna of the Trenches' (1924), in which a soldier simply concludes that real life '*begins* at death'.[43] Kipling further explores the afterlife in 'On the Gate: A Tale of '16' (1926), which does indeed show 'eternity strangely thronged'. It describes harassed angels trying to control entry to heaven, while almost overwhelmed by huge crowds recently destroyed on the battlefields of earth. Wyndham Lewis's fantasy *The Childermass* (1928) develops a similar scenario, describing a purgatorial landscape in which throngs of recent dead await entry to a heavenly city.

The possibility that 'life begins at death' was explored in another tale of 1916, Hugh Walpole's *The Dark Forest*, published that year. Debarred by poor eyesight from joining the British Army, Walpole eventually worked in St Petersburg for British propaganda, but first for the Red Cross in Russia in 1915. Describing work with casualties, his novel shares characteristics with the hospital-based narratives mentioned earlier. Depicting a Russian army hospital unit on the Eastern front, *The Dark Forest* also shares with many accounts of military life a close focus on friendships, frictions, and factions developing among diverse characters, thrown together by the war into intense interaction. In exploring this interaction, Walpole negotiates throughout with the implications of his title, drawn from the Russian proverb that 'the heart (or soul) of another is a dark forest'. His novel opens up an extraordinary number of pathways through such forests. Characters' inner lives are comprehensively illuminated by their eagerness—sometimes barely plausible—to

[42] Richards, *Old Soldiers Never Die*, 183.
[43] Brittain, *Testament*, 408; Rudyard Kipling, *Debits and Credits* (1926; rpt. Harmondsworth: Penguin, 1987), 191.

lend intimate diaries and journals to the narrator, or in other ways to unburden their thoughts and emotions to him, or to each other. These emotions are eventually illumined in a still stranger way—by the novel's transcendent conclusion, strongly suggesting, like Kipling's story, that the truest and most inviolable romance may be consummated only after death.

In this and other aspects, *The Dark Forest* is symptomatic of conditions shaping narrative in 1916, and for some time thereafter. It indicates, first of all, opportunities available more readily to Walpole than many other writers at the time. 'One must remember', Sassoon warns, 'that in 1916 very few candid comments on the war had appeared in print.'[44] There were good reasons why this was so. By 1916, additions made to the Defence of the Realm Act had more or less outlawed statements likely to damage public morale or the conduct of the war. These were banished not only from the newspapers, but also from literature, film, and public discourse generally. In writing about the Eastern Front and the Russian army, Walpole was a little freer, particularly in describing defeats, retreats, and casualties. By contrast, Mary Borden's account of front-line hospital work on the Western Front, *The Forbidden Zone*, completed in 1917, could not find a publisher during the war, and did not appear until twelve years later.

Borden is more candid than Walpole, describing mutilated patients and their wounds in meticulous detail. But Walpole's advantage, in the eyes of publishers, may not have been only in the restraint of his descriptions, but in the directness of his invitation to readers to look away from, or beyond them. Along with the popularity of writers such as Sapper, Donald Hankey, and Gilbert Frankau, *The Dark Forest* suggests that unremittingly candid description—even had censorship allowed it— was not necessarily what much of the public wanted during the war. An element of authenticity was desirable, but preferably in combination with some vision or affirmation which could distract readers from the direr realities of the day. Even Adams's *Nothing of Importance*, so direct and disillusioned in describing the Western Front, ends with a resounding affirmation of its author's Christian faith. The Angels of Mons, and the spiritualist movement, offer further indications of a preference

---

[44] Sassoon, *Siegfried's Journey*, 28–9.

for affirmation—for mythic consolation, offering in fantasy, religion, romance, or the supernatural some compensation for immediate terrors and disappointments. This urge was naturally most in evidence when the war was going badly, during the long retreat from Mons in 1914, or the alarming 'Retirement' of 1918. But it may have been present at some level throughout. It might further account for the oddly doubled thinking Chapter 1 described at work on the Home Front. Often at least partly aware of the nature of the war, through privately acquired information, the home population nevertheless continued to show tolerance, even enthusiasm, for mendacious accounts provided by press and propaganda. These had the obvious attraction of confirming not what readers might privately know or fear, but what they hoped for or wished to believe.

Horrible Realism

As Chapter 1 suggested, tolerance of the press generally did not extend far among serving soldiers, though there is evidence that they occasionally shared in their own way some of the inclinations outlined above. This appears in records of reading material favoured at the Front. Organized by agencies including the British War Library and the YMCA, and facilitated by a book-collection scheme in post offices, as many as 50,000 items were sent out weekly from around September 1915, with a particular demand expressed for action, adventure, mystery, and sometimes romance. There was some enthusiasm for action and adventure centred on the war itself. *Nothing of Importance* remarks that 'this stuff of Ian Hay's is awfully good', though Adams adds—in another version of doubled thinking—that *The First Hundred Thousand* provides 'good readable stuff', which is ideal not for the Front but to 'give to your people at home'. Hay, in Adams's view, chooses to miss too much out—familiar front-line experiences including 'the utter fed-upness and the dullness' and the consequences of being gassed.[45] Yet front-line soldiers were not always readier than civilians to welcome full, candid accounts of what they experienced so painfully in fact. In an article published in the *Guardian* a few weeks after the armistice, taking up the question 'What

---

[45] Adams, *Nothing of Importance*, 225.

did the soldier read during the Great War?', a former combatant suggests that in general 'soldiers avoid war-books when at the front'. He also offers a particular instance, of a soldier in the trenches, twice decorated for distinguished conduct, who nevertheless explained that 'he had tried to read Barbusse's "Le Feu," but that it had frightened him by its horrible realism'.[46]

His comments might have surprised other former soldiers. For Sassoon, and other ex-combatant writers, it was Barbusse's realism, produced powerfully and early in the war, which made his work so appealing and useful for their own. Sassoon found Barbusse's work 'deeply stimulating . . . really revealing the truth about the Front Line', used a quotation from it as epigraph for *Counter-Attack and Other Poems* (1918), and passed it on to Wilfred Owen when they were patients in Craiglockhart Hospital in Edinburgh in 1918. Henry Williamson likewise records his enthusiasm for 'reality, la verité' in *Le Feu*, and its usefulness as a model for his own writing.[47] Yet as the soldier quoted in the *Guardian* suggests—or Sassoon himself, in pointing out the shortage of 'candid' commentary about the war—Barbusse's realism still seemed fairly unfamiliar in 1918, and perhaps unwelcome, even to some of those who had experienced the realities of the war themselves. To the many difficulties confronting Great War narrative, there might therefore be added uncertainty about the existence of audiences for it. Much other evidence suggests that realistic accounts of the war seemed unfamiliar, 'horrible', or otherwise unwelcome not only immediately following the armistice, but for a longer period after 1918.

Some of this evidence is provided by a novel published in the next year—*The Secret Battle*, by A. P. Herbert, also a war poet. His novel is as exemplary as *The Dark Forest*—indicative, in this case, of a wide range of difficulties facing literature about the war in the period following its conclusion. *The Secret Battle* points to the most fundamental difficulty of all, suggesting profound uneasiness in any encounter between imagination and violent action. Herbert's central figure, Penrose, exemplifies the problem later summarized by Dorothy L. Sayers's patrician detective Lord Peter Wimsey in *The Unpleasantness at the Bellona Club* (1928):

---

[46] 'H.W.Y', 'Trench Libraries', *Manchester Guardian*, 31 Dec. 1918, 10.

[47] Sassoon, *Complete Memoirs of George Sherston*, 525; Henry Williamson, *The Wet Flanders Plain* (1929; rpt. London: Faber and Faber, 2009), 136.

that 'the War pressed hardly on imaginative men in responsible positions'. Despite genuine bravery, Penrose is an officer 'cursed with imagination' throughout his service at Gallipoli and on the Western Front,
repeatedly inhibited by 'imagining...hundreds of possible disasters',
and eventually executed, unjustly, for supposedly running away from a
bombardment. As his death follows from a disastrous interaction
between personal susceptibility and hostile circumstance, it seems
almost inevitable rather than—as so often in war conditions—merely
random or unlucky. As a result, *The Secret Battle* is unusually close to the
conventions of tragedy. Central interest in a figure doomed by his
'romantic, imaginative outlook' resembles some of Joseph Conrad's
tragic fiction, *Lord Jim* (1900) especially.[48]

This resemblance indirectly indicates a further problem for Great War
narrative—that after a century without major conflict, and in dealing
with violence on an unprecedented scale, its authors had few literary
models they could draw on or imitate. Popular, patriotic strains of war
fiction could follow the imperial romances of G. A. Henty and other
nineteenth-century writers. For authors intending more realistic, anti-
heroic treatment of the war, or of the moral issues it raised, among recent
writers only Conrad—sceptical of imperial romance and conventional
heroism—offered much promise. Even this was obviously limited in its
appropriateness for description of the trenches. The poet Herbert Read's
memoir *In Retreat* (1925) quotes Conrad before going on to describe the
British army's defeats and withdrawals in early 1918. In *Grey Dawn—Red
Night*, Hodson's protagonist includes *Lord Jim* among novels he takes
with him when embarking for the Front. In *A Test to Destruction* (1960),
Henry Williamson's protagonist rapidly works his way through most of
Conrad's major novels, intrigued in particular by his belief that *Lord Jim*
may address his own dread of cowardice. But Conrad himself wrote
directly about the war only in a few maritime short stories, and para-
digms his earlier novels offer do not figure extensively in the Great War
narrative developing during the 1920s.

Herbert had to wait for some of this development to occur before *The
Secret Battle* enjoyed much success. In a Preface for the second edition,

---

[48] Dorothy L. Sayers, *The Unpleasantness at the Bellona Club* (1928; rpt. London: Hodder
and Stoughton, 2003), 14; A. P. Herbert, *The Secret Battle* (1919; rpt. Oxford: Oxford
University Press, 1982), 128, 11, 5.

published in 1928, Winston Churchill particularly praised the novel for the 'sober truth of its descriptions' and for making public 'the prolonged and measureless torment' endured by the troops. Churchill knew both Gallipoli and the Western Front from his own experience, but he goes on to point out that the 'sober truth' about neither area may have been welcome when the novel was first published in 1919. Instead, he suggests that *The Secret Battle* may have been 'a little swept aside by the revulsion of the public mind from anything to do with the awful period just ended'.[49] In *Blasting and Bombardiering*, Wyndham Lewis recalls Ford Madox Ford remarking, in 1915, that 'when this War's over...one month after it's ended, it will be forgotten. Everybody will want to forget it—it will be bad form to mention it'.[50] Published in the year after the war's end, Herbert's novel suggests a conclusion only slightly at odds with Ford's or Churchill's. The war could not be forgotten. But Herbert's depiction of conflict as 'black and beastly...a necessary but disgusting business'[51] evidently held much less appeal than the containment of war experience, within an account of marital romance and successful business, which Gilbert Frankau offered in the same year in *Peter Jackson*. Read's experience with an early version of *In Retreat*, completed in 1919 and shaped by a 'stern oath of realism' taken during the war, further confirms this view of the public mind at the time. Read explains that he 'tried to publish this short narrative as soon as [he] had written it', but found that 'the state of the public mind, or at least, of that mind as localized in the minds of publishers and editors, refused anything so bleak. The war was still a sentimental illusion: it was a subject for pathos, for platitude, even for rationalization. It was not yet time for the simple facts'.[52] Other authors indicate similar difficulties with publishers and the public. Richard Aldington's *Death of a Hero* was also begun just after the war, but not published for another ten years. Mottram's *Spanish Farm* sequence was rejected several times, leading its author to conclusions about the public's preferences comparable to those Read and Churchill reached in 1919.

These preferences help explain a conclusion, or conundrum, often mentioned in commentary on Great War narrative—by Dominic Hibberd,

[49] Winston Churchill, Preface to Herbert, *The Secret Battle*, vii.

[50] Lewis, *Blasting and Bombardiering*, 185.

[51] Herbert, *Secret Battle*, 43.

[52] Herbert Read, *In Retreat* (London: Hogarth Press, 1925), 7.

for example, when he reflects that 'remarkably little was published about the realities of front-line fighting for nearly a decade after the Armistice'.[53] In this view, ten years of relative silence were followed by the production of war narratives in sudden profusion in the late 1920s and early 1930s. Auto-biographical writing published at the time included Edmund Blunden's *Undertones of War* (1928); Siegfried Sassoon's *Memoirs of a Fox-Hunting Man* (1928) and *Memoirs of an Infantry Officer* (1930); Max Plowman's *A Subaltern on the Somme* (1928); Robert Graves's *Goodbye to All That* (1929); Charles Edmonds's *A Subaltern's War* (1929); Mary Borden's *The Forbidden Zone* (1929); Vera Brittain's *Testament of Youth* (1933); and the translation of Ernst Jünger's *In Stahlgewittern* (1920) as *Storm of Steel* (1929). Fiction appearing around the end of the 1920s included Aldington's *Death of a Hero* (1929); Henry Williamson's *The Patriot's Progress* (1930); Frederic Manning's *The Middle Parts of Fortune* (1929); H. M. Tomlinson's *All Our Yesterdays* (1930); and in the USA, Ernest Hemingway's *A Farewell to Arms*, published in 1929. In the same year, Remarque's *Im Westen Nichts Neues* was translated into English, within a few months of its hugely successful publication in Germany. It was quickly made into a film, one of the first of the talkies, released in Britain in June 1930. A film of Sherriff's play *Journey's End*, first staged in 1928, had appeared earlier in the year.

This profuse output at the end of the 1920s is often attributed to Remarque's success, credited with convincing authors and publishers of an expanding market for realistic narratives, however dark and disturbing. Remarque's popularity was certainly influential. When reviewing *The Middle Parts of Fortune* in 1930, *The Times* pointed out that Manning addressed an audience already 'well read in "All Quiet on the Western Front"'.[54] One opportunistic publisher even approached a freelance writer, Evadne Price, with a proposal for a Remarque parody, 'All Quaint on the Western Front'. Understandably, Price did not think parody appropriate, and produced instead a novel describing nursing service in France, *Not So Quiet...* (1930), based on the diaries of a VAD nurse and published under the pseudonym Helen Zenna Smith. Yet Remarque's success is better understood not as a sole or sudden influence on war narrative at the end of the 1920s—several of the works listed above in any

[53] Dominic Hibberd, *The First World War* (London: Macmillan, 1990), 193.

[54] 'New Novels', *The Times*, 17 Jan. 1930, 8. The review was of the novel's expurgated version, published as *Her Privates We* (1930).

case pre-date *All Quiet on the Western Front*—but in the context of gradual developments throughout the decade. Influential memoirs—Montague's *Disenchantment* (1922), for example, or Philip Gibbs's *Realities of War* (1920), reassessing his work as a war correspondent—had been published in the earlier years of the decade. So had several outstanding novels of war experience. John Dos Passos's account of US infantry training and combat, *Three Soldiers*, appeared in 1921. Ford Madox Ford began publishing his *Parade's End* tetralogy in 1924. In the same year, helped by his mentor John Galsworthy, Mottram had completed and found a publisher for the early parts of his *Spanish Farm* sequence, eventually issued as a single volume in 1927.

The regular appearance of war narratives was accompanied and facilitated by steady changes in 'the public mind'. Remarque and other writers published at the end of the 1920s contributed further to these changes, providing visions of war bleaker than most of those appearing in earlier years, but the appeal of their writing also derived from shifts in outlook which had already taken place. The 'sentimental illusion', pathos, and platitude which Read attributed to publishers was not necessarily shared universally at the end of the war. Returning troops, in particular, may not have retained many illusions about their experience. Yet they did retain some inclination to rejoice or at least feel pride or relief about victory, and to look ahead with some optimism. In the army and among civilians, there was broad support for the conviction expressed in McKenna's *Sonia* (1917)—that 'we've got to get a New Way of Life out of this war'.[55] This often extended into hopes for improved social conditions at home, and, internationally, for the kind of lasting peace H. G. Wells had anticipated in 1914—now apparently achievable through new institutions such as the League of Nations. Many ex-soldiers endured instead years of poor housing and unemployment, which affected around 16 per cent of the working population for much of the 1920s. They also witnessed the failure of the General Strike in 1926, and worsening prospects for European peace. In John Galsworthy's *Windows*, first staged in 1922, a former soldier already reflects that he had 'just missed being killed for three blooming years for no spiritual result whatever'.[56] By the end of the decade, his views were likely to have been widely shared. As Somerset

---

[55] Stephen McKenna, *Sonia: Between Two Worlds* (1917; rpt. London: Methuen, 1920), 372.
[56] John Galsworthy, *The Plays of John Galsworthy* (London: Duckworth, 1929), 690.

Maugham's play *For Services Rendered* (1932) emphasized early in the 1930s, optimism and hopes for a New Way of Life had steadily drained away during the previous decade, for civilian and soldier alike. By its end, the reading public was readier for the 'simple facts' Read mentions, and less likely to be deterred by the bleak vision or 'horrible realism' with which these might be delivered. The public had gone through its own version of the disillusion or *unbildungs* outlined earlier, leaving much more scope for presenting the war as a 'black and beastly...disgusting business', even a futile one in terms of its results. Like many combatants, Bernard Adams knew by 1916 that 'the mask of glory' had been 'stripped from the face of war'. During the 1920s, the general public became more prepared to look at what this left behind.[57]

Developments in authors' minds, as well as the public one, were also required before narratives of the war years could be confidently constructed. In some cases, these developments paralleled the wider disillusion of the age. Vera Brittain's description of a lost generation in *Testament of Youth*, and her 'indictment of a civilisation' which destroyed it between 1914 and 1918, sometimes contrast sharply with the journal she kept during the war.[58] Later published as *Chronicle of Youth: War Diary 1913-17* (1981), this is often more patriotic or enthusiastic about the war than the version of events she completed in the 1930s. Other authors had to overcome another form of disillusion—with the debasement of public discourse Chapter 1 outlined as a feature of the war years. One of these was Sassoon, who recalls wondering in 1917 'what use...were printed words against a war like this?...People who told the truth were likely to be imprisoned, and lies were at a premium.'[59] Such scepticism about words and truthful communication inevitably took time to wear off.

More generally, wartime experience just took time to assimilate or settle into coherent, communicable forms. 'Ordered understanding', Sassoon suggests, could only be 'assembled through afterthought and retrospection', often requiring a period extending long after the events experienced.[60] Recalling the aftermath of the Battle of Arras, he adds in *Memoirs of an Infantry Officer* that any wish to be 'sagely reconstructive

[57] Adams, *Nothing of Importance*, xv.
[58] Brittain, *Testament*, xxvi.
[59] Sassoon, *Complete Memoirs of George Sherston*, 457.
[60] Sassoon, *Siegfried's Journey*, 224.

about [his] experience' was scarcely realizable immediately, when 'minds were still out of breath and our inmost thoughts in disorderly retreat from bellowing darkness and men dying out in shell-holes under the desolation of returning daylight. We were the survivors; few among us would ever tell the truth to our friends and relations in England.'[61] Like A. P. Herbert, Sassoon emphasizes the bludgeoning antipathy of 'bellowing darkness' to imagination or any ordering in the mind. Though the 'sage reconstruction' of writing often played a role in re-establishing this order and restoring the mind's breath and health, it was only a gradual one. 'Writing about war', Wyndham Lewis suggests, 'may be the best way to shake the accursed thing off by putting it in its place', but the shaking was inevitably protracted.[62] Sassoon records 'recurrent dreams...of unmitigated horror' troubling him less only after he had written his account of military service. Graves likewise mentions his use of writing to 'rid [him]self of the poison of war memories', and to escape from daydreams vivid enough to persist as 'an alternate life' almost until his publication of *Goodbye to All That*. Though generally further from the front line than Graves or Sassoon, even Compton Mackenzie recalls that for ten years he 'never seemed able to achieve the necessary detachment' to write about Gallipoli.[63]

For other writers, putting the war in its place threatened to take still longer. In the remark quoted earlier, Sassoon wondered how it might be envisioned, in all its epic scale, even after a hundred years. Soldiers in Henry Williamson's fiction estimate a nearer date, though one still decades away. While 'talking about war correspondents, and the difference between reality and appearances' they agree that 'it will take years to see what's happening now, in perspective...it will take thirty years before anyone taking part in this war, or age, will be able to settle down enough to write truly about the human beings involved in this war, let alone what really happened on the battlefield.'[64] Their conclusion is more than confirmed by the novel in which it appears—*Love and the Loveless*, published in 1958, as the seventh volume, and the fourth to deal with the Great War,

[61] Sassoon, *Complete Memoirs of George Sherston*, 448–9.

[62] Lewis, *Blasting and Bombardiering*, 4.

[63] Sassoon, *Complete Memoirs of George Sherston*, 555; Graves, *Goodbye to All That*, 262, 240; Mackenzie, *Gallipoli Memories*, 29.

[64] Henry Williamson, *Love and the Loveless* (1958; rpt. Stroud: Alan Sutton, 1997), 212.

in Williamson's *Chronicle of Ancient Sunlight* series. Though *The Patriot's Progress* and *The Wet Flanders Plain* had appeared as part of the rush of war narratives at the end of the 1920s, Williamson did not settle down to work on his *Chronicle* until the late 1940s. Compared with this delay, the deferral of many accounts of the war until only ten years after the armistice seems minor. Given the scale and impact of the conflict, and the challenges it presented to genre, chronology, and individual agency, narratives of the war might even be considered to have appeared quite rapidly.

Autobiography and Memoir

These challenges help explain not only delays in the production of war narratives, but also the forms they took when they did appear. Historical events seldom suppress literary imagination altogether, or at any rate rarely for ever. But their pressures inevitably shape the forms and strategies writers adopt, often concentrating imagination around aspects of experience most painful or threatening in fact. As Chapter 4 further considers, some of the mythic, compensatory role identifiable in stories of the Angels of Mons might be seen more widely at work within narrative, though usually with more modest and less fantastical consequences. While certainly challenging for autobiographical writing and personal accounts of the war, in ways discussed earlier, the pressures of military life also encouraged the production of such narratives on a much-expanded scale: though war experiences challenged the significance of the individual, they also provoked its re-assertion. Autobiographies noticeably outnumber novels in the list of major late-1920s publications above. As the next section considers, strongly personal or autobiographical elements also appear in much war fiction. Personal, autobiographical views of the war were further encouraged as a reaction to the numerous official accounts produced by public figures in the years after 1918. The next year alone saw the publication of Sir Douglas Haig's wartime despatches, a memoir by his predecessor as commander of the BEF, Sir John French, and Admiral Jellicoe's account of naval operations, *The Grand Fleet*. Memoirs by senior German generals, Ludendorff and von Falkenhayn, were also translated at the time. Instalments of the multi-volume official *History of the Great War* began to appear in the following year, and the director of the Department of Information from 1917, John Buchan, published his account of the war in 1921.

Quoted earlier, one of the first volumes of the official *History* begins with a warning about the limited reliability of local knowledge and individual testimony. Vera Brittain offers a directly contrary view at the start of *Testament of Youth*, suggesting that it is only an 'attempt to write history in terms of personal life...that might be of value'. She develops this view by quoting a conclusion George Eliot reaches in her novel *Daniel Deronda* (1876)—that 'there comes a terrible moment to many souls when the great movements of the world, the larger destinies of mankind, which have lain aloof in newspapers and other neglected reading, enter like an earthquake into their own lives'.[65] Though the overall movements of the war might be beyond complete containment in any single brain, as Jules Romains warned, they could at least be registered in their specific, seismic effects on single selves. Incentives to do so were further focused by ways the war had not so much 'lain aloof' in newspapers but been misrepresented by them, and in some of the official accounts that followed. Autobiographical writing not only reasserted the primacy of personal experience, it offered a chance to communicate, with the conviction of individuals' eyewitness testimony, 'simple facts' or 'truth about the front line' long suppressed in public discourse. For several writers, authentic communication of this kind was part of a continuing commitment to the dead. Georges Duhamel concludes an imagined dialogue with his dying patients by stressing—in a remark noted by both Graves and Sassoon—'I will not let all your sufferings be lost...and so I record them thus at length...the world must not forget'.[66] For other authors, this urgent obligation to communicate extends into direct demands on the attention of readers. 'Listen', Mary Borden insists in *The Forbidden Zone*:

> you can hear how well it works...the sound of the cannon and the sound of the ambulances bringing the wounded, and the sound of the tramp of strong men going along the road to fill the empty places. Do you hear? Do you understand?

[65] Brittain, *Testament*, xxv, 79.
[66] Duhamel, *New Book of Martyrs*, 32. See also Graves, *Goodbye to All That*, 226.

'I would have you see that little reconnaissance', Edmund Blunden remarks of an action described in *Undertones of War*, 'date yourself 1916, and come'.[67]

Commitment to authentic description—ensuring readers see, hear, or understand as directly as possible—made several war writers suspicious of fictional forms. Graves explains that *Goodbye to All That* originated in work begun in 1916, but completed only after he realized that he had 'stupidly written it as a novel'. He could avoid feeling 'ashamed at having distorted [his] material with a plot', he adds, only by deciding to 'turn it back into undisguised history, as here'. Blunden expresses similar scepticism about art and plot. After describing a friendly sentry being killed by a shell, he remarks that 'in this vicinity a peculiar difficulty would exist for the artist to select the sights, faces, words, incidents, which characterized the time. The art is rather to collect them, in their original form of incoherence.' Mary Borden begins her Preface to *The Forbidden Zone* by explaining 'I have not invented anything in this book.' She goes on to describe her work as a 'collection of fragments...fragments of a great confusion. Any attempt to reduce them to order would require artifice on my part and would falsify them.'[68] Her comments, and Blunden's, suggest that in stressing authenticity and truthfulness—in offering apparently artless versions of experience—autobiographical modes could avoid some of the problems of structure, genre, and closure outlined earlier. Expectations of closure are associated more strongly with fiction than autobiography, which can end adequately simply by bringing the narrative of the author's life up to the time of writing. Like Sassoon in *Sherston's Progress*, many of the autobiographies mentioned above simply conclude at the 'moment...when I write the last words of my book'.[69] Autobiography likewise depends rather less than the novel on continuity and logical progression in the course of its narrative. Instead, it can describe events which follow each other with some of the arbitrariness of life itself—the kind of fragmentariness or 'form of incoherence' Borden and Blunden find particularly appropriate in communicating the great confusion of the war.

---

[67] Mary Borden, *The Forbidden Zone* (London: William Heinemann, 1929), 121–2; Blunden, *Undertones of War*, 83.

[68] Graves, *Goodbye to all That*, 79, 262; Blunden, *Undertones of War*, 141; Borden, *Forbidden Zone*, 3.

[69] Sassoon, *Complete Memoirs of George Sherston*, 656.

Like Graves, Bernard Adams worries in his memoir about distortion or 'desecration' in narrating wartime experience. Reflecting early in *Nothing of Importance* on ways of communicating 'the truth...a complete or proportioned picture' he remarks

> I have not yet found a perfect simile for this war, but the nearest I can think of is that of a pack of cards. Life in this war is a series of events so utterly different and disconnected, that the effect upon the actor in the midst of them is like receiving a hand of cards from an invisible dealer.[70]

The disconnectedness which actors or authors found in the war is often passed on fairly directly in their autobiographies. As Adams's simile suggests, many war narratives record events much as a hand of random cards, in the order of their occurrence, coherent or otherwise, as fate dealt them out to the writer concerned. Military life often seemed extraordinary enough to demand direct recording in this way, without much reorganization or reflection. 'From 10 August 1914, to 5 January 1915', Marc Bloch recalls, 'I led a life as different as possible from my ordinary existence: a life at once barbarous, violent, often colourful...in five months in the field, who would not have amassed a rich harvest of experiences?'[71] The richness or strangeness of this 'harvest' accounts for the enthusiasm of many soldiers for keeping daily journals, and for the continuing interest of these documents in later years. Stuart Chapman's diary—published nearly a century after the war, in 2007, as *Home in Time for Breakfast*—offers a day-by-day record of an artilleryman's experience, uncomplicated and unreflective, vividly confirming Adams's judgement of the utter disconnection between events in wartime. Chapman's entry for Christmas Day, 1916, is typical of random juxtapositions throughout. It records that 'we fired over 200 rounds yesterday between 8 a.m. and 2 p.m. For dinner we are having fried steak, sprouts, greens and potatoes, quarter of a pound of Xmas pudding, custard and figs, walnuts and oranges.' Similar incongruities mark another day-by-day account of events, May Sinclair's *Journal of Impressions in Belgium*, in which she records at one point, in successive lines, that 'my cough has nearly gone' and that 'Antwerp has fallen'.[72]

---

[70] Adams, *Nothing of Importance*, 181, xv–xvi.

[71] Bloch, *Memoirs of War*, 159.

[72] Stuart Chapman, *Home in Time For Breakfast: A First World War Diary* (London: Athena Press, 2007), 27; Sinclair, *Journal*, 258.

Juxtapositions of this kind add pace and immediacy to Sinclair's account of the war's first weeks in Belgium, ones marked by innocence, chaos, and bewilderment among ambulance crews, civilians, and soldiers alike. Yet her *Journal* also records how frustratingly, in her view, members of her ambulance unit try to keep her at a distance from military action and immediate danger. This nevertheless allows—or is matched by—an element of distancing in her journal, more occupied at times by meditations about 'the heroism and agony and waste of war' than by direct descriptions of its events.[73] In this way, Sinclair's writing combines immediacies exemplified in Chapman's journal with the more reflective mode, shaped by longer 'afterthought and retrospection', which distinguishes later memoirs by authors such as Graves and Sassoon. Even their writing, though, alternates between reflectiveness and immediate forms of description, sometimes directly incorporated into their texts in sections reproducing letters or journals contemporary with events described. In *Memoirs of an Infantry Officer*, Sassoon includes the hour-by-hour journal he kept on the first day of the Somme, as if no order other than mere succession could be found for the overwhelming events concerned. 'A small shiny black notebook contains my pencilled particulars', he explains, 'and nothing will be gained by embroidering them with afterthoughts. I cannot turn my field-glasses on to the past.'[74]

Even in sections where Sassoon applies more afterthought to his experience, it rarely embroiders events into patterns much differing from the original order of their occurrence. He remarks in *Sherston's Progress* that 'my procedure has always been to allow things to happen to me in their own time', part of a preference for allowing the 'inevitable sequence of events', rather than personal initiative, to shape his life.[75] His writing follows the same procedure, typical of war autobiography's fairly direct incorporation, into extended narrative modes, of the kind of 'interludes' and 'timeless intervals' which provided such promising material for short stories during the war. Often episodic or journal-like in its construction, war autobiography relies on threads of afterthought or introspection to link together what are effectively vivid short stories, characteristic of successive phases of military life. Chapter 1 suggested

---

[73] Ibid. 257.

[74] Sassoon, *Complete Memoirs of George Sherston*, 332.

[75] Ibid. 563.

that description of the unearthly landscape of the war often relied on a hectic synecdoche, in which the author's attention flits uneasily across battlefields' ruined objects and bodies. War autobiography moves equally restlessly across the landscape of the past, shifting between anecdotes illustrative of earlier experience, yet also, in their disconnectedness, demonstrative of its diversity and the difficulties of assimilating it into orderly vision and understanding. Much war autobiography deals in this way with the discontinuities of 'war time', discussed earlier, by more or less incorporating them into the texture of the narrative.

An anecdotal style also helps communicate the humour which Graves, Adams, and others saw strongly surviving in the war. Individual chapters in Lewis's *Blasting and Bombardiering* often function as complete stories on their own, shaped by their author's highly ironic view of the war. A chapter entitled 'The King of the Trenches' describes a 'new comic gas' infecting the front line, in the form of a deranged officer who prods subordinates into submissiveness with his stick while infuriatingly exclaiming 'Ha! *Ha!*'. 'Hunted with Howitzers' offers another blackly comic anecdote, describing Lewis being shelled, in an oddly '*personal* way', after being observed from a sausage-balloon flaunting 'an impudent air of being *chez soi*, right over our front line…like a strangely levitated black slug'.[76] Paul Fussell sees Graves's *Goodbye to All That* in similar terms—as a 'life in scenes' marked throughout by 'farce and comedy'.[77] Graves is less frivolous than this assessment suggests, but humour figures clearly enough in some of his anecdotes—even in that account of his reported death and subsequent unknown whereabouts. The episode's positioning is also typical of ironies Graves develops through his juxtaposition of disparate recollections. Description of his grievous wounding, and of his family hearing of his 'death', is immediately followed by quotation of the famous propaganda letter, published in the *Morning Post* at the time, from a 'Little Mother' apparently eager for her only son to live and die as 'human ammunition'.[78] Recalling his own near-death with bitter wit, Graves also highlights tensions which had arisen, by 1916, between propaganda or posturing at home and combatants' experience of the Front.

---

[76] Lewis, *Blasting and Bombardiering*, 171, 161–4.

[77] Paul Fussell, *The Great War and Modern Memory* (Oxford: Oxford University Press, 1975), 203.

[78] Graves, *Goodbye to All That*, 189.

Another kind of juxtaposition plays a particular role in accounts of the war. Sassoon explains that 'making one's memoirs...really needs two lives; one for experiencing and another for thinking it over'.[79] As he suggests, all autobiographical writing—even, minimally, in the form of diaries and journals—juxtaposes two selves: an earlier, experiencing one, and the later one, reflective and experienced, who remembers and reconstructs the past. Many autobiographies show these two selves gradually and logically merging into one—their authors recalling how their current identities steadily developed out of previous experience. Typically of its disruption of narrative convention, the war inevitably lowered confidence in such steady, coherent progression. Instead, in dealing with lives 'cut sharply into three sections—pre-war, war, and post-war', memoirists were obliged to re-examine earlier versions of themselves which seemed more than usually different and distant from the present one. 'Was there really any connection between me then and me now', Adams wonders, looking back on the 'dear innocence' that marked his first encounters with the war.[80] Earlier selves sometimes seem distinct and disconnected enough to engage in dialogue or argument with the present one. Though in one way an invitation to readers, the request quoted earlier from *Undertones of War*—to 'date yourself 1916, and come'—also seems part of a conversation between Blunden's wartime self and a later authorial one. This conversation develops further in 'Another Journey from Béthune to Cuinchy', one of the poems used to conclude *Undertones of War*. Blunden's poem sustains at length what it describes as an 'identity- | Argument'—a dialogue between selves, obliged to question even the pronouns and verb tenses in which its own discussions can be conducted, and in which past and present might comprehensibly address each other. 'Do you jib at my tenses? | Who's who? you or I?', the poem enquires, also poignantly requesting that the younger self "ware wire and don't die'.[81] Poignancy of this kind figures as an 'undertone' throughout Blunden's memoir. Along with doubts he explicitly records about expressing incoherent earlier experience, Blunden's tentative, musing style suggests in itself an uncertainty about whether artistic consciousness could survive the war, or communicate effectively its bitter memories.

[79] Sassoon, *Complete Memoirs of George Sherston*, 563.
[80] Adams, *Nothing of Importance*, 278, 15.
[81] Blunden, *Undertones of War*, 231, 228.

One of the solutions Blunden practises is indeed to 'jib at tenses', regularly substituting present verb forms for past tenses in *Undertones of War*. Given Max Plowman's jibbing at tenses—his inclination to 'forget "I shall"'' when faced with the dangers and discontinuities of military life—the present tense might be considered particularly appropriate to the recording of 'war time' experience. Usually credited with adding vividness and immediacy to narrative, it at any rate aptly communicates phases in which, as Blunden expresses it, 'the succession of sensations erratically occupies [the] mind'.[82] A dozen brief clauses, recording fleeting, startled impressions of the 'new world' of the trenches, are in this way crammed pell-mell into a single sentence at the end of Chapter 8 of *Undertones of War*. Similar uses of the present tense appear widely in other autobiographical writing—by Georges Duhamel, Mary Borden, Enid Bagnold, Charles Edmonds, Cecil Lewis, George Coppard, and Max Plowman—as well as in fiction by Remarque, Barbusse, and Dos Passos. Most of these uses communicate what Blunden calls 'the original form of incoherence' of the war—particularly appropriately where the 'timeless confusion' of battle or violent action is involved. Lists of disconnected, momentary impressions, delivered in the present tense, communicate the sense Manning mentions of living 'instantaneously', in a 'timeless interval' of sensations alternating too rapidly or chaotically to allow immediate comprehension. Along with the habit of restlessly surveying ruined landscapes, or moving frequently between diverse anecdotes, such writing is characteristic of narratives of the Great War, and of solutions authors found to its challenges to representation. It is a solution which nevertheless continues to indicate the scale of these challenges. Like the journals and letters incorporated into their memoirs by Graves and Sassoon, passages of present-tense narrative suggest how far war experience—'war time' generally—resisted afterthought or embroidery by a later self. Certain episodes could not be fully focused in field glasses turned on the past. Even years afterwards, overwhelming sensations sometimes still demanded forms preserving some of the incoherence originally encountered by an earlier, experiencing self.

Like Blunden, Sassoon engages explicitly in dialogue with this earlier, wartime self. In the concluding pages of *Sherston's Progress*, he castigates this 'vanished self' for 'taking needless risks...doing his utmost to prevent my being here to write about him', though he acknowledges it was just this rash behaviour which provided something to write about in the first place. Earlier in the volume, Sassoon contrasts his 'contemporary self' not with one but several antecedents, succeeding one another in response to pressures experienced very variously during a life cut unusually sharply into disparate sections by the war.[83] Published anonymously in 1928, *Memoirs of a Fox-Hunting Man* recalls rural tranquillity, during the early years of the century, painfully contrasted with the trench experience, described in *Memoirs of an Infantry Officer* (1930), which eventually led to Sassoon's public refusal to serve any longer in the war. *Sherston's Progress* followed in 1936, further describing military life and the consequences of Sassoon's famous protest. The three volumes were re-issued a year later in a collected edition, *The Complete Memoirs of George Sherston*. Its title emphasizes a further complication in Sassoon's negotiation with various selves—his use of the Sherston persona as the ostensible author of the entire trilogy, with no other name originally attached to its first volume.

Questions arise about how far the experiences recorded were Sassoon's own, and whether *The Complete Memoirs of George Sherston* can be legitimately considered his autobiography. An affirmative answer appears in *Siegfried's Journey*, in which Sassoon straightforwardly explains of the 'inveterate memorizer George Sherston' that 'his experiences were mine'. Yet he adds a qualification, suggesting that 'Sherston was a simplified version of my "outdoor self"', omitting mention of the career as a 'soldier poet' which developed steadily for Sassoon from around 1916. 'It wasn't easy to be a poet and a platoon commander at the same time', *Siegfried's Journey* (1945) explains, and perhaps only sensible to avoid trying to deal with the two occupations within the same memoir.[84] Critics such as Samuel Hynes have nevertheless taken Sassoon too completely at his word, accepting that Sherston differs from his author only in lacking a poetic career. Sherston also differs in being an orphan and an only child. Despite an upbringing by an affectionate aunt, he remains relatively rootless and ready to acquiesce in any supposedly 'inevitable sequence of events' shaping his life—characteristics convenient in illustrating the effects of conflicting influences of war and peace

[83] Sassoon, *Complete Memoirs of George Sherston*, 645, 558.
[84] Sassoon, *Siegfried's Journey*, 69, 5.

shaping his age. A self-professed 'instinct for aloofness' adds further to his usefulness, making him a suitably detached and judicious observer of the war.[85]

Memoirs of a Fox-Hunting Man was initially treated as fiction, and the whole trilogy has sometimes since been considered in this way. Sassoon might more appropriately be credited with employing some of the imaginative techniques and freedoms of the novelist in making his personal story more representative of the experience of his times. Other autobiographies of wartime benefit from similarly free invention and from novelistic approaches to form. As well as reshaping her earlier opinions of war in *Testament of Youth*, Brittain maintains strong elements of suspense by hinting at impending events, such as the loss of her fiancé, while withholding full description of them until their impact can be delivered as powerfully as possible. Graves shows similar sophistication in his apparently casual but often ironic sequencing of events in *Goodbye to All That*. War autobiographies, in other words, were not always as straightforward or artless as they claimed, or as some of the comments quoted from Blunden and Mary Borden might suggest. A semblance of artlessness and 'undisguised history' was essential in replacing official versions of the war with direct eyewitness testimony and supposedly 'simple facts'. Yet effective communication of this testimony obviously required some elements of reconstruction and reflection, as well as raw representation of the bitter experiences concerned. Reconstruction was in any case essential for authors themselves, in helping to neutralize 'the poison of war memories' Graves mentions. Sassoon, in particular, seems to have been able to write about experiences he endured only if these could somehow be imagined as having happened to someone else. As well as offering strong incentives to autobiographical writing, the Great War's challenges shaped it into distinctive narrative forms.

T. E. Lawrence's *Seven Pillars of Wisdom* (1935) was one of the most distinctive of these, and one of the most popular. Its abridged version, *Revolt in the Desert*, quickly sold 30,000 copies in 1927, helped by serialization in the *Daily Telegraph*. Lawrence's work is *so* distinctive, and—set in Arabian desert lands between Mecca and Damascus—so distant from the war zones described in most other literature of the period, that it has often been omitted from accounts of Great War writing. It demands

---

[85] Sassoon, *Complete Memoirs of George Sherston*, 354.

inclusion for the revealing contrasts it provides with this writing, and for its lasting popularity, extended by the film *Lawrence of Arabia*, released in 1962. Subtitled *A Triumph*, *Seven Pillars of Wisdom* owed some of its initial popularity to Lawrence's description of the kind of military success that had long eluded British initiatives on the Western Front. Movement, progress, and change of landscape, so long denied the British army there, feature throughout *Seven Pillars of Wisdom*. For much of its length, until its disturbingly bloody latter stages, changing landscapes are among Lawrence's principal interests. *Seven Pillars of Wisdom* is almost as much travelogue as military memoir, especially in its account of the immense, circuitous journey required to capture Akaba, by surprise, from the east. Landscapes and the titanic natural environment encountered in Lawrence's epic journeys are often as vividly characterized as the individuals involved in his campaigns. 'In all my life objects had been gladder to me than persons', Lawrence remarks, and his descriptions are enlivened, almost literally, by his regular personifications, ascribing agency, usually hostile, to the inanimate rocks and sands around him. Possessed almost of a mind and will of its own, 'the landscape refused to be accessory...and we chattering humans became dust at its feet'. The 'naked desert, under the indifferent heaven' is nevertheless continuously absorbing—for Lawrence himself, and for readers seduced by his intriguing grasp of camel-lore, his breakfasting on ostrich eggs, or just the mind-emptying immensity of land- and sky-scapes, vast and silent as a 'childhood's dream'.[86]

A further appeal of Lawrence's writing derives from its view of his Arab armies and their leaders, dwarfed by the landscape but valorized in action and individuality in ways rarely accorded the 'automatons' of the Western Front. Despite professing indifference to persons, Lawrence records throughout *Seven Pillars of Wisdom* his concern that military discipline threatened 'to mark off soldiers from complete men, and obliterate the humanity of the individual'. He organizes his campaigns on the contrary assumption that 'the essence of the desert was the lonely moving individual', most effective if freed from 'discipline in the sense in which it was restrictive, submergent of individuality'. In guerrilla actions against the Turks, he considers that 'the efficiency of our forces was the

---

[86] T. E. Lawrence, *Seven Pillars of Wisdom* (1935; rpt. Hertfordshire: Wordsworth, 1997), 101, 539, 11, 342.

personal efficiency of the single man … our ideal should be to make our battles a series of single combats, our ranks a happy alliance of agile commanders-in-chief'.[87] Lawrence's organization, in other words, comprehensively reverses the erosion of individuality evident in other areas of military life during the Great War, and a central concern of most of the writers discussed above.

Throughout *Seven Pillars of Wisdom*, this reversal is most spectacularly evident in the persona of Lawrence himself. Granted a largely free hand in his campaigns by General Allenby, Lawrence is the prime mover and principal 'lonely moving individual' in his narratives. He directly admits that his actions, and his accounts of them, are designed to answer a public need for 'legend … book-heroes', and to fulfil his own wish for 'a theme ready and epic'.[88] *Seven Pillars of Wisdom* concludes with his triumphal entry to Damascus strangely sullied by the need to deal with an abandoned hospital, and to dig a trench as a mass grave for the liquefying, rat-gnawed corpses he finds there. Yet in its redolence of the Western Front, where two of Lawrence's younger brothers had died in 1915, this ending highlights contrastively the preceding narrative's success in maintaining the dreams of military success and individual glory, widely shared in 1914, which the trenches had comprehensively destroyed. A near-deliberate strategy on Lawrence's part, this mythic compensation—celebrating British 'agility', individual heroism, imaginative enterprise, and ingenious sympathy with native populations—ensured his own legendary status, though on the basis of a romantic, colourful, triumphant narrative whose truthfulness was questioned by later commentators, including Richard Aldington.

Autobiography and Beyond: War Novels

'A good biography is of course a sort of novel', Wyndham Lewis remarks at the start of his own war memoir.[89] While wartime autobiography sometimes relied on novelistic technique, many Great War novels are strongly autobiographical, including some of the best of them—fiction

---

[87] Ibid. 504, 635, 329–30.
[88] Ibid. 317, 545.
[89] Lewis, *Blasting and Bombardiering*, 1.

by Frederic Manning, R. H. Mottram, Henry Williamson, and Ford Madox Ford. Novel and autobiography sometimes seem almost indistinguishable. Though subtitled *1917: A Novel*, John Dos Passos's *One Man's Initiation* reads more like a memoir. For Dos Passos's friend E. E. Cummings, distinctions between novel and memoir seemed subtle enough to require discussion in *The Enormous Room* (1922), an account of his mistaken imprisonment in France, following work for a US ambulance corps. Cummings spends a paragraph wondering whether this 'great and personal adventure' will seem ' "real" ' to readers, or 'mere fiction', and whether a 'Happy Ending' might assist their view.[90] As Bernard Bergonzi suggests in discussing Great War literature, fiction allows 'a wider angle of vision' than autobiography—usually limited to a 'single thread of personal experience'—and could offer clear advantages in representing the scale and complexity of the war.[91] Yet in the 1920s and later, much war fiction remained necessarily intertwined with the 'single thread' of autobiography. Like autobiography and memoir, novels at the time—those by ex-combatants particularly—sought to resist long-standing misrepresentations of propaganda and official documentation. In order to do so, they had to seem partly real to readers, and not entirely mere fictions. A necessary authenticating element was often provided by suggesting novels' strong basis in fact, and the possibility of reading them as fictionalized versions of events authors had encountered, or might have encountered, themselves.

This authenticating element is sometimes immediately emphasized. Henry Williamson begins *A Fox under My Cloak* with an 'Author's Note' explaining that 'many of the scenes in this novel are authentic... each of the characters in this novel had an existence in the 1914–18 war'. Frederic Manning likewise begins *The Middle Parts of Fortune* with a 'Prefatory Note' explaining that 'the following pages are a record of experience on the Somme and Ancre fronts, with an interval behind the lines, during the latter half of the year 1916; and the events described in it actually happened; the characters are fictitious'.[92] Along with prefaces of this kind,

---

[90] E. E. Cummings, *The Enormous Room* (1922; rpt. New York and London: Liverwright, 1978), 229.

[91] Bernard Bergonzi, *Heroes' Twilight: A Study of the Literature of the Great War* (1965; rpt. Manchester: Carcanet, 1996), 163.

[92] Williamson, *Fox under My Cloak*, [ii]; Manning, *Middle Parts of Fortune*, [viii].

critical studies, reviews—even the back covers of novels—regularly confirm for readers how far Great War fiction might have 'actually happened', or been based on the experience of authors concerned. This possibility is further confirmed by stylistic features of the texts themselves. First-person narratives—such as Barbusse's, Remarque's, or Aldington's in *Death of a Hero*—invite association between the author and the 'I' of the text. In Aldington's case, opinions this 'I' delivers about the war's origins in Victorian hypocrisy are at times extensive enough to overwhelm his account of a hero tortured by experience at home as well as at the Front, leaving *Death of a Hero* almost as much essay as novel. In different ways, third-person narratives often offer equally strong incentives to associate author and fiction. These appear in the focalization of many war novels—including *The Middle Parts of Fortune*, individual sections of Mottram's *Spanish Farm* sequence, Ford's *Parade's End*, and much of Williamson's writing—so firmly around the 'single thread' of a central figure's vision and experience. Readers naturally surmise that figures so thoroughly explored must be based at least partly on the author's own experience and outlook.

Further encouragement to make this connection is offered by forms of private discourse employed in communicating the inner life of the figures concerned. Manning's work provides a good example, though *The Middle Parts of Fortune* might be said to employ 'private' discourse of two very different kinds. When the novel was first published—in the limited edition of 1929, and in expurgated form the following year—its author was named only by Manning's army number, 'Private 19022'. Concentration on the experience of private soldiers extends throughout the novel, which finds in their loyalty and comradeship some compensation for the privations of the Somme campaign, and some refuge from the 'inflexible and inhuman machine' of the war generally. When 'brought to the last extremity of hope', his soldiers find that they can after all rely on rather more than 'nothing; not even their own bodies'. Instead, 'they put their hands on each other's shoulders and said with a passionate conviction that it would be all right, though they had faith in nothing, but in themselves and in each other'.[93] Gritty, residual faith among ordinary soldiers seemed to many authors a rare redeeming aspect of the war. As Chapter 1 explained, the sense of solidarity among Manning's

[93] Manning, *Middle Parts of Fortune*, 205.

privates is communicated particularly powerfully through their language. This is delivered in frequent, extended sections of direct speech, pungently vernacular and copious enough in expletives to have deferred unlimited, unexpurgated publication of *The Middle Parts of Fortune* until 1977.

In developing his central figure, Bourne, Manning employs a different kind of private discourse, reliant not on direct speech, but on intermingling his own narrative voice with the inner register of his character's thoughts. Bourne's disturbing recollections of an earlier battle illustrate the tactics involved:

> Suddenly he remembered the dead in Trones Wood, the unburied dead with whom one lived, he might say, cheek by jowl, Briton and Hun impartially confounded, festering, fly-blown corruption…Out of one bloody misery into another, until we break. One must not break. He took in his breath suddenly in a shaken sob, and the mind relinquished its hopeless business.[94]

The first and last sentences in this passage belong fairly firmly to the author's objective narrative voice. In the second and third—like Blunden's shifty pronouns in 'Another Journey from Béthune to Cuinchy'—'one' and 'we' create a more fluid persona, suggesting a voice no longer exclusively authorial, but evidently belonging in part to the character. Neither sentence is in the form of the direct speech occupying so much of the rest of the novel—there are no inverted commas, or speech cues in forms such as 'he thought' or 'he said'—yet each is close to what Bourne 'might say' himself, either aloud, or more probably inwardly, as part of the 'hopeless business' of the mind. Forms of free indirect discourse of this kind figure throughout *The Middle Parts of Fortune*, alongside Manning's extensive presentation of Bourne's thoughts in more conventional forms of direct description. These tactics ensure for readers an easy assumption that the character's inner experience coincides with the author's own—literally, that the 'one' voice may be used to cover both.

The *Spanish Farm* sequence also has autobiographical aspects, and a firm focus around individual character, though by concentrating on a different figure in each of his three volumes, Mottram moves well beyond the 'single thread' Bergonzi mentions. Mottram further expands his vision of the war through concentration on place as well as character—on the Spanish Farm of the title, whose position close to the Front ensures that 'practically the whole English Army must have passed through or near it at one time or another'.[95] The British army and its activities are viewed from an unusually detached perspective in Mottram's first volume. This centres on the farmer's daughter, Madeleine Vanderlynden, who searches across the war zone for a former lover, while also beginning a new affair, with an English officer, Skene, fluent—as Mottram was—in French. The second volume, *Sixty-Four, Ninety-Four!*, shifts to Skene's perspective, on the war and on his absorbing but unsustainable relationship with Madeleine.

Envisaging the same events through different characters in one way simply diversifies Mottram's view of the war, allowing him to include a French perspective unusual in fiction in English. Yet it is the tensions and disparities between these individual perspectives, as much as what is envisaged in each, that communicates the experience of the war so disturbingly. Even when Skene and Madeleine are at their closest, they barely coincide in their views of the war, the world, or even their own affair. As Madeleine realizes at the end of *Sixty-Four, Ninety-Four!*, only wartime could have allowed such an affair to develop, yet it destroys it just as readily. No intimacy can long remain immune to the war's immense, violent changefulness, overwhelming individual aims and desires. Their frailties are further highlighted in contrast to the long endurance of the Spanish Farm, and to Madeleine's unswerving peasant commitment to it—scarcely distracted by scattered armies drifting across its land, obscure to her in their purposes, vaguely destined death-ward. Like Hemingway in *A Farewell to Arms*, in describing an affair Mottram creates a compelling context in which to explore the war's numbing, destructive effect on personal life and emotion—'reduced and reduced' by the war, the novel suggests, and struggling not to go 'clean out of sight'. Extended and often fairly explicit account of a relationship—though very different from Frankau's comedic approach—also added to the popularity of the *Spanish Farm* sequence, which sold 100,000 copies when it first appeared.

Mottram's third volume, *The Crime at Vanderlynden's*, extends still more widely the view of war developed in the first two. Free indirect

<hr>

[95] Mottram, *Spanish Farm*, 10.

discourse once again contributes to a close focus around a single figure—Dormer, an English Officer required to find the soldier responsible
for vandalism at the farm, a job similar to ones Mottram undertook himself while serving as a liaison officer. As his name half-implies, Dormer is
not the most alert or profound of thinkers: even after several paragraphs
of reflection, he is described as 'no visionary'. Instead, an 'unadventur-
ous mind' makes him an uncomplicated observer of the many experiences and encounters his investigations entail. They occupy months,
'years even, over all those miles', and take him 'in and out of so many
units and formations', including, unusually, in war fiction, some of the
many non-combatant operations—of transport, salvage, support, etc.—
eventually involved in military operations in France. Yet despite their
extent, Dormer's investigations are never satisfactorily concluded.
Description of his pursuit of what may be a 'phantom' culprit, through
so many spheres of military life, helps to make the scale and complexity
of the war less a narrative problem than a pervasive theme in Mottram's
sequence.[96] *The Crime at Vanderlynden's* is in a way an unresolved mystery story, emphasizing the impossibility of sustained moral purpose, or
reasoned understanding, within the indecipherable chaos of wartime.
Ultimately, the crime at Vanderlynden's, and throughout the huge territory Dormer surveys, seems principally the war itself, skewing so many
lives away from sense and normality.

Scale and diversity were among problems earlier considered particularly challenging for accounts of the war. Along with tactics considered
above, part of Mottram's response—like Ford's, in his *Parade's End* tetralogy—is simply to extend fiction on a commensurate scale, exploring
wartime experience not in a single novel, but a sequence of several.
Other Great War novelists work at comparable length. Though a single
volume, H. M. Tomlinson's *All Our Yesterdays* (1930) runs to almost as
many pages as the *Spanish Farm* sequence. Ranging from 1900 to 1919,
its five parts cover widely separate settings and groups of characters,
retracing the war's origins to 'the increasing uproar of progress' after the
turn of the century, and to growing tensions between rival colonial interests at the time.[97] Still more wide-ranging Great War fiction—the
most extensive simply in scale—appears in Henry Williamson's novel

[96] Ibid. 472, 538.
[97] H. M. Tomlinson, *All Our Yesterdays* (London: William Heinemann, 1930), 220.

sequence *A Chronicle of Ancient Sunlight*. Five of his fifteen volumes are set in the war years: *How Dear is Life* (1954), *A Fox under My Cloak* (1955), *The Golden Virgin* (1957), *Love and the Loveless* (1958), and *A Test to Destruction* (1960). In earlier volumes of the sequence—three of these precede *How Dear is Life*—Williamson looks back like Tomlinson at turn-of-the-century London, and at the 'uproar' of progress and modernity threatening tranquil suburban life at the time. Throughout, tactics of free indirect discourse and authorial description, comparable to Mottram's or Manning's, focus on the experience and thinking of a single individual, Phillip Maddison. Initially a rather naïve figure in the war volumes, inhibited by an 'inner core of diffidence',[98] Madison's passivity and openness to experience make him a good observer of his times, like Sassoon's George Sherston, and a good indicator of their influences. Gradually and painfully, the war imposes on him a hesitant maturity, along with self-reliance essential to his promotion, or just his survival, in the infantry.

This survival, and the longevity of his military experience, make him a conveniently comprehensive witness of the war. As Williamson did, Maddison serves throughout the conflict, but he is involved in many more actions than his creator: at the First Battle of Ypres in 1914, at Loos in 1915, on the Somme in 1916, at Passchendaele in 1917, and in the great retreat in the spring of 1918. Various promotions and secondments—as officer in charge of gas, machine guns, or transport—introduce him, like Mottram's Dormer, to a huge range of military duties and personnel. The Christmas Truce of 1914 even allows him an extended bicycle trip behind German lines. Friendship with an exemplarily courageous senior officer offers him insight into the broader management of the war, and even a chance—surely every infantryman's fantasy—to explain conditions around Passchendaele personally to Haig, the Commander-in-Chief. Williamson uses many other means to document the war as widely as possible, including long extracts from the *Wipers Times* and from contemporary newspapers. Maddison's extended periods of leave, recovering from wounds received at Ypres and the Somme, allow an equally wide-ranging account of the Home Front. He encounters profiteering, unrest in Ireland, the remnants of the suffrage movement, Zeppelin raids, and—frequently and painfully—a family scarcely able

[98] Henry Williamson, *A Test to Destruction* (London: Macdonald, 1960), 283.

to comprehend the war or how it has transformed him. 'Father...
Home...belonged to another world, gone for ever', he reflects.[99] It is a
world Williamson nevertheless treats sympathetically, presenting several of the civilians Phillip encounters—including his father, often his
bitterest adversary in views of the war—with some of the inwardness
accorded to the central figure. Ensuring that both war and early-twen-
tieth-century civilian life are so broadly envisaged, and tensions
between the two so extensively explored, Williamson's tactics accord
with an ambition soldiers discuss in *Love and the Loveless*: 'to write a
War and Peace for this age'.[100]

Critics and readers could never much approve the result. Williamson's
reputation was stained by the repellent fascist sympathies he expressed
in the 1930s, and further damaged by their reappearance in later volumes
of *A Chronicle of Ancient Sunlight*. As a result, the earlier stages of his
sequence have not received the recognition they deserve—as the most
comprehensive novelistic account of the Great War and its place in the
history of the twentieth century. His tactics ensure that *A Chronicle of
Ancient Sunlight* offers a version of events sometimes fuller than anything Great War histories provide. Often based on study of these histories, his writing is usually accurate and copious in detail—in outlining,
for example, the British Army's failure at Loos, and its causes in the late,
chaotic despatch of reserves to the Front. As well as describing events,
though, through Maddison's reflections Williamson can suggest, more
intimately than any history, their consequences for the feelings of troops
involved—in this case, ones of burning frustration with British generals,
for throwing away initiatives gained at Loos with so much blood and
pain. Forty years after the armistice, Williamson's fiction brings Great
War narrative around a full circle. In its focus on individuals and their
emotions, *A Chronicle of Ancient Sunlight* reinserts into a broadly historical narrative of the war just those elements of personal experience
excluded from the official *History* and similar accounts published shortly
after 1918.

This achievement obviously does not in itself guarantee favourable
comparison with *War and Peace*, nor even fully answer more general

---

[99] Henry Williamson *How Dear is Life* (1954; rpt. London: Arrow, 1985), 266.
[100] Henry Williamson, *Love and the Loveless* (1958; rpt. Stroud: Alan Sutton, 1997),
212.

criticisms that can be made of Great War fiction, rarely valued as highly in literary terms as the period's poetry. Despite highlighting personal experience and emotion, Manning, Mottram, Williamson, and other war novelists have sometimes been considered to use their central figures as little more than convenient points of view, characterized mostly in order to draw readers into firmly focused vision of a broad landscape of war. Critics such as Evelyn Cobley have commented on strategies which often seem in this way 'predominantly descriptive. Plot and characters frequently function only as convenient devices to motivate description'. This results, she suggests, in narratives that are 'like a series of photographs... connected by a common theme'.[101] Writers concerned might not have resented this judgement of work often motivated—like contemporary autobiography and memoir—by a need to provide truer pictures of the war than were generally available during the conflict, or for some years thereafter. Given the difficulties of finding any language or form equal to this task, providing 'a series of photographs' might seem an adequate achievement—one appropriate to the fragmentary nature of war experience, or even an instance of text matching forms of 'picture story' increasingly influential in the early twentieth century. Yet Great War novels can be judged still more generously in literary terms. As Cobley acknowledges, many of those discussed above communicate wartime experience in ways more productive or profound than emphases on description or 'photograph' suggest. Fiction can outdo the camera's merely visual recording—particularly in an era of still-silent films—in its stronger suggestion of the war's overwhelming uproar and its torrid assaults on all the senses. Private, inward discourses in fiction by Manning or Mottram can also trace the Great War's pressures within another area excluded from the camera's reach—and, as Chapter 1 suggested, from many written accounts of the conflict—the inner reaches of the self. In doing so, their work helps to confirm a resilient individuality surviving despite the overwhelmingly impersonal nature and 'inhuman machine' of the war. At its best, Great War fiction finds literary forms able to both record and partly resist wartime pressures threatening to destroy 'the last shred of individuality'.

---

[101] Evelyn Cobley, *Representing War: Form and Ideology in First World War Narratives* (Toronto: University of Toronto Press, 1993), 11.

There is also Great War fiction, excluded from Cobley's analysis, which particularly resists definition in terms of straightforward photography or description—Ford's *Parade's End* tetralogy. Like *A Chronicle of Ancient Sunlight*, this offers a broad view of life before, during, and after the war. The immediately pre-war period is covered in *Some Do Not...* (1924), and its aftermath in *The Last Post* (1928). The two middle volumes—*No More Parades* (1925) and *A Man Could Stand Up* (1926)—move between the Home Front and the war zone in France. Ford served there in 1916 and 1917, arriving during the early part of the Somme campaign, after enlisting the previous year, when slightly over the regulation age, allowing him to describe himself as the oldest novelist to have witnessed the fighting at first hand. His central figure throughout the tetralogy, Christopher Tietjens, is once again an autobiographical one, though also widely representative. His principled outlook highlights contrastively the declining stability of British society and institutions, exacerbated by the war. Like Montague's hero in *Rough Justice*, Tietjens remains unswervingly committed to long-standing values and morals, and to the idea of a ruling class worthy of its role and responsibility, even as the commercialism and opportunism of pre-war and wartime life comprehensively erode such faiths.

Tietjens's values grow steadily more beleaguered throughout *No More Parades* and *A Man Could Stand Up*. Each demonstrates at length, in Ford's words, 'how modern fighting of the organized, scientific type affects the mind'.[102] Vividly communicated in forms of free indirect discourse, Tietjens's troubled mental processes often conflate 'grey horrors, in front, and behind, amongst the civilian populations', juxtaposing the immediate chaos of the war with recollections of his extraordinarily complicated home life.[103] A painful conversation with General Campion in *No More Parades*, for example, reminds him of difficulties as much domestic as military—of the unfaithfulness of his wife, as well as his feelings of responsibility for the death of one of his soldiers, Morgan. When the General asks him 'Why *don't* you divorce?',

> Panic came over Tietjens. He knew it would be his last panic of that interview. No brain could stand more. Fragments of scenes of fighting, voices, names, went before his eyes and ears. Elaborate

[102] Quoted in Robie Macauley, Introduction to Ford, *Parade's End*, v.
[103] Ford, *Parade's End*, 344.

problems.... The whole map of the embattled world ran out in front of him—as large as a field. An embossed map in greenish *papier mâché*—a ten-acre field of embossed *papier mâché*, with the blood of O Nine Morgan blurring luminously over it. Years before... How many months?... Nineteen, to be exact, he had sat on some tobacco plants on the Mont de Kats... No, the Montagne Noire. In Belgium... What had he been doing? Trying to get the lie of the land... No... Waiting to point out positions to some fat home general.[104]

Fractured phrases—self-questioning, self-contradictory, repeatedly broken off by pauses and ellipses—communicate the flickering uncertainty of Tietjens's thoughts. Similar registers for mental activity, disturbed and fragmentary, figure elsewhere in Great War fiction—occasionally in Patrick Miller's *The Natural Man*, in V. M. Yeates's *Winged Victory*, and in Hemingway's *A Farewell to Arms*. But *Parade's End* uses this register much more extensively, often maintaining it for pages at a time. Unspoken memories and inner reflections, beginning in the passage above, continue for two pages before Tietjens's dialogue with the General is resumed. Along with more conventional descriptions, such passages contribute to an account of wartime which compellingly combines breadth and depth. Surveying a 'whole... embattled world', at home and in France, *Parade's End* shows the bloodiness of the trenches steadily spreading across the entire field of the war, staining British life and society generally, as well as deeply suffusing the consciousness of Tietjens at the Front.

In concentrating his narrative around this consciousness, Ford also finds means of representing the war's infringement of a sense of coherent, progressive temporal order, replaced by the strange, fragmentary 'war time' discussed earlier. Tietjens offers a theory for this aspect of the novel's practice when he remarks that 'you can cut out from this afternoon... to now... cut it out; and join time up'.[105] *Parade's End* regularly resumes remembered periods of the past in this way, cutting out earlier afternoons, or earlier days, and interpolating them into Tietjens's consciousness in the present. Often, as in the passage above, the memories

---

[104] Ibid. 492–3. The ellipses are Ford's.
[105] Ibid. 285.

concerned are mere 'fragments of scenes'—involuntary, momentary flashbacks on experience 'outside sensible time', or too violent or incoherent to be restored into chronological order, or any significant order. Tietjens often finds that he has 'lost all sense of chronology',[106] and, like Bloch's confused recollections of the Marne, his fragmented memories offer only a 'discontinuous series of images, vivid in themselves but badly arranged'. There are, once again, other Great War novels which attempt comparable disruptions. Unnerved by the precise timing regulating much military life, Vernon Bartlett's hero in *No Man's Land* (1930) protests that 'it was lunacy—it was almost blasphemy—for men to try to divide time into months, weeks, hours, minutes . . . neatly ordered days'.[107] The structure of Bartlett's novel likewise relies on memory in order partly to escape this 'lunacy'. There are also, as discussed earlier, many instances in both autobiography and fiction of present-tense narrative suggesting the 'timeless confusion' of wartime impressions as they fall violently upon the mind, before reflection is able to assimilate them. But it is only *Parade's End* that deploys at length a formal representation of the war's challenge to reflection itself—to what the 'brain could stand'. Forms of memory later recognized as characteristic of wartime trauma are reproduced in Tietjens's struggles with gaps and reversals in his recollections, and in his repeated recursion over episodes such as the death of O Nine Morgan. These tactics make *Parade's End* one of the most compelling narratives of the Great War, offering an unusually comprehensive engagement with its disruptive consequences. These are shown eroding not only long-standing British institutions, but the integrity of any consciousness—such as Tietjens's—that might have been directed towards their reconstruction after the armistice in 1918.

War and the Modernist Novel

Ford's emphases on inner consciousness and memory share in modernist initiatives developing, during and after the war, in the work of authors including Dorothy Richardson, Virginia Woolf, and James Joyce. Yet

---

[106] Ibid. 486.
[107] Vernon Bartlett, *No Man's Land* (London: George Allen and Unwin, 1930), 135–6.

Ford was fairly unusual, among modernist authors, in having witnessed the war directly. Only Ford and Wyndham Lewis served as army personnel, though other modernists—such as May Sinclair, John Dos Passos, and Ernest Hemingway—experienced the conflict almost as directly, in the ambulance services. *Parade's End* raises questions in this way about relations between two idioms most strongly emerging in 1920s narrative: modernist fiction, and writing about the war. These questions are further considered in Chapter 4, but an introduction to them can be provided by returning to that edition of *The Times* on 3 July 1916. Headed 'Roll of Honour', almost all of page 12 is devoted to the daily list of casualties, including in this case more than 1,500 names (Fig. 9). Yet within this huge array of dead and wounded, space has also been found for honours of a very different kind. A single small column headed 'Oxford Honours Lists' records the results of university examinations announced on 1 July, the day the Battle of the Somme began. In 'Class I' of English Language and Literature, the list includes 'A. L. Huxley'—Aldous Huxley, whose short-sightedness exempted him from military service. His first publication, a book of poems, appeared a few weeks later, and he went on in several broadly modernist 1920s novels to satirize shifting morals and outlooks marking the war's legacy in the society of the time.

On this evidence, writers who remained at home and those who directly witnessed the war might be seen simply as contained within the same huge field of death—one extending across a whole embattled world, surrounding soldier and civilian alike. Yet there is obviously a world of difference—one of many huge gaps separating the experience of soldiers and civilians at the time—between direct experience of the Somme and the completion of an Oxford degree on the day the battle began. In *Jacob's Room* (1922), Virginia Woolf develops this kind of gap into a theme of her fiction, dramatizing contradictions between the inescapable influence of the Great War and the impossibility, for most of the domestic population, of directly experiencing or even imagining its nature. References to the mowing down of armies, or to a young man who 'feeds crows in Flanders', hint at the realities of the conflict.[108] Yet the elusiveness of the novel's principal character ensures that the war figures only as a kind of black hole—a space whose gravity influences

---

[108] Virginia Woolf, *Jacob's Room* (1922; rpt. London: Panther, 1976), 93.

everything, while remaining incompletely visible itself. Though the suggestively named Jacob Flanders is a centre of attention throughout, he is rarely presented directly, but figures instead mostly as an absence, represented only through the words, thoughts, and regrets of other characters, inevitably distanced from his life and death in the war.

Other novels by Woolf and her fellow modernists likewise show the war as an absent cause—an experience both distant yet painfully immediate in its effects. In *Mrs Dalloway* (1925), Woolf goes on to represent the war's impact more extensively, but still only in its later effects, mostly on a suicidal, shell-shocked, ex-soldier. In the novel he was drafting during the Battle of the Somme, *Women in Love* (1921), D. H. Lawrence barely mentions the war directly, though occasionally hinting at its influence on the dislocated society he portrays. 'What people want is hate— hate and nothing but hate', one character remarks. 'In the name of righteousness and love…they distil themselves with nitro-glycerine'. The hint is expanded in the novel's concluding paragraphs, when another character recalls 'the Kaiser's: "*Ich habe es nicht gewollt*"' (I did not want this)—a denial of responsibility he addressed to the German people to coincide with the first anniversary of the war's declaration. It was recorded with scepticism throughout the British press at the time.[109] Still widely remembered in the early 1920s, the remark invites contemporary readers to connect the loss and destructiveness at the end of *Women in Love* with vivid memories of the war itself.

For later readers especially, the war might nevertheless seem no more than a distant echo in the novels mentioned—as disturbing, yet vague, as the hollow, desolate 'ou-boum' that resounds through the Marabar Caves in E. M. Forster's *A Passage to India* (1924). Though the war's effects continued to resound throughout the literature of the 1920s, its actual scenes and subject matter inevitably lay beyond the experience or even imagination of modernist authors such as Lawrence and Woolf. Yet literary judgement obviously looks further than subject matter, particularly when assessing modernism, usually defined principally in terms of innovations in form and style. In these areas, modernist writing can be

---

[109] D. H. Lawrence, *Women in Love* (1921; rpt. Harmondsworth: Penguin, 1971), 141, 539. See, for example, 'Manifesto by the Kaiser: Germany the Victim', *The Times*, 2 Aug. 1915, 5, which translates the Kaiser's original remark—'Ich habe den Krieg nicht gewollt' as 'I did not will the war.'

seen as substantially shaped by the war, though in ways still sharply distinguished from the work of writers, considered throughout this chapter, who witnessed its action directly. Most of the latter shared motives Sassoon mentions, or Max Plowman sums up when he remarks that accounts of the war 'must be as candid and truthful as the writer can make them'—part of a responsibility to close gaps between combatant experience and civilian complacency.[110] Such motives inclined many authors concerned towards the most straightforward, familiar forms available. When more innovative styles do appear—in the fragmented thoughts of *Parade's End*, or the restrained descriptive directness of Hemingway's prose—they often extend these motives, offering still more immediate contact with experience of the war, communicated by disturbed thought patterns, or the implied difficulties of reflection of any kind. For modernist writers such as Lawrence and Woolf, innovative styles were employed more regularly, but with very different motives— not as ways of making the war more immediate, but in order instead to distance it; to find means of ensuring its terrible experiences could be imaginatively reformed and contained.

That page in *The Times* might once again help define pressures and processes involved. Huxley could hardly have welcomed finding his early intellectual success reported in the middle of a sea of names of the dead. The experience might explain why he went on to write fiction in which enclaves of cultured individuals often flourish only through isolation—essential but precarious—from the vicissitudes of a wider society. In *Brave New World* (1932), for example, this isolation is made as decisive or literal as possible by exiling intellectual communities into confinement on distant islands. In one way or another—usually less literal—much modernist fiction favours similar forms of isolation or containment. These figure paradigmatically in Woolf's *To the Lighthouse* (1927), which describes the Ramsay family's holiday on one island, and its ambitions to reach another, on which the eponymous lighthouse stands. As in *Jacob's Room* and *Mrs Dalloway,* many hints and references ensure that the war remains strongly present to readers, particularly in the novel's middle section, bleakly summarizing decay and destruction in the family home during the years of its duration. Set around 1910, the first section is more tranquil, ending in a form of Victorian or

---

[110] Plowman, *Subaltern*, vii.

Edwardian comedic closure. By the end of their long summer's day, harmony has been restored to the Ramsay's marriage, and among the social circle of their acquaintances. Describing how 'one by one the lamps were all extinguished', the second section opens very differently, echoing a comment made by the foreign secretary, Sir Edward Grey, in early August 1914, and recalled in memoirs he published two years before Woolf's novel appeared. 'The lamps are going out all over Europe', Grey is said to have remarked, 'we shall not see them lit again in our lifetime.'[111] Several of the Ramsay family certainly do not. As part of the 'profusion of darkness' the second section describes, it records that '[A shell exploded. Twenty or thirty young men were blown up in France, among them Andrew Ramsay, whose death, mercifully, was instantaneous].'[112]

Conventions of pre-war literature are extinguished equally decisively in the latter stages of *To the Lighthouse*—the war destroying the lives, and the wider social cohesion, through which any comedic conclusion might have been reached. Yet the novel ends affirmatively, moving from darkness back to the light in several other ways. The family finally realize their ambition of sailing to the lighthouse, though their achievement is subsidiary to the artist Lily Briscoe's accomplishment in completing her painting. Finding herself 'losing consciousness of outer things' and that 'the Lighthouse had become almost invisible, had melted away into a blue haze', she finishes her picture with the addition of a firm central line, dividing it, like the novel in which she appears, into three sections.[113] Square brackets surrounding description of Andrew Ramsay's death, in the quotation above, already hint at its framing within artistic vision. By the end of the novel, this artistic containment is largely complete, the war and its explosions fading into a haze of forgetfulness and blue distance. This conclusion suggests that after the destruction of so many people, institutions, faiths, and social conventions during the war, coherence and harmony may no longer be discoverable in 'outer things'—in life itself, or in realistic representations of it. Instead, coherence and affirmation may be found only in some still-tranquil, isolated depth of

---

[111] Virginia Woolf, *To the Lighthouse* (1927; rpt. Harmondsworth: Penguin, 1973), 143; Grey, quoted in Samuel Hynes, *A War Imagined: The First World War and English Culture* (1990; rpt. London: Pimlico, 1992), 470.

[112] Woolf, *To the Lighthouse*, 143, 152.

[113] Ibid. 181, 236.

inner consciousness, or in abstract forms of imagination (perhaps facilitated by wartime detachments of language from straightforward 'semblance'), or through the shaping, ordering potential of art itself.

To the Lighthouse is by no means the only 1920s novel to offer this suggestion. Throughout A Son at the Front (1923), Edith Wharton considers
the potentials of wartime experience 'clarified and transmuted into
vision'.[114] Dos Passos's Three Soldiers is likewise only in part a novel about
the war, moving in its latter stages into descriptions of the bohemian
artistic milieus that developed in Paris after its conclusion. Its hero likewise moves towards faith in musical composition as his only means of
escaping mechanical military discipline, or of imposing some sense of
order on his painfully chaotic experience of the war. 'One page that I felt
was adequate', he considers, would compensate for the loss of 'every joy
in the world'.[115] Each novel helps to show how destruction of 'joy in the
world' led towards contrary but cognate emphases in 1920s writing—
ones as close, yet distinct, as those columns in The Times on 3 July 1916.
Greater realism was favoured by most writers who had experienced the
war and its losses directly, while the majority of modernists, who had
not, pursued more abstract, complex visions in their efforts somehow to
find 'a page that was adequate'. Ex-combatants sought above all to bear
witness: modernists to distance the unbearable. In either case, awareness of the unbearable, unspeakable, or unaccountable—of experience
potentially beyond narration, or what 'brain could stand'—remained a
key influence on writing emerging in the 1920s. Further implications for
narrative forms, and for the period's literature generally, are considered
in Chapter 4.

---

[114] Edith Wharton, A Son at the Front (1923; rpt. DeKalb: Northern Illinois University
Press, 1995), 203.
[115] Dos Passos, Three Soldiers, 234.

| 3 |

Unfamiliar Lines

The sweet o'the morn and the sweet o'the year;
Fresh, young airs and a wondering light...
. . . .
The winsome, farewell glance of the last lone star
Where the gates of Heaven wait ajar.

But all the Heaven my sense doth know:
—Three lemonade boxes in a row;
And the muddled dream I left an hour ago.

George A. C. Mackinlay,
'Sentry-Go' (April 1915)[1]

Last lone stars and fresh young airs still graced much poetry in the spring
of 1914. But the stars soon faded, and the young airs expired. Less romantic visions, and more banal objects—like those lemonade boxes—began
to appear more regularly even a year or so later. By 1918, a new generation

---

[1] George A. C. Mackinlay, *Poems* (Glasgow: Lyon, 1919), 53.

of poets had developed: writers whose direct experience of military life and combat left the sweetness of morns, or of years, often only muddled or muddied dreams.

Including Edmund Blunden, Ivor Gurney, Wilfred Owen, Isaac Rosenberg, Charles Hamilton Sorley, Siegfried Sassoon, and Edward Thomas—later canonized as 'war poets'—this new generation came to seem a distinctive, influential grouping in English poetry. Yet at some stages in the war, especially during its opening phases, new developments in poetry had seemed unlikely. Instead, it sometimes seemed that not only sweetness but poetry itself might be squeezed out of existence. A war threatening to overwhelm *any* established literary language or form might naturally have been considered especially challenging for the formalized, artificed discourse of poetry. 'Rent or furled | Are all Art's ensigns. Verse wails', Wilfred Owen worried in '1914'.[2] In a poem written at the end of that year, 'A Jingle on the Times', Thomas Hardy likewise questions whether the war left any role for the arts, wondering if the public might simply have concluded:

> —Poets we read not,
> Heed not, feed not,
> Men now need not
> What they do.[3]

Even in its early stages, though, there were strong signs—ones Hardy might have registered well before the end of 1914—that the war expanded demand for poetry, or at any rate greatly encouraged its writing. As Samuel Hynes records in *A War Imagined*, during August 1914, and for some time thereafter, *The Times* received as many as a hundred war poems every day, nearly all written by civilians. Other newspapers and journals were similarly inundated. Looking back in 1917, E. B. Osborn—editor of the anthology *The Muse in Arms*—wryly remarks on a 'huge harvest of war poetry by civilian verse-makers', adding that the 'bombardment

---

[2] Wilfred Owen, *Wilfred Owen: The Complete Poems and Fragments*, ed. Jon Stallworthy (London: Chatto and Windus, Hogarth Press, and Oxford University Press, 1983), I: 116. The poem was drafted late in 1914.

[3] Thomas Hardy, *The Complete Poems of Thomas Hardy*, ed. James Gibson (1976; rpt. London: Macmillan, 1991), 947. The poem was not published until 1917.

of defenceless persons by "concealed batteries [of] poets" had added a new terror to warfare'.[4]

Song and Spirit

Several factors contributed to this huge harvest, and to a continuing or expanding role for poetry in wartime. One of the most fundamental was simply the well-established role of poetry, and of linguistic artifice generally, throughout the life and imagination of the times. Though the cinema's popularity was growing rapidly, verbal as well as visual media maintained a strong position in leisure and entertainment during the early years of the century. Formalized language, its tricks and rhythms, were disseminated not only in printed literature, but much more widely through performance, popular recitation, and song. In music halls and theatres, in concert parties—or played on the 'eternal gramophone' Max Plowman recalls hearing everywhere, even in the trenches[5]—song and recitation played a huge part in entertaining both civilians and soldiers at the time. The attractions of song overlapped or were shared with those of contemporary poetry, and often celebrated in it. 'O sing us the songs, the songs of our own land', Siegfried Sassoon implores in 'Concert Party', describing 'hunger' among soldiers for

> God send you home; and then *A long, long trail*;
> *I hear you calling me*; and *Dixieland* ....
> Sing slowly...now the chorus...one by one
> We hear them, drink them; till the concert's done.[6]

'Hunger' for song was regularly satisfied by soldiers themselves, as many of them describe. In *The Red Horizon* (1916), Patrick MacGill defines his comrades as 'men who sing in the trenches, in the billet, and on the march...men who glory in song on the last lap of a long, killing journey in full marching order'. Edwin Campion Vaughan's wartime journal notes the 'magical' effect of songs on the morale even of exhausted men.

---

   [4] E. B. Osborn (ed.), *The Muse in Arms* (London: John Murray, 1917), xiv.
   [5] Max Plowman ['Mark VII'], *A Subaltern on the Somme: in 1916* (1927; rpt. New York: E. P. Dutton, 1928), 13.
   [6] Siegfried Sassoon, *Collected Poems: 1908–1956* (London: Faber and Faber, 1961), 100.

'So far as I know there were no poets or writers among us', George Coppard recalls of marching towards the Somme, but 'on we went, singing the bawdy songs we loved so well, towards one of the greatest, most terrible and frustrating battles in history'.[7]

Similar delight in song is recorded in the wartime poetry of Robert Service, better known as the author of pioneer ballads—'wild-west verses', in Edmund Blunden's description.[8] Service worked for the Canadian Red Cross and celebrates one of the most famous of wartime songs in 'Tipperary Days', suggesting that its singing offered a way of being 'battle-bound and heart-high'—of confronting danger while 'solaced…with scraps of song' ('Foreword'). Stress and danger accompanying these 'scraps' ensured that they were often deeply engraved on memory. 'Damn this jingle in my brain | I'm full of old songs', Harold Monro's disoriented soldier complains in 'Retreat'. Siegfried Sassoon likewise recalls that during a 'cannonading cataclysm' at the Front, he could not get out of his head the half-remembered advertising jingle '*They come as a boon and a blessing to men*, | *The Something, the Owl, and the Waverley Pen*'. Many soldiers, on both sides of the battlefield, lived and even died with such songs and jingles turning over in their minds—as Robert Graves suggests in 'It's a Queer Time', perhaps

> ….passing straight
> From Tipperary or their Hymn of Hate
> To Alleluiah-chanting, and the chime
> Of Golden harps…[9]

The war years, in other words, still lived and died—far more than later decades—under the sway of rhythmic forms of language. Yet this obviously does not account wholly for the flood of poetry at the start of the war, nor for continuing demand in the years that followed. This followed

---

[7] Patrick MacGill, *The Red Horizon* (London: Herbert Jenkins, 1916), 40–1; Edwin Campion Vaughan, *Some Desperate Glory: The World War I Diary of a British Officer, 1917* (1981; rpt. New York: Henry Holt, 1988), 176; George Coppard, *With a Machine Gun to Cambrai* (1980; rpt. London: Macmillan, 1986), 78.

[8] Edmund Blunden, *Undertones of War* (1928; rpt. Harmondsworth: Penguin, 1986), 8.

[9] Robert Service, *The Collected Poems of Robert Service* (1940; rpt. New York: G.P. Putnam's Sons, 1993), 291, 318; Dominic Hibberd and John Onions (eds), *The Winter of the World: Poems of the First World War* (London: Constable, 2008), 21; Siegfried Sassoon, *The Complete Memoirs of George Sherston* (1937; rpt. London: Faber and Faber, 1972), 331; Robert Graves, *Over the Brazier* (1916; rpt. London: St James Press, 1975), 30.

not only from the familiarity of formalized language, but from perception of poetry's particular powers in addressing difficult, 'heart-high'
times. Rather than being overwhelmed by the war, poetry sometimes
seemed the only means of confronting its challenges, or one at any rate
better adapted to them than other genres of writing. Though Henry
James had long sought to convince readers and critics of the aesthetic
qualities of fiction, it was still not always seen as a form of high art. As
George Bernard Shaw lamented in his introduction to *Heartbreak House*
(1919), drama was usually treated in the same way, particularly during
the war, when popular entertainment dominated the stage. Poetry, on
the other hand, continued to occupy a role in the literary sphere—like
the Royal Navy in the military one—as the Senior Service, the genre
most appropriate to serious emotion and the exalted stirrings of spirit
and soul. Poetry seemed the natural vehicle for patriotic effusions reaching *The Times* and other journals in August 1914. Its exalted potentials
were emphasized by the Poet Laureate at the time, Robert Bridges, in
The Spirit of Man (1916), a popular anthology he assembled in the early
years of the war and dedicated to the King. Half a dozen years later,
George Mallory continued to find the anthology suitably uplifting, reading it aloud to fellow climbers on the British Everest expeditions in 1922
and 1924.[10] 'Man is a spiritual being', Bridges remarks in his Preface, adding that from 'miseries, the insensate and interminable slaughter, the
hate and filth, we can turn to seek comfort only in the quiet confidence
of our souls; and we look instinctively to the seers and poets of mankind,
whose sayings are the oracles and prophecies of loveliness.'[11]

Though usually less effusive, many commentators confirm the wartime appeal Bridges outlines. In *Testament of Youth* (1933), Vera Brittain
records that 'all through the War poetry was the only form of literature I
could read for comfort', with Wordsworth and Shelley—authors strongly
favoured in Bridges's anthology—among those most likely to provide
the consolation she sought. The same poets were accorded a central role
by the *Times Literary Supplement* in 1916, in its analysis of 'Literature and
the War'. This described a new demand for poetry as 'the most striking

---

[10] See Wade Davis, *Into the Silence: The Great War, Mallory and the Conquest of Everest*
(London: Bodley Head, 2011), 416, 507.
[11] Robert Bridges (ed.), *The Spirit of Man* (London: Longmans, Green, 1916), [i–ii],
[iii–iv].

thing of all' among trends in reading and book purchase at the time, adding that it was as much in evidence among soldiers as civilians. 'Poetry counteracts the deadening influence a good deal', one serving soldier—Vera Brittain's brother Edmund—reported from the Italian Front.[12] Edmund Blunden was among many other soldiers who praised poetry's powers in dealing with deadening or deadly feelings—even when it had to be read under fire in a pillbox fortification. Forms of 'profound eighteenth-century calm' Blunden favours, or Wordsworth's intimations of immortality, naturally seemed alluring at a time when death and destruction were so ubiquitous. 'No man could be destroyed, once he had discovered poetry, the spirit of life', Henry Williamson's central character in *A Chronicle of Ancient Sunlight* concludes of his war experience. Though often sceptical and satirical in his attitudes to the war, even Sassoon suggests that 'the only answer to death is the life of the spirit'— one in which he considered poetry and 'the utterance of inspiration' to play substantial roles.[13]

A strong role in contemporary life and education ensured that poetry was seen not only as reading material by soldiers, but also written by many of them, on a scale eventually matching the 'huge harvest' from civilian writers. An episode in Ford Madox Ford's novel sequence *Parade's End* (1924–8) illustrates ready familiarity with poetry among new, well-educated officers in Kitchener's volunteer armies. Ford's hero Tietjens finds even the most exacting demands of poetic composition a welcome distraction from the stresses of the trenches, challenging a fellow officer to 'give me the fourteen end-rhymes of a sonnet and I'll write the lines. In under two minutes and a half.' Successful completion of this challenge confirms Tietjens's exceptional mental powers, emphasized throughout the novel, but his fellow officer is equally adept poetically. 'Of course I know what a sonnet is', he replies, promising to turn any composition Tietjens completes 'into Latin hexameters...in *under* three minutes'.[14] The *Wipers Times* of March 1916 suggests similar enthusiasms

[12] Vera Brittain, *Testament of Youth: An Autobiographical Study of the Years 1900–1925* (1933; rpt. London: Virago, 2004), 112, 362–3; 'Literature and the War', *Times Literary Supplement*, 1 June 1916, 253.

[13] Blunden, *Undertones of War*, 170; Henry Williamson, *A Test to Destruction* (London: Macdonald, 1960), 461; Siegfried Sassoon, *Siegfried's Journey: 1916–1920* (London: Faber and Faber, 1945), 193.

[14] Ford Madox Ford, *Parade's End* (1924–8; rpt. Harmondsworth: Penguin, 1982), 315.

were widely shared among officers, recording that 'an insidious disease is affecting the Division, and the result is a hurricane of poetry. Subalterns have been seen with a note-book in one hand, and bombs in the other absently walking near the wire in deep communion with the muse.' The editor goes on to hope that quartermasters might cease to break into song, and that 'a few of the poets would break into prose as a paper cannot live by "poems" alone'.[15] Subalterns were not the only victims, or sources, of this 'hurricane of poetry'. It was also widely produced by ordinary soldiers—even if, as George Coppard suggests, song may often have been enough for them while on the march. Among the war's canonical poets, both Isaac Rosenberg and Ivor Gurney were private soldiers. A private who served in the Royal Sussex Regiment on the Western Front recalled a more relaxed version of Tietjens's competition, in which—during 'blessed days of rest'—he and his fellow soldiers 'flung bits of poetry to each other and...teased to say what we had quoted'. Blunden describes finding a private soldier writing poetry while very far from blessed rest—while 'sitting on an ammunition box' in a saphead position, some way in advance of the front line.[16]

War Time and the Lyric

As these descriptions suggest, part of poetry's appeal in wartime, to all ranks, was the possibility it offered of reading or composition almost anywhere, in any corner of spare time which military duties might allow. The subtitle of George A. C. Mackinlay's 'Sentry-Go'—'Lines written in Springfield Goods Station, Falkirk'—emphasizes the use that could be made even of moments snatched from other duties. E. J. L. Garstin's 'Lines written between 1 and 2.30 a.m. in a German Dugout' offers a more extreme example.[17] Poetic opportunism of this kind suggests

---

[15] Patrick Beaver (ed.), *The Wipers Times: A Complete Facsimile* (London: Macmillan, 1973), 45.

[16] Alfred Wilcox, 'A July Day at St Julien', in C. B. Purdom (ed.), *True World War I Stories: Sixty Personal Narratives of the War* (1930; rpt. London: Robinson, 1999), 126; Edmund Blunden, Foreword to Brian Gardner (ed.), *Up the Line to Death: The War Poets 1914–1918: An Anthology* (1964; rpt. London: Methuen, 2007), vii.

[17] In Galloway Kyle (ed.), *Soldier Poets: Songs of the Fighting Men* (London: Erskine Macdonald, 1916), 25–6.

that some of the difficulties confronting war narratives, discussed in Chapter 2, can be seen either as relatively unproblematic for poets or even as positive advantages. Narrative manuscripts are bulky to carry around, and require extended periods—and their author's long survival—to complete. For soldiers necessarily travelling light, and lacking confident expectancy of long life, poetry's brevity offered obvious attractions. Descriptions in the *Wipers Times* of subalterns with notebook in one hand and bombs in the other were not altogether extravagant, as Garstin's poem confirms. Naturally, combatant poets completed much of their writing during periods of leave, convalescence, or relative safety. Yet many found it possible, like Robert Service, to continue 'tinkering' at 'bits of rhymes | In weary, woeful, waiting times', even while at or near the Front.[18] Rosenberg was obliged to do so, as he was much less favoured than officers with periods of leave. In a letter of May 1917, he explains that his 70-line poem 'Daughters of War' was started around eight months previously, and that 'it is only when we get a bit of rest and the others might be gambling or squabbling I add a line or two, and continue this way'.[19] His opportunism even extended to writing a poem on toilet paper, though this was later lost, in circumstances not recorded. Among officer-poets, Blunden mentions similar determination, describing his work on 'numerous pieces' while waiting for an attack in the summer of 1917, though all of these later 'vanished in the mud'.[20] The discovery of some of the war's most influential poems in Charles Hamilton Sorley's kit, after his death in October 1915, sadly confirms what could be achieved by war poets managing closely to combine composition and combat.

They were helped not only by poetry's brevity and relative quickness of completion. Poetry's brief, concentrated visions were also ideally appropriate to the fragmentary yet powerful experiences the war often offered. Chapter 2 quoted Bernard Adams's view of war service as 'a series of events so utterly different and disconnected' that they were encountered as if 'receiving a hand of cards from an invisible dealer'.[21] Though difficult

[18] Service, 'Foreword', *Collected Poems*, 291.

[19] Isaac Rosenberg, letter postmarked 27 May 1917 to Edward Marsh, *The Collected Works of Isaac Rosenberg: Poetry, Prose, Letters, Paintings and Drawings*, ed. Ian Parsons (London: Chatto and Windus/Hogarth Press, 1984), 255.

[20] Edmund Blunden, Preface to *The Poems of Edmund Blunden* (London: Cobden-Sanderson, 1930), v.

[21] See p. 95.

to accommodate within narrative conventions of connectedness and causality, this 'hand of cards' could be aptly represented in individual poems, each shaped by intense moments of wartime experience. As Galloway Kyle emphasizes in introducing *Soldier Poets: Songs of the Fighting Men* (1916), 'fine poetry' regularly arose from 'intensification of feeling and concentration of expression developed by military service...under extraordinary conditions'.[22] The war exposed combatant poets to huge diversities of feeling, sometimes alternating between confidence and despair, life and death, rapidly enough to endow even individual instants with extraordinary vividness. For Blunden, the chaos described in 'Third Ypres' left 'each moment puffed into a year with death'.[23] In 'The End of a War', Herbert Read's meditative officer recalls an 'edge':

> a ridge between eternal death and life eternal
> a moment of time, temporal.
> The universe swaying between Nothing and Being
> and life faltering like a clock's tick
> between a pendulum's coming and going.
> The individual lost: seventy years
> seventy minutes, have no meaning.[24]

A similar 'ridge' figures in Max Plowman's 'Going into the Line', which describes a world

> ... sharply cut in two. On one side lay
> A golden, dreamy, peaceful afternoon,
> And on the other, men gone mad with fear,
> A hell of noise and darkness, a Last Day.[25]

In 'Spring Offensive', probably one of his last poems, Wilfred Owen describes soldiers likewise poised between life and death, waiting on the final ridge of an advanced position, 'knowing their feet had come to the end of the world', immediately before an order to attack.[26] Owen's poems, and those of other canonical war poets, are often similarly edgy, envisaging lives swaying or faltering between 'Nothing and Being' in

[22] Kyle (ed.), *Soldier Poets*, 8.
[23] Blunden, *Poems*, 156.
[24] Herbert Read, *Collected Poems* (London: Faber and Faber, 1966), 111.
[25] Gardner (ed.), *Up the Line*, 101.
[26] Owen, *Complete Poems*, I: 192.

self-contained episodes occupying a few minutes, or at most a few hours. In 'Dulce et Decorum Est', Owen describes a few fleeting moments during a gas attack—leaving a soldier, barely awake at first, instead barely alive—and in 'The Sentry' concentrates on a few equally disastrous hours in a captured German trench. Being and nothingness are as swiftly juxtaposed in Sassoon's 'A Working Party', depicting a soldier who 'three hours ago...stumbled up the trench' but 'will never walk that road again' after 'the instant split | His startled life with lead, and all went out'.[27] These and many other poems demonstrate the effectiveness in recording war experience of the lyric form—war poets exploiting its capacity to focus intense feelings within split instants, or brief, particular moments of vision.

Losses in the present and the uncertainty of future survival encouraged many poets to play out another hand of cards, likewise endowed with intense feeling, but drawn from memories of a happier past. In 'Reverie', Richard Aldington worries that 'Tomorrow, maybe, I shall be one of them, | One in a vast field of dead men'. He escapes instead into a different field, a 'fair land' described as 'inviolable behind the walls of death', and based on vivid 'dreams of my love, |...she bending by the pale flower | And I beside her'. The same fleeting, remembered gesture consoles Rose Macaulay, recalling in 'Peace' a soldier dead and buried in France, yet still seen 'brown and alive...| As you stoop over the tall red foxglove'.[28] For Sassoon, such vivid, fragmentary memories of lost comrades are part of what characterizes war time, defined in 'Picture-Show' by analogy with the flickering new technology of cinema. 'Time spins so fast, and they've no time to stay | Beyond the moment's gesture of a lifted hand', Sassoon reflects of lost acquaintances. They come back to mind only as 'an endless picture-show, | Where wild or listless faces flicker on their way'.[29]

The war's highlighting of memories, and of a sense of loss, also figures in much of Edward Thomas's poetry, and might even account for a change of direction in his writing career during the war years. Juvenilia apart, all Thomas's poems were written between late 1914 and his departure for the

[27] Sassoon, *Collected Poems*, 20.
[28] Richard Aldington, *The Complete Poems of Richard Aldington* (London: Alan Wingate, 1948), 101; Hibberd and Onions (eds), *Winter*, 270.
[29] Sassoon, *Collected Poems*, 99.

trenches in January 1917, suggesting he might be considered a war poet as much for the timing of his output as for its interests. These continued the concentration on country life established in his extensive earlier prose writing, and include little direct commentary on the war. Yet in 'As the team's head-brass' and many other poems, Thomas suggests that much may be happening for the last time, in the poet's own life and in the wider life of the land. Anticipated loss heightens the intensity of memory—famously, in 'Adlestrop', his most celebrated poem, written in January 1915. Thomas recalls in it an unexpected 'lonely fair' moment, experienced the previous June, when 'a blackbird sang | Close by' and suddenly, 'for that minute', opened up for the poet, waiting in a briefly halted train, the life and birdsong of a whole sunny countryside. Like a later poet also writing with war much in mind—Louis MacNeice, in 'The Sunlight on the Garden' (1938)—in 'Adlestrop' and several other poems Thomas forlornly attempts to 'cage the minute | Within its nets of gold'. In 'As the team's head-brass', each time the plough-horses begin a new furrow, there is a moment when their 'head-brass flashed out on the turn'.[30] Like the horses, the rural world Thomas envisages is on the turn, from peace to war, and from old ways toward an uncertain future. In this darkening world, sunlit remembered moments—of a warm late June, in 'Adlestrop', or a mellow autumn in 'As the team's head-brass'—flash out with particular brilliance. Remembered, momentary gestures and individual instants of intense emotion—powerful 'cards' the memory deals out—may be less readily communicated in extended prose, and Thomas may have been drawn to the genre of lyric poetry partly in order to record them. More generally, his example confirms that in throwing isolated episodes upon the mind—whether from memory or immediate experience—the flickering, faltering temporalities of 'war time' could be productive as well as problematic for contemporary poets.

The lyric form offered further advantages in wartime, particularly in meeting challenges which military life and discipline imposed upon individual autonomy and self-respect. Poets were certainly as alert as prose writers to the difficulties concerned. In a letter of 1916, Isaac Rosenberg defines the army as 'the most detestable invention on this earth',

---

[30] Edward Thomas, *The Annotated Collected Poems*, ed. Edna Longley (Northumberland: Bloodaxe, 2008), 51, 123; Louis MacNeice, *Collected Poems* (1966; rpt. London: Faber and Faber, 1979), 84.

adding that only a private 'knows what it is to be a slave'.[31] 'Who sent us forth? Who takes us home again?', Charles Hamilton Sorley demands in 'A hundred thousand million mites we go', describing soldiers merely as innumerable insects, 'wheeling and tacking o'er the eternal plain' in 'blindness and great blindness'.[32] Similar anonymity and apparent aimlessness dominate Owen's poem about departure for the war, 'The Send-Off'. Decked in flowers more suggestive of funerals or sacrifice than lovers' gifts, Owen's soldiers are pressed into 'close darkening lanes', then into a train boarded almost as cattle rather than as humans—from a 'siding-shed' rather than a platform. They depart 'secretly, like wrongs hushed-up'.[33] If any manage to return, it will be anonymously, with no sense of honour, purpose, or belonging. Meantime, no one seems to know where they are going, or to be responsible for sending them. They are despatched instead not by human agency, but by railway machinery that has apparently usurped its role—by signals that nod, and a lamp that winks.

Resistance to such anonymity is explored directly in a few war poems—such as Owen's 'With an Identity Disk', which rejects conventional trappings of fame and public honour in favour of limited, ephemeral survivals of personal significance, based on individual loyalty and affection. A more fundamental, comprehensive resistance inheres in the lyric form itself—in its concise, concentrated communication not only of individual episodes, but of the thoughts and feelings of individuals experiencing them. Chapter 2 described the distortions of propaganda and the pressures of military life encouraging autobiographical narrative, able to offer the authenticity of direct witnessing and personal response to the war. Strongly autobiographical—either in describing its author's own experience and inner life or in delivering a personal vision of wider events—lyric poetry offers concise, intense forms of the same potential. This ensured an appeal in wartime at least as strong among serving soldiers as civilians, and a harvest of poetry, from the battlefields, eventually as extensive as any appearing on the Home Front in 1914.

[31] Letter of 11 March to Lascelles Abercrombie, *Collected Works*, 230.

[32] Charles Hamilton Sorley, *The Collected Poems of Charles Hamilton Sorley*, ed. Jean Moorcroft Wilson (London: Woolf, 1985), 74.

[33] Owen, *Complete Poems*, I: 172.

Pastoral

In his memoir *Undertones of War* (1928), Edmund Blunden indicates another aspect of poetry's contemporary appeal—and of its potential in confronting the challenges of the war—when he talks of 'coincidence of nature without and nature within'. These challenges were regularly resisted in war writing through literature's long-established connection of inner life and imagination with the natural world. Describing himself as 'a harmless young shepherd in a soldier's coat', Blunden explores these pastoral connections throughout *Undertones of War*, celebrating pleasures discoverable in nature even quite close to the trenches. 'Lawny coolness three kilometres from the line' allows the summer of 1916 'to multiply his convolvulus, his linnets and butterflies', while 'acres of self-sown wheat glistened and sighed...the lizard ran warless in the warm dust; and the ditches were trembling quick with odd tiny fish'. 'Life, life abundant sang here and smiled', Blunden remarks, finding nature's allures heightened by their proximity to 'the last sharp turnings into the unknown'.[34] Many other writers—of prose as well as poetry—record this allure, both during the war and in its immediate aftermath. A. D. Gristwood's novel *The Coward* (1927) describes moving even a short distance from the Front as an escape 'from the dust and roar of the bombardment into another world—the old familiar world of trees and fields and sunshine. Behind us lay the Abomination of Desolation'.[35] Many such moments of escape figure in the account of the war in Williamson's *Chronicle of Ancient Sunlight*. It was a form of escape Williamson practised extensively himself in later years. Most famous as the author of *Tarka the Otter* (1927), he was inspired—like Edward Thomas and many of his contemporaries—by the nature writing of Richard Jeffries, retiring after the war to rural Devon, an experience reflected in his *Flax of Dream* novel sequence (1921–8). Ford Madox Ford attempted a similar retreat, moving in 1919 to a cottage in rural Sussex, described in the war reminiscences he published as *No Enemy: A Tale of Reconstruction* (1929).

The 'world of trees and fields and sunshine' these authors favour probably remained more widely familiar in the early part of the twentieth

---

[34] Blunden, *Undertones of War*, xi, 191, 24, 21.
[35] A. D. Gristwood, *The Somme: Including Also the Coward* (1927; rpt. Columbia: University of South Carolina Press, 2006), 160–1.

century than in its later, more urbanized years. War correspondents—such as *The Times* journalist quoted at the start of Chapter 1—still found it worth mentioning sunshine, mists, herbage, and islands of cloud even in the course of describing an 'Abomination of Desolation' on the Somme. Huge numbers of volunteers joining Kitchener's armies soon found themselves engaged in outdoor life, whether familiar or not, and often showed an imaginative readiness to appreciate the attractions it offered. George Ramage's journal lists by name a dozen wild flowers blooming near the Front in May 1915, and regularly describes splendours of landscape and sky, such as the way a 'gorgeous, golden, immense, egg shaped moon rose behind a thin line of gaunt trees'. He also indicates careful appreciation of nature surviving even under the rough conditions of army life in France. His journal mentions 'a nest which contains a very tame & spry bird with four chicks—prominent on the bush is the notice "Be careful, bird's nest"—soldiers watch it feed its young'.[36]

Widely evident in prose accounts of the war, appreciation of nature was still more pervasive in contemporary poetry. Early in the twentieth century, a newcomer to English literature might have been forgiven for thinking poetry somehow a branch of botany, or biology. For those familiar with literary history, contemporary writing obviously remained firmly shaped by traditions of pastoral and nature writing extending back to the Romantic poets and beyond. Blunden, for example, recalled that when he began writing poetry around the war years—as 'a picturesque interpreter of the English countryside'—it was in awareness of 'so rich a literature…already in that field', and one thoroughly familiar to writers and contemporary audiences alike.[37] Along with Wordsworth and Shelley, Romantic or late-Romantic writers such as Keats and W. B. Yeats predominate in Bridges's 1916 *Spirit of Man* anthology, favoured presumably for an oracular 'loveliness' particularly resistant to 'slaughter…hate and filth'. Pastoral preferences among contemporary readers and authors were further served by anthologies of 'Georgian' poetry appearing between 1912 and 1922 and enjoying wide sales at the time. Edited by Edward Marsh, supported in their early stages by Rupert

---

[36] 'The Rather Tame War Experiences in Flanders 1915 of Lance Corporal George Ramage, 1st Battalion, Gordon Highlanders'. National Library of Scotland MS944–7, II: 1–2; I: 82; III: 41–2.

[37] Blunden, *Poems*, vii.

Brooke, and published by Harold Monro through his Poetry Bookshop, the five anthologies were intended to support the work of new and innovative writers. Early volumes did fulfil some of the Georgians' wish for more authentic treatment of ordinary speech and daily life—occasionally, in the work of Wilfrid Wilson Gibson and others, set in the cities. Later ones included some of the first published work of war poets such as Blunden, Rosenberg, Sassoon, and Graves. Generally, though, and increasingly as the sequence went on, Georgian poetry continued to look at the areas W. H. Davies favours in 'A Great Time'—ones 'beyond the town, where wild flowers grow'—and to offer conventional, often prettily pastoral views of rustic life, cuckoos, rainbows, and flowers.[38]

Poets who began writing during the Great War, in other words, usually did so—like Blunden—in awareness of pastoral–Romantic influences both long-standing and popularly contemporary. Appearing widely, and in a range of uses, these influences require extended discussion. They illustrate the established strengths of poetry in 1914, as well as the ways these were taken to the limit, and ultimately greatly changed— away from emphases on spirit and 'loveliness'—by the challenges combatant poets had to confront as the war went on. In its early stages, one of the first uses of pastoral was in consolidating—almost literally, in grounding—patriotism and a hesitant sense of purpose during the uncertain late summer of 1914. In 'August 1914', one of the Georgian poets, John Masefield, draws on Wordsworth and other Romantic writers in describing 'an endless quiet valley' in Berkshire, graced at sunset by memories of 'heartfelt things, past-speaking dear | To unknown generations of dead men'. Though these local men had left reluctantly to serve, and die, 'in foreign lands | For some idea but dimly understood', their heartfelt love for this countryside remains, for Masefield, an undying spirit ennobling its twilit fields and still deeply infused in the evening glow that falls upon them.[39] Implicitly, in this way, 'August 1914' encourages any reader considering enlistment and possible death abroad, suggesting in vague but exalted terms—half-pastoral and half-spiritual— what they might be fighting for.

---

[38] Edward Marsh (ed.), *Georgian Poetry: 1913–1915* (1915; rpt. London: The Poetry Bookshop, 1918), 69.

[39] Hibberd and Onions (eds), *Winter*, 14–15.

Similar suggestions figured in several other poems, at the time and later, though not always with the sombre eloquence marking 'August 1914'. With logic less subtle than Masefield's—or just less comprehensible—Geoffrey Howard claimed in 1915 that 'Malvern men must die and kill | That wind may blow on Malvern Hill' ('Without Shedding of Blood...').[40] In 'Battle', Robert Nichols likewise proposes that 'English downs' and 'scenes and sounds of the countryside' deserve to be 'enriched by blood'.[41] Though less bloodthirstily, Ford Madox Ford continued to explain in 1918, in 'Footsloggers', that

> ... it is for the sake of the wolds and the wealds
> That we die,
> And for the sake of the quiet fields,
> And the path through the stackyard gate.[42]

Typically, the 'wolds and wealds' and pastoral scenery on which patriotism is based in these poems are specifically English, and mostly southern. Other areas of Britain are less often represented, though poets such as Nowell Oxland, in 'Outward Bound' return to the Cumberland landscapes beloved of the early Romantic poets. Scottish war poets, such as Sorley and E. A. Mackintosh, show fewer or different commitments to the pastoral, though an elegiac consolation is drawn extensively from nature in John Buchan's 'On Leave', mourning the dead of 1916. In the later view of W. H. Auden's 'In Praise of Limestone' (1951), 'granite wastes' may suggest only 'how permanent is death', perhaps making some northern landscapes less appropriate for pastoral poetry in general, and its wartime versions particularly.[43] At any rate, war poets seeking 'coincidence of nature without and nature within' seemed to find it most readily in the long-domesticated fields and farms of Berkshire, Oxfordshire, and Gloucestershire (Fig. 10).

Edward Thomas's poetry shares this southern setting, and occasionally the patriotic feelings other writers attached to it. 'This is no case of petty right or wrong', in particular, describes patriotic commitments

---

[40] Ibid. 73.

[41] Robert Nichols, *Ardours and Endurances* (1917; rpt. London: Chatto and Windus, 1918), 28–9.

[42] Hibberd and Onions (eds), *Winter*, 209.

[43] W. H. Auden, *Collected Shorter Poems* (1966; rpt. London: Faber and Faber, 1971), 240.

FIG 10 Late in 1915, the central figure of Rose Allatini's *Despised and Rejected* (1918) notices a new recruiting poster depicting 'a pink-kneed Highlander with arm outflung against a highly-coloured patchwork of field and hedge' (p. 200). As he suggests, the poster shows a conspicuously Scottish solider defending what appears to be the Cotswolds.

© Imperial War Museums (Art. IWM PST 0320)

which the poet emphasizes are owed not to the rhetoric of newspapers and politicians, but to the very dust of the land beneath his feet. Thomas's attitude in this poem—literally down-to-earth—is typical of a vision of rural life generally harsher and more authentic than the Georgians', despite the intentions their movement professed. Thomas was friendly with several of those involved, and sometimes wrote poems as botanical or flower-strewn as theirs—'October', for example, names seven flowers and seven other plants in its twenty-one lines. But his work did not appear in the Georgian anthologies, and usually avoids the pretty coincidences of nature and humanity favoured by many of the authors who were included. Instead, in poems such as 'A Private', 'February Afternoon', 'The Owl', or 'Man and Dog' Thomas envisages a countryside newly disturbed by the pressures of the war, and often hostile or indifferent to human desires. Its aloofness nevertheless offers consolations of its own. 'February Afternoon' invokes recurrences and endurances— 'making as a day | A thousand years'—which reach far beyond the poet's concerns about transience in his own life or in the rural community.[44] Thomas's work often resembles Hardy's, and the eternal recurrences suggested in the latter's 'In Time of "The Breaking of Nations"' also appear in 'As the team's head-brass'. Like Hardy, Thomas suggests a fertile vitality in the reiterated movements of ploughing, and of lovers who vanish into and return from a wood. These movements counterpoint immediate threats of loss and destruction—storms that fell trees across the fields; distant battles that fell men who laboured on their soil. Like much of Thomas's work, 'As the team's head-brass' indicates involutions of nature, landscape, war, loss, and recurrence troublingly unresolved for the poet, yet profoundly compelling for his poetry, contributing to the strongest development of the pastoral idiom in the early twentieth century.

Ivor Gurney admired Thomas's work, grew up close to the areas of Gloucestershire in which some of it is set, and recalled this landscape vividly during his time serving abroad. These memories are deployed quite systematically in his poetry, remembered scenes repeatedly offering the 'resort' he describes in 'First March', helping 'the mind to

[44] Thomas, *Annotated Collected*, 109.

escape...its vain | Own circling greyness and stain'. The title of his first collection, *Severn and Somme* (1917), emphasizes the importance of this mental resort, described in 'Strange Service' as a 'daily being' in the poet's 'deep heart', and a basis for a landscape-based patriotism comparable to Thomas's. Addressing England in the same poem, Gurney accepts that 'you bore me | Under the Cotswold hills beside the water meadows, | To do you dreadful service, here, beyond your borders'. Yet even while remaining firmly loyal to 'hills of home, woodlands, white roads and inns' ('Crickley Hill'), Gurney also relishes the potential of foreign landscapes in allowing 'the mind to escape'. Landscapes of Severn and Somme were after all not so unalike. Close to the battlefields in France and Belgium, the countryside often appeared conveniently comparable to the southern English landscapes wartime pastoral most favoured. Though acknowledging that it was difficult to find 'what is sweet | Of Ypres plains', Gurney nevertheless praises 'autumn sunlight and the fleet | Clouds after rains, || Blue sky and mellow distance softly blue' ('Memory, Let All Slip').[45]

Many war poets shared this readiness to find redeeming, restorative features not only in remembered landscapes but even in close proximity to the battlefields. Like Gurney's, several poems Blunden wrote during the war return entirely to remembered English scenes, sometimes described in conventional, fanciful pastoral images of 'lilied lakes', 'wood fairies', and 'bubbling brooks of elfin song' ('The Unchangeable'). Yet these poems alternate with others set close to the Front—often in rest areas, like those described in *Undertones or War*, just to the rear of the trenches. Quiet days described in 'Bleue Maison' offer Blunden, like Gurney, an opportunity to 'attune [his] dull soul... | To the contentment of this countryside', and to notice 'poppies flaring', 'blossomed bean and clover', and 'rifts of blue above the trees'. 'At Senlis Once' likewise records 'reviving' offered by finding 'green grass thriving' within walking distance of 'clay and...death' in the front line. Much of Blunden's poetry even describes nature continuing to thrive, and console, not only behind the trenches, but on the battlefields themselves. 'War Autobiography' recalls 'sunny times... | Even in shattered Festubert', and that in 'many a

---

[45] Ivor Gurney, *Collected Poems of Ivor Gurney*, ed. P. J. Kavanagh (Oxford: Oxford University Press, 1982), 75, 31, 56, 53.

valley of death | Some trifling thing has given me breath'. Among moments 'puffed into a year with death' in 'Third Ypres', Blunden still records an escape from 'the abyss of madness' offered by the way 'a score of field-mice nimble, | And tame and curious look about them; (these | Calmed me, on these depended my salvation)'.[46] Wilfred Owen sometimes indicates similar powers in some 'trifling thing' in the natural world. Though soldiers in 'Spring Offensive' know 'their feet had come to the end of the world', the poem also describes how 'buttercups | Had blessed with gold their slow boots coming up'. While 'marvelling' at the extremity of their position, Owen's soldiers also have time to register 'the long grass swirled | By the May breeze, murmurous with wasp and midge'.[47]

Skies and Stars

Pastoral vision, in other words, was by no means entirely suppressed by the life and death of the front line. But it was often encouraged to follow new directions, or, literally, to develop new angles. Max Plowman explains that he borrows from Ruskin the idea that 'the upper and more glorious half of Nature's pageant goes unseen by the majority of people', and goes on to remark that 'the trenches have altered that. Shutting off the landscape, they compel us to observe the sky'. As he suggests, the trenches offered good reasons to turn affirmative views of nature through ninety degrees, from horizontal towards the vertical. Looking straight out over the parapet of a trench invited death by a sniper's bullet, and in any case revealed only the 'shell-stricken waste' Plowman describes in *A Subaltern on the Somme* (1927), largely devoid of vegetation or of living creatures.[48] A cosmopolitan rat turns up in Rosenberg's 'Break of Day in the Trenches', but Blunden's calming mice are among few other instances of earth-bound wildlife appealing to war poets. Looking up was a different matter. Flocks of clouds, in war poetry, or more often of birds, replace the flocks of sheep beloved of conventional pastoral. Nine separate species are named in 'Magpies in Picardy', T. P. Cameron

[46] Blunden, *Poems*, 48, 43, 144–5, 169, 155.
[47] Owen, *Complete Poems*, I: 192.
[48] Plowman, *Subaltern*, 72.

Wilson's description of birds which 'flicker down the dusty roads' leading to the Front, catching 'the sunlight that sings | And dances in deep shadows', heightening 'the beauty of the wild green earth'. Lost beauty is likewise restored in Blunden's 'Les Halles d'Ypres' by pigeons that continue to 'flaunt and preen, | And flicker in playful flight', even among the ruins. Henry L. Simpson's 'Consequences' similarly celebrates a cuckoo and other birds that 'all day long…over and under | And in among the interminable moan | Of shells, sing and are happy and build and love'.[49]

Above all, though, the imagination of war poets is transfixed by the indomitable flight and song of larks—used as a metaphor for war poetry itself, in Kyle's Preface to *Soldier Poets* in 1916. Edward Thomas's diary entry for 7 April 1917, the day before he was killed, records larks—along with partridges, sparrows, and magpies—much in evidence despite 'continuous shelling'. In 'The Iron Music', written within days of first arriving near the Front in July 1916, Ford Madox Ford immediately notices larks singing above the noise of the guns. For Robert Service, they provide a 'leaping rapture' and 'a fusillade of melody' ('The Lark').[50] Their fame spread among civilians, including Wilfrid Wilson Gibson, in 'The Lark', or Muriel Elsie Graham, inspired by a French newspaper account of the front line to write another admiring poem, 'The Lark above the Trenches'. John W. Streets uses much the same title for one of his poems, and further celebrates the lark's 'immortal ode' in another, 'Shelley in the Trenches'.[51] As his reference to Shelley suggests, larks were already endowed with a long lineage in English poetry, stretching back to the Romantics, and might have replaced poppies in later memorialization of the Great War had they offered a more conveniently portable symbol. The two regularly appear together in war writing—such as Cecil Lewis's memoir *Sagittarius Rising* (1936), in which lark and poppy crystallize a moment's vivid memory, a vision of nature 'undaunted by the desolation, heedless of human fury and stupidity'.[52] They also figure together in John McCrae's 'In Flanders Fields', which quickly became

[49] Hibberd and Onions (eds), *Winter*, 101–2, 230; Blunden, *Poems*, 40.

[50] Edward Thomas, *The Collected Poems of Edward Thomas*, ed. R. George Thomas (Oxford: Oxford University Press, 1981), 194; Service, *Collected Poems*, 310.

[51] John W. Streets, 'A Lark above the Trenches', in Frederick Brereton (ed.), *An Anthology of War Poems* (London: Collins, 1930), 150; Vivien Noakes (ed.), *Voices of Silence: The Alternative Book of First World War Poetry* (Stroud: Sutton, 2006), 83.

[52] Cecil Lewis, *Sagittarius Rising* (1936; London: Warner, 1998), 113.

one of the most famous of all Great War poems, and the one most responsible for poppies' eventual centrality in remembrance. Published late in 1915, a time of growing war-weariness, the poem's original success was owed not only to its celebration of undaunted nature—of blowing poppies, and larks that 'still bravely singing, fly'—but also to McCrae's implication that similar resilience should be maintained in the war effort.[53]

Flocks of birds and the song of larks were only part of the appeal of the sky, alluringly inviolate when compared to the war-torn earth. Describing 'Sad, smoking, flat horizons, reeking woods' in 'Prelude: The Troops', Sassoon suggests that in a 'land where all | Is ruin...nothing blossoms but the sky'. In 'Bombardment', Aldington likewise records that after days in which the landscape was 'rent and torn | By bursting steel', his comrades are still able to gaze 'above the wreckage of the earth | To where the white clouds moved in silent lines | Across the untroubled blue'.[54] As well as the blue of broad daylight, war poetry regularly celebrates the skies at sunrise and sunset. There were particular reasons for doing so, even beyond the appeal of colourful cloudscapes. As Paul Fussell explains in his extended discussion of pastoral in *The Great War and Modern Memory*, each of these times was one of heightened activity in the trenches. All soldiers in the front line were required to 'stand-to' at both dusk and dawn, in readiness for attacks frequently timed to take advantage of evening or—more often—morning twilight. Along with 'In Flanders Fields', one of the most popular Great War poems is Laurence Binyon's 'For the Fallen'—anticipating that the dead will be remembered 'at the going down of the sun and in the morning'. First published in September 1914, 'For the Fallen' actually preceded most trench warfare and its settled patterns of duty, though these soon became thoroughly familiar to serving soldiers. For civilians at the time, and since, sunset and sunrise naturally suggest transition, poignantly associating ephemeral human life with the evanescent shades of the sky.

'For the Fallen' goes on to describe stars, 'moving in marches upon the heavenly plain'.[55] For soldiers experiencing an outdoor life for the first time, periods between sunset and sunrise offered most novelty, revealing

[53] Hibberd and Onions (eds), *Winter*, 56.
[54] Sassoon, *Collected Poems*, 67; Aldington, *Complete Poems*, 105.
[55] Brereton (ed.), *Anthology*, 39–40.

a heavenly plain they might have had little reason or opportunity to notice in civilian life. As the wounded soldier in Wilfred Wilson Gibson's 'Between the Lines' reflects, when 'Serving in the shop, | Stars didn't count for much…|…| You didn't see much but the city lights'. At the Front he finds instead that 'he'd never in his life seen so much sky', nor stars 'so thick-sown, | Millions and millions'.[56] Many authors shared Max Plowman's pleasure in the 'calm serenity' of this prospect, 'beyond the power of weak and petty madness' since the armies 'cannot shoot the stars'.[57] For poets, the night sky offered still more distanced aloofness than the blue vault of daylight, and one still more compelling. 'The untroubled blue' that appeals to Aldington in 'Bombardment' is more than matched by the nightly return of the moon, 'haughty and perfect', and by the way 'night after night the Pleiades sing | And Orion swings his belt across the sky' ('In the Trenches').[58] The same preferences figure widely in Ivor Gurney's work, the editor of his *Collected Poems* even suggesting that if Gurney 'is to be given a locality, he could with more justice be called a sky-poet' than a Gloucestershire one. As he remarks, the sky provides a 'resort' as promising as memories of the Gloucestershire countryside—a nightly opportunity, described in 'The Battalion Is Now on Rest', to 'watch the stars and find | Some peace like the old peace, some soothe for soul and mind'. Such peace seems possible even in 'Half Dead', Gurney's record of stumbling out 'dazed into half dark' when suffering from dysentery, yet finding 'still were the stars bright—my sick mind hung on them even'. 'Hunger and weak body' are tempered by visions that can 'drown sorrow deep'—by looking 'for Argo or Sirius in the east skies or for Regulus'.[59]

Gurney would have known the constellations and their names since his youth. New-found interests in the heavenly plain, among Kitchener's armies, account for a puzzle mentioned in the *Times Literary Supplement* in 1916. Along with resurgent demand for poetry, its survey of 'Literature and the War' notes 'a curious increase in the sale of books on astronomy', attributing it to 'the airmen's new familiarity with the stars'.[60] Royal

---

[56] Wilfrid Wilson Gibson, *Battle* (London: Elkin Matthews, 1916), 44.

[57] Plowman, *Subaltern*, 46.

[58] Aldington, *Collected Poems*, 82.

[59] P. J. Kavanagh, Introduction to Gurney, *Collected Poems*, 1, 46, 81–2.

[60] *Times Literary Supplement*, 1 June 1916, 253.

Flying Corps poets such as Paul Bewsher, Gordon Alchin, and Jeffrey Day regularly celebrate the beauties of the sky, and Cecil Lewis offers a vivid account of the first night flights in *Sagittarius Rising*. But stars and the heavenly plain probably appealed still more strongly to ordinary, earth-bound infantrymen—obliged, as Frederic Manning describes in 'The Trenches', to look up at 'the sky, seen as from a well', and often the only open space they could look at safely.[61] This appeal extended naturally enough towards astronomical or scientific interests.

Occasionally, it extended further, towards religious ones. For Robert Service, the lark's flight was an encouragement to look upward not only towards a 'bit of blue', but to 'lift shining eyes, see Heaven too' ('The Lark'). Generally, the war provoked a sharp decline in conventional religion, though for different individuals, its pressures could concentrate either faith or scepticism, leaving heaven seeming either closer or more distant than ever. Edward Thomas's 'February Afternoon', for example, envisages a God wholly unmoved by war—one who 'sits aloft...|...stone-deaf and stone-blind'. Leslie Coulson implies similar insentience in 'Who Made the Law?'—in bitter questions such as 'who made the Law that men should die in meadows?', or 'who spread the hills with flesh, and blood, and brains?'[62] For Robert Bridges, on the other hand, in his preface to *The Spirit of Man*, 'trust in God' seemed more than ever indispensable. For poets lifting shining eyes heavenward, some of this trust was replaced—or extended—by an enlargement of pastoral imagination towards a kind of pantheism. 'Help me to Die, O Lord', William Noel Hodgson prays, straightforwardly enough, in 'Before Action'—a poem whose impact was much increased by its author's death on the Somme, two days after its first publication. But Hodgson asks for his prayers to be fulfilled as much by the powers of the natural sphere as the divine one—

> By all the glories of the day
> And the cool evening's benison,
> By that last sunset touch that lay
> Upon the hills when day was done.[63]

[61] Martin Stephen (ed.), *Never Such Innocence* (1988; rpt. London: Dent, 2003), 90.

[62] Service, *Collected Poems*, 310; Thomas, *Annotated Collected*, 109; Hibberd and Onions (eds), *Winter*, 133.

[63] Hibberd and Onions (eds), *Winter*, 98.

Several other poets describe death contained or transcended through this everlasting natural world. Robert Nichols's 'Sonnet: Our Dead' suggests that the dead 'have not gone from us' but 'flame in every star', 'chant on every wind', and 'return | In the long roll of any deep blue wave'. In 'To "My People" before the "Great Offensive"', E. F. Wilkinson reflects on endurance beyond death 'in the wind that hurries by' or 'in the voice of birds, the scent of flowers, | The evening silence and the falling dew | ... every throbbing pulse of nature's powers'.[64] In one of his popular sonnets of 1914, 'Safety', Rupert Brooke likewise describes himself as 'armed against all death's endeavour' by 'all things undying, | The winds, and morning... | The deep night, and birds singing, and clouds flying'. Similar consolations are offered by Julian Grenfell's 'Into Battle', another poem much admired in the early months of the war. 'The fighting man', in Grenfell's view, 'shall from the sun | Take warmth, and life from the glowing earth', enjoying the 'high comradeship' of 'The Dog-Star, and the Sisters Seven, | Orion's Belt and sworded hip'. Even when 'death moans and sings' all around him, he can be assured that his fate is part of a 'Destined Will', and that 'Day shall clasp him with strong hands, | And Night shall fold him in soft wings'.[65]

Against Nature

Poems such as Grenfell's, or several others quoted above, confirm what a powerful resource pastoral could provide during the war, and how far it allowed some poets to extend the optimism and exalted vision embodied in Bridges's *Spirit of Man*. Yet affirmative pastoral visions inevitably proved harder to sustain as the war continued, and more and more soldier-poets witnessed its worst conditions for themselves. Several of the more idealistic writers working in its earlier years were killed, Grenfell and Brooke included, and new soldiers arriving at the Front were as likely to find hills and meadows 'spread... with flesh and blood and brains' as any last evening touch of the sun. The natural world continued to prove absorbing, but often as a context for disillusion rather than

---

[64] Nichols, *Ardours*, 66; Kyle (ed.), *Soldier Poets*, 106.
[65] Rupert Brooke, *The Complete Poems* (1932; rpt. London: Sidgwick and Jackson, 1945),147; Hibberd, and Onions (eds), *Winter*, 52–3.

idealism. Even before encountering violent action, new soldiers were likely to find an outdoor life at least as full of privations as pleasures. Scepticism of pastoral poetic conventions was sometimes a direct result. 'We have been living in a sort of rustic bower', R. L. Mackay's diary of life at the Front records, 'such as the poets sing about—until they have to live in one in a rainstorm'. George A. C. Mackinlay seems to have had his ideals similarly dampened. Known for a few nature poems, much in the Georgian manner, published in the *Glasgow Herald* before the war, he reflects in 'Route March Roundelay' that life in the army still allows him to admire grasses, dew, and clover, but leaves him just as often 'layer deep in dust, blasphemy deep in sweat'.[66]

Changed attitudes towards pastoral convention are symptomatic of the wider move in war poetry, away from romantic idealism, mentioned earlier and typified by Mackinlay's shift of attention from lone star to lemonade box. Any disillusion in 'Route March Roundelay' or 'Sentry-Go', though, is mild compared with some of the views of canonical war poets. Unlike Sassoon and other writers quoted above, in 'Recalling War', Robert Graves remembers neither 'blossom' nor any other affirmation to be found even in the sky. Instead, he envisages the whole conflict as 'an infection of the common sky | That sagged ominously upon the earth', perhaps recalling Blunden's description in 'The Zonnebeke Road' of how 'the low sky like a load | Hangs over—a dead weight'.[67] Graves might equally have had in mind Owen's view, in 'Exposure', that soldiers 'only know war lasts, rain soaks, and clouds sag stormy'. 'Exposure' also describes the 'merciless iced east winds that knive us', and a 'poignant misery of dawn'—grey, sunless, and thoroughly remote from Binyon's nostalgic sunrises and sunsets.[68] As poems such as 'Exposure' and 'The Zonnebeke Road' emphasize, skies could hardly offer uninterruptedly a blue vault of daylight, or star-strewn heavenly plains at night. On the contrary, men froze to death in winter, as Owen describes in 'Futility', summer heat could be overwhelming, and the rain—often endured without the protection even of a 'rustic bower'—sometimes so constant

---

[66] The War Diary of Lieut. R. L Mackay, 11th and later 1st/8th Battalions, Argyll and Sutherland Highlanders, September 1916 to January 1919. National Library of Scotland, Acc. 12350/18, 30 July 1918, 74; Mackinlay, *Poems*, 57.

[67] Jon Silkin (ed.), *The Penguin Book of First World War Poetry* (Harmondsworth: Penguin, 1981), 121; Blunden, *Poems*, 147.

[68] Owen, *Collected Poems*, I: 185.

that many British soldiers believed it was somehow directed upon them by the enemy.

Even on good days—perhaps especially then—unbridgeable distances seemed troublingly to intervene between earth and sky, nature and imagination. Georges Duhamel describes a sunny interlude in the summer of 1915 as 'one of those days when the supreme indifference of Nature makes one feel the burden of war more cruelly, when the beauty of the sky seems to proclaim its remoteness from the anguish of the human heart'.[69] For many writers, the war seemed more than sufficiently *un*natural—destructive of all generative potentials—to deny any affirmative 'coincidence of nature without and nature within'. Coincidence or correlation were replaced in their work by forms of counterpoint, conflict, or just complete separateness and disconnection. Views very close to Duhamel's reappear in the work of a very different writer—in the middle section of Virginia Woolf's *To the Lighthouse* (1927), set in the war years. Anyone walking on a beach at that time, Woolf suggests, might find soiled, staining traces of naval action disturbingly at odds with 'the usual tokens of divine bounty', making it difficult to maintain any idea that 'beauty outside mirrored beauty within', or might 'reflect the compass of the soul'. 'Did Nature supplement what man advanced?', *To the Lighthouse* goes on to ask, 'did she complete what he began?' The novel's reply—'with equal complacence she saw his misery, condoned his meanness, and acquiesced in his torture'—sums up a new sense of fracture and failure in pastoral imagination, troubling many poets at the time.[70]

Distances between nature and the human sphere, earth and the heavens, were highlighted even after a few weeks of the war. Published in its third month, Alice Meynell's 'Summer in England, 1914' recalls the year's famously glorious weather—also celebrated in Masefield's 'August 1914'—mentioning 'benignant skies' and 'moon after moon ... heavenly-sweet'. Yet her poem adds that 'the armies died convulsed' nevertheless, shattered into 'one wet corruption'.[71] Incongruities of this kind were expressed still more bitterly as the war continued. Geoffrey Dearmer's

[69] Georges Duhamel, *The New Book of Martyrs* (1917), trans. Florence Simmonds (London: William Heinemann, 1918), 129.

[70] Virginia Woolf, *To the Lighthouse* (1927; rpt. Harmondsworth: Penguin, 1973), 146, 152, 153.

[71] Hibberd and Onions (eds), *Winter*, 17.

account of a battle on the first day of the Somme, 'Gommecourt', praises 'the beauty of the Earth' and 'sacraments the Summer yields', but adds that the 'silent dignity' of the moon and 'the vast star-soldiered army of the sky' simply 'scorned the petty tragedy of Man'.[72] Even the feathered friends war poets so favoured could prove fickle, or indifferent, to soldiers' 'petty tragedy'. T. P. Cameron Wilson begins 'Magpies in Picardy' with an uncertainty—that 'the magpies in Picardy | Are more than I can tell'—which extends disturbingly into the rest of the poem. The magpies do prove hard to 'tell', or to fit within the poem's apparently straightforward conjunction of 'the beauty of the wild green earth | And the bravery of man'. Nature and man instead seem subject to divergent fates. The magpies enjoy a confidence in continuing life, from bird to egg to bird, unavailable to the men on whom they 'cast a magic spell'—'men who march through Picardy, | Through Picardy to hell'. Creatures of ill omen, they 'flicker down the dusty roads' with a sunny freedom denied to the men marching along them—their airy vitality counterpointing the doom of the earth-bound soldiers.[73]

Contrasts between doomed mortals and 'wild green earth' are highlighted by other poets almost through a form of colour-coding. 'Return to greet me, colours that were my joy, | Not in the woeful crimson of men slain, | But shining as a garden', Sassoon asks in 'To Victory'. Contrary to his wish, nature was only too often overrun by the crimson of the slain, or incarnadined of itself in the colours of blood. Pleasantly affirmative of a 'last sunset touch' in its opening stanza, Hodgson's 'Before Action' nevertheless moves on to describe how 'sunsets spill | Their fresh and sanguine sacrifice', and to figure the noonday sun as a sword.[74] Sunrises could appear just as bloody. Blunden starts his description of a dawn attack in 'Zero'—eastwards, as always, towards the German line—by admiring the 'rosy red...torrent splendour' of the sunrise that 'hangs behind the goal'. Any 'artist's joy' in its colouration is soon dispelled, the poet finding instead that a wounded soldier's 'red blood now is the red I see', lividly highlighted against his pallor of 'swooning white'. Even in 'Vlamertinghe: Passing the Chateau', Blunden's celebration of roses and

[72] Noakes (ed.), *Voices*, 198, 200.
[73] Hibberd and Onions (eds), *Winter*, 101–2.
[74] Sassoon, *Collected Poems*, 13; Hibberd and Onions (eds), *Winter*, 98–9.

'poppies by the million' is tainted by his reflection that something closer to the colour of blood than the 'damask…vermillion' of the flowers might have been appropriate for those 'coming to the sacrifice'.[75]

Gurney's 'To His Love' is similarly colour-conscious. Like many of his poems, it begins with quiet memories of the Cotswolds, continuing equably enough, within conventions of pastoral elegy, in asking for a dead soldier to be covered with 'violets of pride | Purple from Severn side'. Gurney's last stanza, though, is altogether more urgent:

> Cover him, cover him soon!
> And with thick-set
> Masses of memoried flowers—
> Hide that red wet
> Thing I must somehow forget.[76]

Rather than introducing any concluding consolation, the stanza's exclamatory first line worries that the 'red wet' of the corpse—a 'thing', no longer human—may overwhelm the purple of the flowers and erupt out of any containment nature, convention, or the poet's consciousness can find for it. Like several writers mentioned above, Gurney moves within a single poem from affirmative engagement with pastoral conventions towards exposure of their inadequacies in confronting the violence of the war.

The same movement appears in several of Isaac Rosenberg's poems. Like so many other poets, in 'Returning, We Hear the Larks' Rosenberg celebrates the birds' elevation of eye and mind beyond the ruined landscape of the trenches—in this case, a 'poison-blasted track' along which soldiers struggle homeward after a night's work at the Front. Yet in comparison to the weary tones of the rest of the poem, the language of Rosenberg's celebration—'but hark! joy—joy—strange joy. | Lo!'—sounds more artificial or parodic than genuinely elevated. The larks themselves, Rosenberg goes on to reflect, may offer a distraction similarly inauthentic, or at any rate as dangerous as it is delightful, for 'death could drop from the dark | As easily as song'. Exalted views of nature's solaces are similarly qualified in 'Break of Day in the Trenches'. The poem opens with Rosenberg insouciantly pulling 'the parapet's poppy | To stick

[75] Blunden, *Poems*, 143–4, 152.
[76] Gurney, *Collected Poems*, 41.

behind [his] ear', and the last line describes it is as still safe there, 'just a little white with the dust'. But Rosenberg also recalls that the poppy's 'roots are in man's veins', connecting them less with life-affirming beauty than the same dusty destiny the poet knows to be his own—one already shared by many of his comrades, 'sprawled in the bowels of the earth'. In these poems, written in the trenches in 1916 and 1917, the pastoral emblems most widely used during the war—lark and poppy—take on roles very different from those affirmed in McCrae's 'In Flanders Fields' in April 1915.[77]

Rosenberg anticipated the war's denaturing influences from its beginning—as an 'infection', in Graves's terms, not just of 'the common sky', but of a whole natural world. As he describes in 'On Receiving News of the War: Cape Town', Rosenberg was in South Africa at the time, figuring the news as 'ice and frost and snow' in 'this Summer land', and as an 'ancient crimson curse' corroding the universe's 'pristine bloom'. In '1914', Wilfred Owen likewise describes war's outbreak blighting nature and initiating 'the Winter of the world'.[78] Like Rosenberg—or Gurney and Blunden—Owen sometimes works within pastoral conventions only to challenge or discard them later in the same poem. Soldiers enjoying their murmurous May moment in 'Spring Offensive' nevertheless know that they must soon turn away from the sun, as if from 'a friend with whom their love is done', and the poem itself takes a similar turn. Charging over the ridge leaves them murderously exposed, though to forces whose source, as in many of his poems, Owen does not ascribe directly to enemy action. Instead, it is 'the whole sky' which 'instantly...burned | With fury against them', while 'earth set sudden cups | In thousands for their blood'. Earth and sky, so beneficent in the poem's early lines, now seem to have offered only a sunny seduction towards utter destruction. Buttercups that had 'blessed with gold' the soldiers' boots seem ready instead, in their thousands, to provide cups for their blood. So indifferent, even betraying, nature's role in the poem allows the 'Offensive' of its title to be read as adjective rather than noun, briskly reversing spring's conventional, long-established promise in pastoral poetry. The same reversal figures even more strongly in Owen's

---

[77] *The Poems and Plays of Isaac Rosenberg*, ed. Vivien Noakes (Oxford: Oxford University Press, 2004), 138–9, 128.

[78] Ibid. 83–4; Owen, *Complete Poems*, I: 116.

description, in 'Futility', of vain attempts to revive a soldier in the warmth of the sun. Though the sun 'wakes the seeds', and first stirred into life the whole 'cold star' of planet Earth itself, it has no power to revivify the frozen soldier's cooling corpse. The poet is left questioning any purpose in nature or creation: 'Was it for this the clay grew tall? | —O what made fatuous sunbeams toil | To break earth's sleep at all?' 'Futility' comprehensively inverts Julian Grenfell's confidence that 'the fighting man shall from the sun take warmth'. For Owen, the 'kind old sun'—even nature itself—seem instead former friends 'with whom... love is done'.[79]

Movements away from pastoral imagination, in war poetry, sometimes extend into direct, explicit criticism of its conventions, or of their contemporary relevance. Though sensitive in so much of his writing to the natural world, Blunden does acknowledge some limits to its promise in the area of the battlefields. In a 'whole sweet countryside amuck with murder', any 'coincidence of nature without and nature within' may reflect only the symmetries of 'soul and soil in agonies'.[80] Consequences for his own poetry are considered in 'Premature Rejoicing'. This begins by looking at a scene of desolation on the Somme, Thiepval Wood, in terms of the pastoral imagery of Shakespeare's *A Midsummer Night's Dream*, reflecting that it may be ten years before life and greenery reappear. In the meantime, the poet is sternly warned:

> … it's a shade too soon
> For you to scribble rhymes
> In your army book
> About those times.[81]

Similarly explicit doubts about poetic practices and their appropriateness appear in Owen's writing. 'Insensibility' warns that 'the front line withers. | But they are troops who fade, not flowers, | For poets' tearful fooling'. Owen is also sceptical of pastoral idioms in his own work in 'A Palinode'. Written in October 1915, it criticizes earlier poetic habits, such as describing the sun 'blessing all the field and air with gold', or nature, more generally, as 'so sympathetic, ample, sweet, and good'.[82]

---

[79] Owen, *Complete Poems*, I: 192, 158.
[80] Blunden, 'Third Ypres', 'Festubert: The Old German Line', in *Poems*, 156, 8.
[81] Ibid. 142.
[82] Owen, *Complete Poems*, I: 145, 77.

Earthy Powers

An element of this self-criticism extends into 'À Terre', questioning the Romantic influences which still shaped poetry so strongly—including, for a time, Owen's own—in the early years of the twentieth century. For Robert Bridges, Shelley remained an oracle and prophet of 'loveliness' ideal for inclusion in his *Spirit of Man* anthology. In the early years of the war, it was still possible for John W. Streets to imagine 'Shelley in the Trenches'—even, as his poem with this title suggests, to flee 'with Shelley, with the lark afar, | Unto the realms where the eternal are'.[83] 'À Terre', on the other hand, suggests that if confronted with the trenches, their occupants and their outlook, 'Shelley would be stunned'. Paradoxically, this shock might result from the widespread popularity of one of his own ideas. 'À Terre' (literally, 'To Earth') is subtitled 'being the philosophy of many soldiers', a philosophy explained by a line quoted from Shelley's pastoral elegy *Adonais* (1822), 'I shall be one with nature, herb, and stone'. 'The dullest Tommy hugs that fancy now', the poem adds, '"Pushing up daisies" is their creed'.[84]

This 'creed' has some wide-ranging implications for war poetry, in its pastoral phases particularly. As 'À Terre' suggests, it was certainly shared widely, and not only among ordinary Tommies. Lt Col E. W. Hermon offers an officer's version it—or of Rosenberg's description of 'poppies whose roots are in man's veins'—when he blithely concludes one of his letters to his wife:

> the whole spur was one mass of the most lovely poppies & cornflowers and looked simply lovely. There's plenty to fertilise them up there, bones & remnants of French & Germans absolutely cover the ground.
>   Well, goodnight old dear.[85]

'À Terre' likewise emphasizes the vestigial, redemptive fertility which the creed of 'pushing up daisies' implies—the badly wounded speaker of Owen's dramatic monologue exhorting 'to grain, then, go my fat, to buds

---

[83] Noakes (ed.), *Voices*, 83.

[84] Owen, *Complete Poems*, I: 178-9.

[85] Lieutenant Colonel E. W. Hermon, *For Love and Courage: The Letters of Lieutenant Colonel E.W. Hermon from the Western Front 1914-1917*, ed. Anne Nason (London: Preface, 2009), 239.

my sap'. Concerns about his soul are superfluous, he concludes, since he will simply be better off in the soil, 'with plants that share | More peaceably the meadow and the shower'. As this conclusion and much of 'À Terre' suggest, pastoral connections with nature might be sustained in wartime not only by looking up, at skies, stars, or clouds. They could also be developed productively, though very differently, by looking in the opposite direction—downwards, at the earth and its fertile interment of bodies, bones, and veins. Owen evaluates the two directions contrastively in 'Asleep', written in November 1917, a few weeks before he began 'À Terre'. The 'deeper sleep' of death might in one way be envisaged as

> ... shaded by the shaking
> Of great wings, and the thoughts that hung the stars,
> High-pillowed on calm pillows of God's making
> Above these clouds, these rains, these sheets of lead.

On the other hand, the 'thin and sodden head' of Owen's dead soldier may just as well be envisaged merging 'more and more with the low mould, | His hair being one with the grey grass'.[86]

For several poets, this 'low mould' offers a more authentic promise than any 'high-pillowed' calm imagined among the stars. In T. P. Cameron Wilson's 'A Soldier', the figure who begins the poem admiring 'great clouds' and 'the unceasing song of the lark' ends only as 'a red ruin of blood and guts and bone'. Yet the poem also identifies 'within those shattered tissues, that dim force, | Which is the ancient alchemy of Earth, | Changing him to the very flowers he loved'.[87] The same 'ancient alchemy' figures in Herbert Read's 'Auguries of Life and Death', which offers the belief that death will 'adorn | tragically the earth with flowers', since

> ... no devastation can
> utterly kill:
> in the burnt blackness of earth
> built from invisible beginnings
> womb-warmth will engender
> an animate thing ...

A still starker version of this belief is expressed in *Seven Pillars of Wisdom* (1935), T. E. Lawrence remarking that human bodies 'reached their

---

[86] Owen, *Complete Poems*, I: 179, 152.
[87] Hibberd and Onions (eds), *Winter*, 100–1.

highest purpose, not as vehicles of the spirit, but when, dissolved, their elements served to manure a field'.[88]

The fullest version of Owen's 'creed', though, appears in the work of Charles Hamilton Sorley, who remarks in a letter late in 1914 that 'the earth even more than Christ is the ultimate ideal of what man should strive to be'.[89] In Sorley's poetry, such striving even seems unnecessary, so surely is ultimate dissolution in the earth guaranteed. In 'All the hills and vales along', he suggests that if 'the clay grew tall', this is at best a temporary condition, a mere interlude before returning to its origins. Serenely confident of ingesting, sooner or later, all 'bones & remnants', the earth is in other ways utterly indifferent to human fate. It registers only 'death, not tears'. As the poem reminds its marching, singing soldiers,

> Earth that blossomed and was glad
> 'Neath the cross that Christ had,
> Shall rejoice and blossom too
> When the bullet reaches you.

Though Sorley's singing soldiers are 'the chaps | Who are going to die perhaps', they are urged to rejoice nevertheless, entirely secure in the knowledge that 'teeming earth' will absorb them, 'glad, though sleeping'.

Sorley finds a strange insouciance in the inevitability of despair, favouring an approach to 'the gates of death with song', and his weirdly cheerful tone makes 'All the hills and vales along' one of the most haunting of war poems.[90] Along with similarly down-to-earth poems by Owen, Read, Rosenberg, and Cameron Wilson, it might also be considered among the most positive, extending pastoral coincidences of humanity and wild green earth—interanimations of self with 'nature, herb and stone'—towards unexpected forms of fertility and affirmation. Yet in other ways these poems mark a climacteric—corresponding to Woolf's description of the disappearance of 'divine bounty' from nature during the war—rather than an affirmative expansion of pastoral imagination. Each poet exposes, almost literally, the roots of Romantic

---

[88] Read, *Collected Poems*, 51; T. E. Lawrence, *Seven Pillars of Wisdom* (1935; rpt. Hertfordshire: Wordsworth, 1997), 460.

[89] Letter to A.E. Hutchinson, 14 Nov. 1914, *The Collected Letters of Charles Hamilton Sorley*, ed. Jean Moorcroft Wilson (London: Woolf, 1990), 200.

[90] Sorley, *Collected Poems*, 68–9.

symbologies of poppies or cornflowers, in a way calling a bluff inherent in pastoral imagination itself. Interfusions of self and nature in conventional pastoral are always, inevitably, metaphoric. In pushing pastoral beyond its usual conventions, under the pressures of war, Owen and others demonstrate that in any absolute unity with nature—literal rather than metaphoric—humans are merely matter; dust and earth without identity or individuality; soil without soul. Pastoral offered many strengths and opportunities to war poets, and some consolations remain even in the earthy aspirations of 'À Terre' or 'All the hills and vales along'. But these poems and others mentioned above also indicate the genre's limits in dealing with experience of the war, emphasizing how comprehensively its violence overwhelmed life and spirit—convincing many soldiers that dissolution into the surrounding mud was their likeliest fate, perhaps even a welcome release.

Ideals Unravelled

Such thoughts might, on the other hand, be construed as neither wholly new nor specific to growing disillusion with the Great War. They could instead be considered as old and conventional as the Bible's warning of 'return unto the ground...for dust thou art, and unto dust shalt thou return'.[91] Thoughts about 'return unto the ground' reappeared in Rupert Brooke's poetry even within a few weeks of the war's outbreak, probably under the influence of a still earlier use by Thomas Hardy, in his Boer War poem 'Drummer Hodge'. Describing his eponymous soldier's burial on the South African veldt, Hardy suggests an earthy fertility which will ensure that some

> ... portion of that unknown plain
> Will Hodge for ever be
> His homely Northern breast and brain
> Grow to some Southern tree.

Brooke may have drawn on Hardy's idea in 'The Soldier', written in October 1914, in which he demands

---

[91] Genesis 3:19.

> If I should die, think only this of me:
> That there's some corner of a foreign field
> That is for ever England. There shall be
> In that rich earth a richer dust concealed.

Yet neither Hardy's poem, nor—still less—Brooke's, much correspond to the dissolution envisaged by Owen and others. The corpse of Hardy's Hodge still confers some identity, albeit a lost and lonely one, on remote foreign fields where 'strange-eyed constellations reign | His stars eternally'. For Brooke, much more affirmatively, foreign fields are made forever familiar by a 'richer dust' eternally extending the spirit of England—a land, his sonnet goes on to explain, blessed by pastoral pleasures and a patriotism sanctioned by heaven.[92] Brooke rejoices in thinking death and decay will preserve and even extend identity. Owen and other poets, later in the war, welcome instead the thought of utter dissolution—an earthy annihilation ultimately unravelling not just individual identity, but even the constituent molecules of body and self.

Brooke and Owen, in other words, employ a comparable imaginative idiom towards thoroughly different ends. Contrasts between the vision of 'The Soldier', in 1914, and Owen's in 'À Terre', in 1918, encapsulate in this way radically shifting priorities in pastoral poetry during the war. They also introduce a wider discussion: of changes from idealism to disillusion, innocence to experience, ignorance to knowledge, which were more generally evident in the development of poetry between 1914 and 1918. At the time of the war's outbreak, very few British poets knew anything of military action from personal experience. Though Rudyard Kipling had been in South Africa in 1900, and briefly witnessed some of the fighting, most poets who wrote about the Boer War had done so, like Hardy, from the safety of home. Inevitably, poetry early in the Great War had to rely on ideas, and ideals, drawn not from direct experience but from previous writers. These were often authors who had worked at second-hand themselves—such as Henry Newbolt, or Alfred, Lord Tennyson, moved by a report in *The Times* from the Crimea to write 'The Charge of the Light Brigade' in 1854.

Something of Tennyson's heroic, patriotic style reappears in the work of poets most in the public eye when the Great War was declared, and

---

[92] Hardy, *Complete Poems*, 91; Brooke, *Complete Poems*, 150.

naturally expected to comment on it and to support the nation's cause. Many did so almost immediately, adding to the 'huge harvest' of verse provided by the general public at the time. As Poet Laureate, Bridges was naturally one of the first. His 'Wake Up, England!' appeared in *The Times* four days after war was declared, rousingly recommending that mirth and play should be renounced in favour of honour, 'God guard[ed] ... Right', and the pursuit of 'beauty through blood'. Published in *The Times* three weeks afterwards, Kipling's 'For all we have and are' likewise welcomes the thought that a somnolent, decadent world had 'passed away | In wantonness o'erthrown', to be replaced by 'steel and fire and stone' and 'iron sacrifice | Of body, will, and soul'.[93] A week later, in 'Men Who March Away', even Hardy was ready to celebrate the 'faith and fire' of soldiers, and the prospect of victory for the just. As recently as April 1914, in 'Channel Firing', he had instead been highly sceptical of the madness of 'red war'.[94] Published in *The Times* on 9 September, 'Men Who March Away' may already have been influenced by C. F. G. Masterman's Propaganda Bureau. Its first convocation of celebrated authors had taken place a week earlier, on a day whose fading, late-summer sunshine left a lingering impression in Hardy's memory.

A late-summer mood of bright idealism and patriotic resolve extended into the sonnets, including 'The Soldier', which Brooke wrote in October 1914 and collected in *1914 and Other Poems*, published early the following year. Like Bridges and Kipling, Brooke looks back in the first of these sonnets, 'Peace', on 'a world grown old and cold and weary' and thanks God for an hour that has awakened the young, sharpened their powers, and made them 'swimmers into cleanness leaping'. In a third sonnet, 'The Dead' he likewise rejoices that 'honour has come back, as a king, to earth'—accompanied by Love, Pain, Nobleness, and the readiness to pour out 'the red | Sweet wine of youth'.[95] By April 1915, Winston Churchill was ready to describe Brooke's writing as 'more true, more thrilling, more able to do justice to the nobility of our youth in arms engaged in this present war, than any other'. Catching enthusiasms widely shared at the time, Brooke's sonnets might in any case have acquired this kind of esteem. Their hold on the public's imagination was nevertheless greatly

[93] Hibberd and Onions (eds), *Winter*, 3, 8–9.
[94] Hardy, *Complete Poems*, 538, 305.
[95] Brooke, *Complete Poems*, 146, 148.

strengthened by the fate of their author. 'The Soldier' had received widespread attention after it was quoted by the Dean of St Paul's Cathedral in a patriotic Easter sermon on 5 April. Less than three weeks later its author was dead—of blood poisoning, on his way to join the Gallipoli campaign. The praise for his work, quoted above, appeared in an obituary in *The Times*, signed by Churchill, on 26 April.[96]

His life and death seeming to follow his art, even to be predicted by it, Brooke's posthumous reputation expanded very rapidly. In *Testament of Youth*, Vera Brittain recalls finding Brooke's 'famous sonnets... unhackneyed, courageous, and almost shattering in their passionate, relevant idealism'. By May 1915, she records, they were 'beginning to take the world's breath away'.[97] Another strong testimony—though apparently a stranger one—appears in George Ramage's journal. Within a week of Brooke's death, Ramage had copied into his diary, while on his way to the Front, Brooke's lines about 'a foreign field | Forever England'—an odd reflection for a Scottish soldier to favour. David Trotter offers some explanation, identifying a 'political synecdoche' early in the twentieth century which 'substituted England for Britain and Englishness for Britishness'—despite the involvement in the war of so many soldiers from Scotland, Wales, and Ireland. 'Britain', Robert Graves records, was 'a word not yet in current use' in 1914, though 'Britain' and 'British' came to be accepted as standard terms in most of the official histories published in the 1920s.[98] Some of the earlier 'synecdoche' still strangely survives in the work of critics such as Samuel Hynes, inclined to describe the Great War as a conflict exclusively between England and Germany. In addition to Scottish, Welsh, and Irish soldiers, large numbers from Canada, India, Australia, and New Zealand also served on the Western Front, and elsewhere. By 1918, troops from these latter countries and other parts of the British Empire made up around 20 per cent of the BEF, joined by steadily growing numbers from the USA.

Vera Brittain goes on to account further for Brooke's popularity and 'relevant idealism', suggesting that his sonnets 'must have nerved many a reluctant young soldier to brave the death from which body and spirit

[96] 'Death of Mr Rupert Brooke', *The Times*, 26 April 1915, 5.

[97] Brittain, *Testament*, 133

[98] David Trotter, *The English Novel in History 1895–1920* (London: Routledge, 1993), 155; Robert Graves, 'The Kaiser's War: A British Point of View', in George A. Panichas (ed.), *Promise of Greatness: The War of 1914–1918* (New York: John Day, 1968), 4.

shrank'. Many other testimonies during and after the war support this view. Like Brittain, J. L. Hodson's narrator in *Grey Dawn—Red Night* (1932) reflects that 'Brooke must have made dying easier for a lot of men.'[99] The Colonel in Ernest Raymond's popular novel *Tell England* (1922) offers lines from Brooke's sonnets to console young officers mourning a former schoolfellow. Later generations have been less convinced of the relevance or validity of Brooke's idealism. Instead, his work has often been criticized as a reflection of a leisured, privileged background, a lack of actual experience of war, and a late-Romantic imagination—half in love with easeful death in ways which had merely become more topical or respectable by late 1914. Brooke deserves a fuller appreciation, not least for what this suggests about the evolution of war poetry more generally. A Fabian socialist, he was far from exclusively patrician in politics or attitude. A brisk cynicism is directed upon the upper middle classes in 'Sonnet Reversed', for example, and on romantic love in 'A Channel Passage', which equates love-sickness with sea-sickness, the latter graphically described. The same scepticism might eventually have been directed on the war, had Brooke lived to experience more of it—contrary to many critics' assumptions, he had taken part briefly in military action, during the early, unsuccessful campaign to defend Antwerp.

Brooke was after all not the only war poet still steeped in late Romantic influences in 1914. Much the same might be said of Owen, eventually moved by the war to amend or unlearn allegiances to Shelley and Keats. Some evidence of comparable movement is discernible in the 'Fragment' Brooke wrote on the way to Gallipoli, shortly before his death. Less abstract and idealistic than the sonnets of six months earlier, this looks instead on his fellow servicemen as no more than 'coloured shadows' or 'perishing things and strange ghosts—soon to die', leaving their bodies 'broken, | Thought little of, pashed, scattered'.[100] Several commentators—admirers and near-contemporaries included—speculate on how far additional experience of war might have developed writing of this kind, already moving beyond the idiom of the sonnets. Brittain wonders whether Brooke could have long continued writing about 'Holiness and

[99] Brittain, *Testament*, 314; J. L. Hodson, *Grey Dawn—Red Night* (London: Gollancz, 1929), 138.
[100] Brooke, *Complete Poems*, 152.

Nobleness and Honour'. In the *Flax of Dream* novel sequence, begun shortly after the war, Henry Williamson extends this speculation to include Julian Grenfell, whose poem 'Into Battle' was written in late April 1915 in response to news of Brooke's death, and shortly before his own. 'What would Grenfell and Brooke have written had they lived through the Somme and Third Ypres with the P.B.I.—the poor bloody infantry', Williamson's central character wonders. He concludes that 'different songs' would have been the likeliest result, closer to the idiom of Sassoon's poems, described as 'the true voice of a soldier'. Much the same conclusion reappears in Williamson's *The Golden Virgin* (1957), set in 1916. Serving soldiers reflect that 'Into Battle' and Brooke's sonnets 'could only have been written before Gallipoli and the Somme', though they acknowledge that in its recent stages the war had moved almost beyond imagination or any form of conventional description.[101]

These conclusions accord with a widely shared critical view, summed up by John Lehmann when he remarks that 'poetry of the First World War can, roughly, be divided into two periods'. Until the Battle of the Somme in 1916, he suggests, war poetry was characterized by 'simple, heroic vision of a struggle for the right, of noble sacrifice for an ideal of patriotism and country'. Thereafter, 'dreams were shattered...despairing hope almost buried beneath the huge weight of disillusionment'.[102] As earlier chapters noted, the Somme did mark a decisive stage in the war's movement from idealism towards disillusion—a movement broadly evident throughout contemporary writing. Yet as Lehmann warns, any division of war poetry into the two periods he identifies can only be a rough one. Poems written both before and after 1916 often thoroughly contradict his broad characterizations of each of these periods. In the later one, many poets still sustained heroic visions of a just and noble struggle. R. E. Vernède fought through the Battle of the Somme, yet in 'Before the Assault', prays 'not now, Lord, we beseech thee | To grant us peace', insisting instead, like McCrae's 'In Flanders Fields', on honouring the dead by carrying on their struggle.[103] In 'Peace Upon

---

[101] Brittain, *Testament*, 134; Henry Williamson, *The Flax of Dream: A Novel in Four Books* (1921–8; rpt. London: Faber and Faber, 1936), 701–2; Henry Williamson, *The Golden Virgin* (1957; rpt. Stroud: Alan Sutton, 1996), 360.

[102] John Lehmann, *The English Poets of the First World War* (1981; rpt. London: Thames and Hudson, 1984), 8–9.

[103] Hibberd and Onions (eds), *Winter*, 142.

Earth', also written in 1916, E. A. Mackintosh likewise prays exclusively to a 'God of battles' and roundly disparages 'the straight, flat road of peace'. Though 'In Memoriam' goes on to reflect more sombrely, after the Somme, on 'ghosts of old songs and laughter', several of Mackintosh's other poems continue in 1917 to celebrate, the 'joy' and 'glow' of battle, or, like Brooke, 'the red wine of War'.[104]

'Different songs', and strong elements of doubt or disillusion, can likewise be identified long before 1916. Incipient scepticism about the war was evident even in its first few weeks, and not only in pastoral poems, such as Alice Meynell's, discussed earlier. Neither Harold Monro, founder of the Poetry Bookshop, nor Wilfrid Wilson Gibson—a lodger in it at the time—had direct experience of military life abroad. Each relied instead, rather like Tennyson, on newspaper reports of the war's early stages—the retreat from Mons in particular—but used them to produce poems favouring realistic description rather than the ideals of patriotism and sacrifice shaping 'The Charge of the Light Brigade'. Written in the autumn of 1914, Monro's 'Youth in Arms' grimly describes 'marching slow' because 'there's so much blood to paddle through'.[105] Likewise depicting death as sudden, banal, and pointless, Gibson's 'Breakfast'—first published in October 1914—is typical of poems included in his collection *Battle* (1915). Early encounters with urban poverty had focused Gibson's attention—more closely than that of most Georgians—on ordinary life and speech, and *Battle* is distinguished throughout by its brief, idiosyncratic visions of ordinary soldiers' daily existence, down-to-earth anxieties, and quirky memories of home. Scarcely aware of 'Holiness and Nobleness and Honour', Gibson's soldiers wonder instead about a beer tap left open, the likely fate of a sick cow, or the weirdness of flocks of butterflies dithering through a bombardment. One of the first collections to focus on ordinary soldiers, and on an unadorned, non-idealistic account of their experience, *Battle* appealed to several poets later attempting realistic treatments of the war, Rosenberg in particular.

---

[104] E. A. Mackintosh, *A Highland Regiment* (London: John Lane, Bodley Head, 1917), 45, 51; 'War, the Liberator' and 'Ghosts of War' in *War, The Liberator: and Other Pieces* (London: John Lane, Bodley Head, 1918), 13, 39.

[105] Hibberd and Onions (eds), *Winter*, 21.

For some of these poets, Brooke also remained an influence, though an inverted one—a popularizer of views and styles their own work sought to resist. Such resistance sometimes appears only in hints or allusions. Whereas Brooke's third sonnet exhorts army bugles to 'blow out... over the rich Dead',[106] Edward Thomas's 'No one cares less than I' endows the same instrument with resounding indifference towards his destiny, his grave, or humanity generally. In 'To a Dead Soldier', written in 1915, E. A. Mackintosh may be deliberately challenging Brooke's view of foreign fields—and confirming differences between Scottish and English pastoral—when he claims that a Highland soldier 'cannot rest so far from home' if buried in 'alien lowland clay' in Flanders.[107] Rosenberg expressed more explicit doubts about Brooke's 'begloried sonnets', ones shared by Charles Hamilton Sorley. In a letter written shortly after Brooke's death, around the time Brittain considered his sonnets were 'beginning to take the world's breath away', Sorley was already questioning their 'sentimental attitude', and ways it was 'clothed... in fine words'.[108] Sorley's criticisms are still clearer in 'When you see millions of the mouthless dead', a sonnet found in his kit after his own death, six months later. Like Brooke in 'The Soldier', Sorley offers instructions about how to think or speak of the dead, but warns his readers to 'say not soft things as other men have said'. Instead, he replaces Brooke's 'think only this' with the instruction 'say only this, "They are dead"'. 'It is easy to be dead', he adds. 'Mouthless', blind and deaf, the millions of dead are entirely beyond contact with the living: beyond their praise, tears, honour, or even curses—beyond anything other than the direct, declarative honesty of stating that they are dead.[109] While Sorley's earth-hungry 'All the hills and vales along' is one of the most desolate, if cheerful, of war poems, 'When you see millions of the mouthless dead' is one of the starkest, demanding a new, bare, directness from language in wartime. Both poems were written well before the Somme, the former possibly as early as 1914. Each was included in Sorley's posthumous collection *Marlborough and Other Poems*, published in 1916 and more broadly influential

    [106] Brooke, *Complete Poems*, 148.
    [107] Mackintosh, *Highland Regiment*, 18–19.
    [108] Rosenberg, undated letter of 1916 to Mrs Herbert Cohen, *Collected Works*, 237; Sorley, letter of 28 Apr. 1915 to his mother, *Collected Letters*, 219.
    [109] Sorley, *Collected Poems*, 91.

on later poets than Gibson's work. Robert Graves gave a copy to Sassoon, who passed it on to Wilfred Owen.

Sorley's poems, and Gibson's, are early instances of the emergence of what became canonical war poetry, sceptical rather than supportive of the ideals of 1914, and of the abstract, elevated language in which these had been framed. This growing scepticism contributed to a wartime subgenre of poetry-about-poetry, or poetry-about-rhetoric, directly critical or parodic of authors who were popular during the war's early phases, but whose work seemed inadequate or irrelevant to the experience of combatant poets in Kitchener's armies. In 'The Charge of the Light Brigade: Brought Up to Date', E. A. Mackintosh extends this criticism back to Tennyson, often the model for early patriotic poems about the war. Though inclined in much of his own poetry to celebrate the joy of battle, Mackintosh was firmly realistic about the conditions in which it was experienced, and scathingly parodic of exalted rhetoric and vision. Though retaining Tennyson's question—'was there a man dismayed?'—Mackintosh provides a different answer:

> Yes, they were damned afraid,
> Loathing both shot and shell,
> Into the mouth of Hell,
> Sticking it pretty well,
> Slouched the six hundred.[110]

Herbert Read provides a similarly ironic updating in 'The Happy Warrior', returning to the idealized figure described in Wordsworth's 1806 poem and depicting him instead as 'his wild heart beats with painful sobs' and 'bloody saliva | Dribbles down his shapeless jacket'.[111] Similarly dismissive views of recent writing figure strongly in 'War Poets', by Arthur Graeme West, also remembered for 'The Night Patrol' and for the disillusioned views of his journal, published posthumously as *Diary of a Dead Officer* in 1919. As in 'The Night Patrol', West includes in 'War Poets' copious details of the 'sickly foetor' and 'muddy brown monotony' of life at the Front. These are juxtaposed with criticism and parodies of poetry by optimistic young officers—ones whom university education had equipped with a potential as versifiers, like Christopher Tietjens's,

---

[110] Mackintosh, *War, the Liberator*, 91.
[111] Read, *Collected Poems*, 35.

and a readiness, like Brooke's, to profess themselves 'happy to have lived these epic days'. West sees no cause for optimism either in their work or their 'epic days'. 'Pious poetry blossoms on [their] graves' only because it has been published posthumously, after their early deaths in action, by their grieving families. 'God! How I hate you, you young cheerful men', West remarks of these poets.[112]

More temperate disdain—though sustained at greater length—shapes Gilbert Frankau's 170-line poem 'L'Envoi: The Other Side', written in October 1917. In his novel *Peter Jackson* (1919), Frankau criticizes, like West, 'the let-me-like-a-hero-fall category' of soldier-poets and their convenient appeal to civilians. In 'L'Envoi', these criticisms take the form of a long letter from 'Major Average', thanking a former subaltern for sending his recently published book of war verse, but complaining it offers only 'eyewash stuff | That seems to please the idiots at home'. The Major reminds his former officer of genuine details of trench life—'mud, cold, fatigue, sweat, nerve-strain, sleeplessness | The men's excreta viscid in the rain'—and longs for poetry that might offer a 'picture true to life' and give

> ... civilian-readers an idea
> Of what life *is* like in the firing line ...
>
> .   .   .   .
>
> ... something real, vital; that should strip
> The glamour from this outrage we call war.

He adds that 'the newspapers are bad enough' without having to encounter yet again, in his subaltern's work, 'the same old tripe we've read a thousand times'—about laughing heroes, cheery wounded, and great adventures.[113]

Similar contempt for newspaper clichés—'old familiar phrases | ... in the Press'—appears in another poem from October 1917, Osbert Sitwell's 'Rhapsode'.[114] As Frankau and Sitwell indicate, as the war went on poets were compelled to criticize much more than the limitations of earlier poetry. They were also obliged to resist the rhetoric and clichés—'foisted platitudes', as Herbert Read calls them—more widely used to describe

[112] Hibberd and Onions (eds), *Winter*, 135.
[113] Gilbert Frankau, *Peter Jackson: Cigar Merchant: A Romance of Married Life* (London: Hutchinson, 1920), 149; Noakes (ed.), *Voices*, 388–91.
[114] Hibberd and Onions (eds), *Winter*, 186.

the war in newspapers, propaganda, and the public domain generally.[115] An early instance of this resistance appears in Robert Graves's 'Big Words'. Graves begins conventionally enough, in the voice of a soldier heroically ready to welcome death, but recants in the last two lines, added after the Battle of Loos in 1915: 'on the firestep, waiting to attack, | He cursed, prayed, sweated, wished the proud words back.'[116] Scepticism of 'proud words' matches Ernest Hemingway's suspicion of 'abstract words' in A Farewell to Arms (1929)—words made obscene by their over-use in public rhetoric and propaganda. Similar scepticism is expressed in the short but insightful 'Preface' Owen drafted for a planned volume of his poems, shortly before his death in 1918. This warns that war poetry should have nothing to do with 'glory honour … might, majesty, domin-ion or power'.[117] His list of exclusions is comparable to Hemingway's, and obviously much at odds with the preference for capitalized abstractions—such as Holiness, Love, Honour, and Nobleness—promi-nent in Brooke's sonnets in 1914.

Scepticism of abstractions and 'big words' is particularly emphasized in Sassoon's later war poetry, possibly because conventional ideals had long retained some appeal to him, still evident in poems such as 'The Kiss', 'Absolution', or 'France'. In any case, much of his poetry came to be marked by sharp satire of propaganda and official representations of the war. '"They"' travesties the Bishop of London's claim that troops would 'not be the same' after the war, listing terrible mutilations which consti-tute—rather than the Bishop's supposed spiritual enhancements—the real change war has imposed on them. 'The Hero' mocks the mendacities of letters of condolence, 'Conscripts' the conventional niceties of poetry, 'How to Die' the public's preference for sanctified accounts of violent death, and 'Editorial Impressions' newspaper clichés about 'the amazing spirit of the troops'. In 'Memorial Tablet', Sassoon likewise focuses on untold anguish underlying epitaphs of 'proud and glorious memory', and in 'Suicide in the Trenches' on the immeasurable distance that lies between the 'smug-faced crowds' who cheer departing troops and these soldiers' eventual destination—'the hell where youth and laughter go'.[118]

[115] Read, 'Auguries of Life and Death', Collected Poems, 50.
[116] Graves, Over the Brazier, 27.
[117] Owen, Complete Poems, II: 535.
[118] Sassoon, Collected Poems, 23, 104, 78.

The need to develop 'compassionate and challenging realism' and 'humanized reportings of front-line episodes' in order to bridge distances between soldier and civilian, and to communicate the realities of the war, were among concerns Sassoon shared with Owen during their time in Craiglockhart Hospital in Edinburgh late in 1917.[119] In determinedly rejecting rhetoric, as his 'Preface' demands, Owen shares with Sassoon a readiness to stress what his poetry is *not* saying, and what it refuses to practise in terms of euphemism or consolation. This is evident in Owen's scepticism of conventional forms of pastoral, discussed earlier, and in his wry parody of newspaper language in 'Smile, Smile, Smile'. It also figures strongly in one of his most celebrated poems, 'Anthem for Doomed Youth', which itemizes and rejects a whole range of conventional devices of mourning, elegy, religious funerary, and military honour. In Owen's view, neither bells, prayers, candles, flowers—nor the bugles Brooke envisaged honouring the 'rich dead'—offer much more than mockery to soldiers 'who die as cattle'.[120]

Rhetoric is rejected equally vehemently in his account of a gas attack in 'Dulce et Decorum Est'. In draft versions, the poem was addressed to Jessie Pope, author of several volumes of war verse in 1915 and 1916 and a regular contributor of patriotic poetry to the *Daily Mail*. She might still be identified as the 'friend' addressed in the final version and invited to stop disseminating to children and others 'the old Lie: Dulce et decorum est | Pro patria mori' (it is sweet and meet to die for one's country). But Owen's criticism is also directed more widely on misleading ways of seeing and speaking about the war—occlusions which he finds disturbingly graphic ways of representing. 'Vile, incurable sores on innocent tongues' can be read as an effect of poison gas, but almost as readily suggest the results of the poisonous 'old Lie' in speaking of the war to children. The gas's effects are represented as an agony not only beyond the ordinary comprehension of civilians, but barely apprehensible even by the poet himself. From relative safety within his goggled gas-helmet, he witnesses the gassed soldier's 'drowning' only dimly, 'through the misty panes and thick green light, | As under a green sea'. His 'helpless sight' returns to torment him in dreams, and it is only 'smothering dreams', he reflects,

---

[119] Sassoon, *Siegfried's Journey*, 60.
[120] Owen, *Complete Poems*, I: 99.

which might allow his audience—Jessie Pope or more generally—somehow to see the victim's 'white eyes writhing in his face', or his blood, 'gargling from the froth-corrupted lungs, | Obscene as cancer'.[121]

Owen's implication is that such obscenities *must* somehow be truly witnessed, lies about them eliminated, and the war's real nature brought within civilians' range of vision. His 'Preface' stresses the responsibilities that this need for truthful witness places on contemporary poetry. 'All a poet can do today is warn. That is why the true Poets must be truthful', Owen suggests.[122] Many fellow war poets reiterate this straightforward conviction, often directly stated in their poetry. 'We are poets, | And shall tell the truth', Sassoon's friend Osbert Sitwell asserts in 'Rhapsode' in 1917, promising an end to 'old familiar phrases' and newspaper clichés about the war. In 'Poem for End', Ivor Gurney likewise describes himself as 'a war poet whose right of honour cuts falsehood like a knife'.[123] This shared emphasis on truth—on Sassoon's 'challenging realism' in 'reporting front-line episodes'—placed many war poets close to the position of narrative writers outlined in Chapter 2. Like these authors, combatant poets found themselves in the same situation as the 'secret men' Owen describes in 'Smile, Smile, Smile'—sharing a knowledge of conditions at the Front apparently almost esoteric in nature, so far did it seem beyond the awareness of civilians at home.[124] Like prose writers, poets were inevitably inclined towards modes of communication which might—as Frankau's Major Average hoped—communicate to 'civilian-readers an idea | Of what life *is* like in the firing line'. For several poets, this naturally involved adopting tactics similar to those used in narrative. Both Owen and Sassoon concentrate in challenging detail on shocking immediacies of death, wounding, and misery in the trenches. These are often assembled through the kind of hectic synecdoche earlier chapters described: through accumulated fragments, assembled as if by a nervous gaze sweeping across a shattered landscape and registering—like Major Average in 'L'Envoi'—details of mud, cold, excreta, horses dead and stiff-legged by the roadside. Listings of this kind figure particularly regularly in Sassoon's poetry—typically, in the enumeration in 'The Rear-Guard' of

[121] Ibid. I: 140.
[122] Owen, *Complete Poems*, II: 535.
[123] Hibberd and Onions (eds), *Winter*, 186; Gurney, *Collected Poems*, 201.
[124] Owen, *Complete Poems*, I: 190.

'tins, boxes, bottles, shapes too vague to know; | A mirror smashed, the mattress from a bed'.[125]

A form of synecdoche—developing a full picture from individual fragments—works just as effectively between Sassoon's poems as it does within them. Poetry he produced between 1915 and 1919 covers the diverse experiences of military life very widely—such as night work in No Man's Land ('Wirers'), going over the top ('Attack'), and sniper fire and sudden death in the trenches ('Counter Attack', 'Trench Duty', and 'A Working Party'). The title poem of the collection he published in mid-1919, 'Picture-Show', thus offers more than only a metaphor for the processes of memory the poem describes—or, incidentally, an indication of writers' awareness of the growing powers of 'picture-stories' offered by cinema and new visual technologies. The title also sums up Sassoon's whole poetic practice, and the potential Virginia Woolf identified in it, for showing 'the terrible pictures which lie behind the colourless phrases of the newspapers'.[126] Owen's poetry is similarly wide-ranging and diverse in describing life and death at the Front, with much the same effect. Work by each poet benefits further from characteristics of the lyric mode discussed earlier—from its compelling concentration on brief, self-contained experiences and the powerful emotions these engender. Each affecting in itself, poems by Sassoon, Owen, and other canonical war poets are powerful and diverse enough to communicate, collectively, a broad landscape of war, accumulated through vivid depiction of local, particular detail. Poetry also turned to good use, in representing life and death at the Front, other strengths earlier identified in the lyric form. Relative ease of composition, quickly encapsulating intense individual experiences, not only allowed poetry to offer the kind of 'picture true to life' Frankau and others thought so urgently required, but ensured that this picture developed a good deal sooner than it did in other genres of writing. Realistic war narratives emerged only gradually after the armistice and during the twenties, and not in substantial numbers until the end of that decade. By 1918, or even earlier, poetry had already developed a potential to bridge distances separating combatant and civilian

---

[125] Sassoon, *Collected Poems*, 69.

[126] 'Two Soldier Poets' [review of Sassoon's *Counter-Attack and Other Poems*], *Times Literary Supplement*, 11 July 1918, 323.

visions of the war, and to offer first-hand knowledge contradicting the romantic or abstract ideals of 1914.

Occasions, Techniques, and Legacies

Distances and earlier ideals nevertheless remained influential for some time after the armistice. Though the war poetry discussed above had developed strong potentials by 1918, it had not yet reached a wide readership. Much of it had to wait for many years before doing so—often for just as long as it took the reading public to accept narratives offering disillusioned accounts of the war. Sassoon was fairly unusual in having published three collections by 1919, and in the measure of public interest that his poetry had attracted, helped by a lecture tour to the United States. A better indication of contemporary preferences appears in the very different receptions accorded Brooke and Owen, during and after the war. Only a handful of Owen's poems had appeared by 1918, and Sassoon's selected edition of his work, published at the start of the 1920s, had scarcely sold a thousand copies by the end of the decade. His poetry began to attract a wider public only when Edmund Blunden edited a new collection, published in 1931 during the period of renewed interest in war writing, ten years or so after the armistice. In contrast, as Samuel Hynes records, Brooke's *1914 and Other Poems* had gone through twenty-eight impressions by 1920, and his *Collected Poems* went through another sixteen in the ten years following their publication in 1918.

Another measure of contemporary taste appears in the popularity of John Oxenham's work, easily outstripping even Brooke's sales. Mixing strong patriotism and unshakeable religious belief, Oxenham's poetry was reputed to have sold a million volumes by 1918. His collection *'All's Well!': Some Helpful Verse For These Dark Days of War*, for example, went through fourteen editions and sold over 100,000 copies within two years of its publication in November 1915. Oxenham's title, and the success of his work, and of Brooke's, suggest that poetry was subject to another version of the doubled thinking Chapters 1 and 2 identified affecting writing during the war, and for several years thereafter. For many readers at this time, inclinations to look directly at 'dark days of war' were likely to be deflected simply by the distress involved in doing so. Bridges's *Spirit of Man* anthology—which included Brooke and Julian Grenfell among its few contemporary writers—offers further evidence of an urge to look away instead. Poetry which followed Bridges's inclination to 'seek comfort'—'helpful verse', in its way—naturally maintained a broader appeal, for a time, than the 'helpless sight' of the war offered by Sassoon or Owen. The Angels of Mons once again offer an emblem of these preferences for affirmation rather than realism—ones also explored by Thomas Hardy in 'The Oxen', published in *The Times* on 24 December 1915. Describing the old notion that cattle kneel in obeisance to Christ, at midnight on Christmas Eve, Hardy acknowledges that 'so fair a fancy few would weave | In these years'. Yet he adds that if anyone did invite him to visit kneeling cattle, he would still 'go with him in the gloom, | Hoping it might be so'.[127] Mingled hope and scepticism in 'The Oxen' sums up transitions much more widely apparent in poetry, and in ways it was appreciated, between 1914 and the 1920s. In the gloom of those years, the appeal of nature, romance, fancy, idealism, or religious consolation still resisted the disillusioned realism emerging as the dominant style of combatant authors, postponing full appreciation of writing which eventually came to be accepted as the canonical poetry of the war.

Edward Thomas offers another perspective on these transitions in an article published in December 1914, surveying that 'huge harvest' of early poetry about the war, most of it patriotic and idealistic. 'Few of the poems now appearing in the press can be taken seriously', an editorial in *Poetry and Drama* had concluded in September 1914. Writing three months later, in the same journal, Thomas judged poems concerned so specific to their time—and so driven by immediate needs to shape public opinion—that they might best be categorized as 'occasional verses', unlikely to appeal to posterity.[128] Valued for what it said to its own times, rather than anything it offers later ones, Oxenham's poetry—even some of Brooke's—might be most accurately or generously designated as 'occasional'. Yet it is a categorization which also raises wider questions about war poetry, including work by canonical writers. As Tim Kendall points out in *Modern English War Poetry* (2006), this work has often been criticized as 'occasional' itself—'circumscribed by events' and bereft of 'more universal concerns'. Such

---

[127] Hardy, *Complete Poems*, 468.

[128] 'Varia Notes News', *Poetry and Drama*, 2(7) (Sept. 1914), 250; Edward Thomas, 'War Poetry', *Poetry and Drama*, 2(8) (Dec. 1914), 343.

accusations were quickly in evidence. The critic J. Middleton Murry complained in 1918 that Sassoon's poetry lacked artistic objectivity, orderliness, and control, and therefore expressed 'nothing, save in so far as a cry expresses pain'. W. B. Yeats offered similar reasons for omitting all the war poets from his 1936 edition of *The Oxford Book of Modern Verse*, arguing in his Introduction that 'passive suffering is not a theme for poetry'.[129] The reputation of most war poets developed strongly after mid-century, yet similar reservations continued to appear even in favourable accounts of their work. In *British Poets of the Great War* (1988), for example, Fred D. Crawford claims that the combatant writers he examines had 'the advantage of immediacy', but that this inevitably entailed some of 'the failings of other occasional poets'. Crawford sums up a further criticism regularly made of war poets when he suggests that their use of 'the poetic medium produced little that was new', and that Owen had been more influential for 'what [he] had to say...than how he said it'.[130] In this view, the war poets lacked formal or technical imagination, encountering a historical crisis of unprecedented severity—challenging the very possibility of description and communication—yet attempting to express it within conventional language, tidy metres, and traditional poetic forms.

These criticisms are useful in assessing war poetry's achievement and value, and might not in any case have much troubled the authors involved. Owen's 'Preface' claims that 'above all I am...not concerned with Poetry. My subject is War, and the pity of War'. Sassoon's straightforward style, emphasis on 'reportings', and determination 'to make known...the war as seen by the fighting men', likewise indicate preferences for directness over considerations of poetic art. Rosenberg, on the other hand, firmly prioritizes art over context, stressing in a letter to Laurence Binyon his determination that 'this war, with all its powers for devastation, shall not master my poeting'.[131] Much of this 'poeting' does

[129] Tim Kendall, *Modern English War Poetry* (Oxford: Oxford University Press, 2006), 3; John Middleton Murry, 'Mr Sassoon's War Verses' [review of *Counter-Attack and Other Poems*], rpt. in *The Evolution of an Intellectual* (London: Richard Cobden-Sanderson, 1920), 71; W. B. Yeats (ed.), *The Oxford Book of Modern Verse: 1892–1935* (Oxford: Clarendon Press, 1936), xxxiv.

[130] Fred D. Crawford, *British Poets of the First World War* (London: Associated University Presses, 1988), 10, 23, 88.

[131] Owen, *Complete Poems*, II: 535; Sassoon, *Siegfried's Journey*, 60, 203; Rosenberg, undated letter to Laurence Binyon, autumn(?) 1916, *Collected Works*, 248.

treat the war less as a subject in its own right than an appalling enigma, demanding subtle, distanced artistic perspectives for its understanding. Rosenberg can be as immediately, shockingly detailed as Owen or Sassoon—in his description in 'Dead Man's Dump', for example, of 'a man's brains splattered on | A stretcher-bearer's face'. Yet his cryptic instruction in another poem, 'break in by subtler nearer ways; | Dulled closeness is too far', is typical not only of his often-aphoristic style, but suggestive of tactics his poetry generally sought to pursue ('Break in by subtler nearer ways'). Even in 'Dead Man's Dump', Rosenberg practises styles subtler than Sassoon's realism, seeking transcendence as well as 'closeness' or representation of the immediate. Evident from the poem's opening, envisaging rusty stakes transported to the Front 'like many crowns of thorns', this extends into descriptions of the soul's 'fierce imaginings', and of the bodies of the dead as merely 'their soul's sack, | Emptied of God-ancestralled essences'.[132] Like John Donne, whose work he admired, Rosenberg regularly frets at the ligatures of body and soul, mortality and transcendence. Something of Donne's ability to find near-transcendent meaning even in a flea reappears in Rosenberg's extended account of lice—a perennial, infuriating irritant to soldiers in the trenches, nevertheless dignified by their naming as 'The Immortals' in the title of one of his poems.

Hunger for transcendence is clearest in 'prophetic gleams' shaping 'Daughters of War', which Rosenberg considered his most important poem. These gleams reflect an almost sexual desire moving the soul to transcend the 'doomed earth', in response to a seductive beckoning from the beyond that draws 'each soul aghast from its crimson corpse'. 'Daughters of War' is unusual among contemporary poems in configuring the conflict as a doom visited upon earth from some vaster realm of myth, or as some perverse consequence of unassuaged desires and 'hankering of hearts' within the mortal sphere.[133] David Jones's epic In Parenthesis— completed long after the war, and published in 1937—is one of few other works to attempt a comparably mythic vision. Like Rosenberg, Jones had trained as an artist before the war, and much of In Parenthesis is distinguished by exact, often earthy detail in its descriptions, divided

---

[132] Rosenberg, Poems and Plays, 139–41, 89.
[133] Ibid. 142, 145.

between verse and prose. Though carefully realistic in this way, *In Parenthesis* is also highly abstract, drawing on Jones's admiration for T. S. Eliot's *The Waste Land* (1922) and envisaging the Great War in the context of centuries of history, art, and myth.

Despite emphasis on war as his exclusive interest, Owen's own poetry often avoids as clearly as Rosenberg's any categorization as 'occasional'. 'The Send-Off' was described earlier in terms of its vision of anonymous individuals trapped within an unfeeling, inexorable military machine. Yet machinery of this kind did not cease operation in 1918. On the contrary, powers of government and bureaucracy, augmented by the war, continued to expand throughout the twentieth century and beyond. 'The Send-Off' is an early engagement with resulting alienations and anonymities—anxieties about the individual's autonomy and agency extending long beyond the Great War's conclusion. Several of Owen's other poems likewise remain immediately relevant long after the war. 'Strange Meeting' offers another example of movement beyond 'occasion'—from a real or partly imagined incident of war towards reflections appropriate to later ages in which, just as in wartime, 'none will break ranks, though nations trek from progress'.[134]

Along with several other poems, including 'Futility' and 'À Terre', 'Strange Meeting' also shows Owen developing new rhyme schemes which go well beyond conventional uses of 'the poetic medium', suggesting a more active interest in poetic art than his Preface professes. 'Strange Meeting' begins by describing escape down a tunnel 'scooped | Through granites which titanic wars had groined', passing places where 'encumbered sleepers groaned'. The poem continues to employ rhymes similarly skewed—'moan'/'mourn'; 'spoiled'/'spilled'; 'mystery'/'mastery'; 'killed'/'cold'. Retracing this use of half-rhyme into Owen's earlier writing, Blunden suggests that in its fullest development in 'Strange Meeting' it concentrates feelings of 'remoteness, darkness, emptiness, shock, echo, the last word'.[135] As he suggests, much of the unearthly, visionary quality of 'Strange Meeting' derives from the part-thwarted, part-fulfilled expectations such half-rhymes foster—evoking a world no longer ruled by normal conventions, but knocked partly askew by the

---

[134] Owen, *Complete Poems*, I: 148.
[135] Edmund Blunden, 'Memoir', *The Poems of Wilfred Owen*, ed. Edmund Blunden (London: Chatto and Windus, 1931), 29.

wounding powers of 'titanic war'. The development of such unfamiliar lines and rhymes might in this way be construed as an echo at a formal level of the conditions of conflict Owen witnessed on the Western Front. Lines of trenches ran from the North Sea to Switzerland more or less in parallel, yet in utter opposition and hostility. The expectation that lines should match each other without friction and conflict—in words or in the world—may have seemed a convention destroyed or outdated by the war. In introducing half-rhyme to English poetry—at any rate on a new scale—Owen encompasses the specific time and place of his writing, creating sonorous evocations and formal equivalents for the shattered, nearly indescribable prospects he had to confront.

Innovations in form and style figure in the work of several other poets during the war, sometimes extending interests developing shortly before its outbreak. Under Ezra Pound's determined direction, Imagism was the most progressive movement at the time, committed much more firmly than the Georgians to the modernization of poetic diction and practices. The movement's new stylistic priorities, as these had developed by 1915, are summed up in the Preface to *Some Imagist Poets*, published that year. Along with preferences for 'the language of common speech' and the creation of new rhythms through free verse, this emphasizes the need for sharp, exact images and economic expression, 'hard and clear' and shunning sentimentality and abstraction.[136] Aldington was among authors included in the anthology, and extends priorities its Preface expresses into war poetry appearing in his collections *Images* (1915) and *Images of War* (1919). In the former, 'Sunsets', for example, offers a vivid image of another violently bloody sky, describing 'the wind | Blowing over London from Flanders' and how

> The white body of the evening
> Is torn into scarlet,
> Slashed and gouged and seared
> Into crimson.[137]

---

[136] Richard Aldington, H.D., John Gould Fletcher, F.S. Flint, D. H. Lawrence, Amy Lowell, *Some Imagist Poets: An Anthology* (Boston/New York: Houghton Mifflin, 1915), vi.
[137] Aldington, *Complete Poems*, 68.

Depicting 'white faces | Like helpless petals on the stream', Helen Dircks's 'London in War' also employs Imagist tactics, close to Ezra Pound's use of haiku, in describing wartime conditions.[138] In the work of combatant poets involved with Imagism—T. E. Hulme, Read, and Ford, as well as Aldington—the movement's emphases often coincide with tactics employed more widely in describing the war. Successions of barely connected images, unsentimentally recorded, evoke the ruined landscape of the trenches—and the uneasiness of its observer—through much the same kind of synecdoche discussed earlier. In Hulme's 'Trenches: St Eloi', for example, dispassionate details of 'making paths in the dark, | Through scattered dead horses, | Over a dead Belgian's belly' impel the poet's bleak conclusion that 'nothing suggests itself. There is nothing to do but keep on'.[139] Concentration on intense, individual images assorted with other characteristics of life at the Front discussed earlier—in particular, its engraving on imagination of isolated, momentary experiences. Whether or not poets had been closely involved with the movement, in other words, tactics close to the Imagists' often appeared in their work. Frederic Manning knew Pound and Aldington before the war, and some of his poetry is as terse and sharply defined as Imagist writing—such as his description in 'The Face' of a 'red mist of anger', out of which appears 'suddenly, | As a wraith of sleep, | A boy's face, white and tense'.[140] Rosenberg, on the other hand, was barely acquainted with the Imagists. His background as a visual artist, rather than literary influences, may have shaped the chromatic exactness of his descriptions—such as those in 'Marching', of

> ... ruddy necks
> Sturdily pressed back, —
> All a red brick moving glint.
> Like flaming pendulums, hands
> Swing across the khaki—
> Mustard-coloured khaki—
> To the automatic feet[141]

---

[138] Catherine W. Reilly (ed.), *Scars upon My Heart: Women's Poetry and Verse of the First World War* (1981; rpt. London: Virago, 2009), 30.
[139] Hibberd and Onions (eds), *Winter*, 58.
[140] Stephen (ed.), *Never Such Innocence*, 90.
[141] Rosenberg, *Poems and Plays*, 123–4.

Elements of Imagist style, along with Owen's inventive half-rhyme, offer specific instances of war poetry's development of the poetic medium. Yet its most significant innovations—and most lasting influences— evolved in more general ways. One of these, already discussed, was its amendment or abandonment of Romantic and pastoral conventions, part of a wider movement towards realism and away from poetry's established role, in Bridges's terms, as celebrant of spiritual values and as oracle and prophecy of 'loveliness'. In 'Premature Rejoicing', Blunden 'looks ahead ten years' to a time when nature itself—and, with it, pastoral poetry—might have recovered from the devastation of war.[142] Rather as he suggests, though pastoral did not altogether lose its appeal after the war—continuing to be written by older poets such as Hardy and Walter de la Mare—it fared poorly in the decade that followed, particularly in the modernist poetry developing influentially at the time. Modernist authors were more deliberately innovative and unconventional than the war poets, though they nevertheless drew upon some of the latter's idioms and concerns. These figure in Ezra Pound's account in *Hugh Selwyn Mauberley* (1920) of a 'botched civilization' and the death of a 'myriad' for 'old lies'—the same old lies of '"dulce"… "et decor"' so disturbing to Owen.[143] Further affinities appear in *The Waste Land*. In one way, Eliot's poem belongs to a subgenre of pastoral writing, in which intense melancholy denies the speaker any of the consolations which might still be found in nature. For the most part, though, *The Waste Land* simply resists pastoral convention as determinedly as any poem in English, and in ways often comparable to war writing. Though the war is scarcely mentioned directly, the landscape of the trenches is strongly recalled by the bone-strewn, rat-infested alley Eliot employs as a metaphor for the modern condition—in particular, for a post-war period still overwhelmed by thoughts of the dead. The poem's opening section, 'The Burial of the Dead', finds spring offensive in ways familiar from Owen's poetry, April's 'cruelty' appearing in renewed fertilities either at odds with exhausted human desires or merely indifferent to them. The section's concluding description—of planting a corpse, in the expectation that it may 'sprout' or 'bloom'—also recalls the 'ancient alchemy of earth' envisaged in poems such as Owen's 'À Terre'. Often described as the most influential poem of its age, *The Waste Land* ensured that wartime scepticisms of Romanticism and pastoral were powerfully extended into later literature. Florid idioms and absorptions with 'loveliness' marking much poetry at the start of the twentieth century were displaced by earthier realisms of war writing, remaining suppressed in the years that followed.

Another of war poetry's influences extends from its realism of voice, as well as vision—from its rejection not only of the inflated rhetoric of newspapers, but of the elevated language of 'oracle and prophecy' often found in poetry itself. Instead, the pace, tone, and idioms of ordinary spoken language are in various ways unusually conspicuous in war poetry, even predominating at times over conventional constraints of form. Direct speech figures frequently in Edward Thomas's work. Even when it is not present, the rhythms of a musing inner voice extend freely over his line endings—an extravagant enjambment at odds with tidier end-stopped verses favoured by acquaintances among the Georgians, and closer to the conversational idiom of his close friend, the US poet Robert Frost. Both Gurney and Rosenberg incline at times towards speech rhythms rather than conventional metre. Rosenberg described 'Break of Day in the Trenches' as 'surely as simple as ordinary talk', and suggests speech patterns in other poems through variable line lengths, ranging from five to twelve syllables in 'Returning, We Hear the Larks', for example.[144] Gurney uses variable or strangely extended line lengths to similar effect in poems such as 'De Profundis'. Imagist war poets also regularly demonstrate their movement's allegiance to 'common speech', leaving some poems by Aldington and Read distinguishable from prose only through fairly tenuous free-verse rhythms. Several poets further highlight the spoken word through their use of the vernacular—often in the cockney dialect which Rudyard Kipling's work persuaded the reading public represented the true voice of all soldiers. It figures throughout entire poems, such as Owen's 'The Letter', a soldier's report to his wife, seconds before being mortally wounded, that 'I'm in the pink at present', or 'The Chances', recording how 'us five got talkin'; we was in the know'.[145] Other poets reproduce soldiers' conversational voice either more

---

[144] Letter of 4 Aug. 1916 to Edward Marsh, *Collected Works*, 239.
[145] Owen, *Complete Poems*, I: 137, 171.

briefly—Sassoon in 'Died of Wounds', '"They"', and 'In the Pink'—or even in single lines, such as Gurney's in 'The Silent One', or Blunden's in 'Vlamertinghe: Passing the Chateau'.

All these poems illustrate a wider determination—anticipated in Kipling's work, early evident in Wilfrid Wilson Gibson's *Battle*, and eventually extending to most war poets—to treat as speaking subjects the kind of ordinary soldiers previously included in poetry, if at all, as distanced objects of description or comment. This brought into poetry the 'genius' and inventiveness in colloquial language celebrated in Blunden's '"Trench Nomenclature"' and discussed in Chapter 1. Slang and vernacular forms vigorously resist and distance official discourse, immediately implying—even in single lines, as in 'Vlamertinghe: Passing the Chateau' and 'The Silent One'—a set of alternative attitudes, generally reductive of rhetoric and falsity. The polite but 'finicking' tones of an officer are sharply contrasted in this way, in Gurney's poem, with 'infinite lovely chatter of Bucks accent'. Conflicting attitudes are highlighted still more concisely in 'Vlamertinghe'. Florid pastoral effusions are briskly arrested by the reductive, colloquial interjection—'But if you ask me, mate'—introducing the more sombre views which conclude the poem.[146] As well as highlighting distances between attitudes, colloquial forms could help to maintain some distance from war experience itself— through 'the hoarse oaths that kept our courage straight' mentioned by Owen in 'Apologia Pro Poemate Meo', or even phrases such as 'pushing up daisies', discussed in 'À Terre'.[147] In another way, slang and vernacular forms also helped to *reduce* a distance, democratizing the language of poetry and bringing it closer to a general readership. Appropriately, when describing his wish to reach such an audience—in a letter to Sassoon shortly before he died—Owen turned to army slang to emphasize his point, remarking 'I don't want to write anything to which a soldier would say No Compris!'[148]

Fuller use of ordinary, everyday language had been an interest of British poetry at least since the ambitions Wordsworth and Coleridge expressed, following Robert Burns, in their Preface to *Lyrical Ballads* in

[146] Gurney, *Collected Poems*, 102; Blunden, *Poems*, 152.
[147] Owen, *Complete Poems*, I: 124, 179.
[148] Letter of 22 Sept. 1918: see Owen, *Complete Poems*, I: 193.

1802. War poetry's developments of this ambition were widely signifi-cant for writing later in the twentieth century, with *The Waste Land* once again offering early evidence of new directions that were followed. At one stage, Eliot considered naming his poem with a quotation from Charles Dickens: 'He Do the Police in Different Voices'. The title would have been appropriate to the polylingual, multi-voiced, diversely dialec-tal nature of the finished work. It would also have emphasized Eliot's recognition—perhaps a reluctant one—of the diminished cultural authority of any singular voice, the need to represent instead a range of attitudes and social strata within the *polis*, and the convenience in doing so of the vigorous, diverse colloquialism war poetry developed. Though poetry in the 1930s was generally less innovative than modernist writ-ing, and more democratic in its politics, it was all the more firmly indebted to war authors. Louis MacNeice considered that 'the nineteen-thirty school of English poets…derives largely from Owen'—from the 'diction and attitude' W. H. Auden particularly admired.[149] Work by the war poets appealed naturally to writers—such as Auden, Stephen Spender, and MacNeice himself—who were once again troubled by the dishonesties of public discourse, and in need of direct, down-to-earth styles that could add conviction to their own alternative views.

The potentials of dialect and colloquialism in creating this conviction continued to appeal to later generations of writers, extending some of the legacies of war poetry much further in the twentieth century. Ted Hughes, for example, greatly admired Owen's work, remained vividly aware of the Great War's impact through the experiences of his father, a survivor of Gallipoli, and continued to write war poems of his own, such as 'Six Young Men' (1957). Hughes also pointed out how vigorously, despite other linguistic influences, 'your dialect stays alive in a sort of inner freedom, a separate little self'.[150] Part of what kept Great War poetry so alive for later generations was its development of this personal voice—never more needed than between 1914 and 1918, when public ones were so mendacious, and wartime pressures so threatening to the life and

---

[149] Louis MacNeice, *Selected Literary Criticism of Louis MacNeice*, ed. Alan Heuser (Oxford: Clarendon Press, 1987), 63.

[150] Quoted in Neil Corcoran, *English Poetry since 1940* (London: Longman Group, 1993), 114.

freedom of the individual. In this way, and others considered above, war poetry deserves to be valued not only for what it said, but for how it said it—for new forms and for new colloquial straightforwardness, communicating the vital, idiosyncratic immediacy of speech and saying.

Value

Evaluation of Great War poetry needs to consider not only its accomplishments of voice and vision, but the circumstances in which these developed—ones scarcely conducive to artistic effort, or even to writing at all. Poems may have been easier to complete than narrative accounts of the war, but formidable challenges remained, as Ivor Gurney emphasizes in 'War Books':

> What did they expect of our toil and extreme
> Hunger—the perfect drawing of a heart's dream?
> Did they look for a book of wrought art's perfection,
> Who promised no reading, nor praise, nor publication?
> Out of the heart's sickness the spirit wrote
> For delight, or to escape hunger, or of war's worst anger.[151]

Along with the discouragements Gurney enumerates, many other factors inhibited war poets' 'perfection' of their work, or their achievement of 'wrought art'. These obviously included the extreme youth and inexperience of many authors, and the untimely ending of their lives. Some of the war poems that came to be most widely admired—probably including Owen's 'Strange Meeting' and 'Spring Offensive'—were either incomplete at the time of their author's death or incompletely revised. Though lyric poets' best writing is sometimes undertaken while they are still relatively young, in different circumstances even poems which were satisfactorily completed and revised during the war might have come to seem juvenilia—work surpassed as a career developed. Robert Graves was inclined to this view of his own wartime writing, generally excluding from later collections poems he had begun to publish in 1916 in *Over the Brazier*—a volume containing, not untypically, poems written at school alongside more recent ones about the war.

[151] Gurney, *Collected Poems*, 196.

Many war poets did not live long enough to discriminate in this way. Another mixture of school and war poetry appeared in 1916, Sorley's *Marlborough and Other Poems*, published after his death, aged twenty, at the Battle of Loos, in October 1915. Rosenberg died during the German spring offensive in April 1918, and Owen while trying to fight his way across the Sambre canal, a week before the armistice. In addition to Grenfell and Brooke, among other poets mentioned in this chapter T. E. Hulme was killed while with his artillery battery in September 1915, and Lesley Coulson, William Noel Hodgson, and John W. Streets during the Battle of the Somme, the latter two on its first day. Edward Thomas died from a shell blast at Arras in April 1917, the same month as R. E. Vernède and Arthur West. George A. C. Mackinlay and E. F. Wilkinson died later in 1917, during the Battle of Passchendaele, and E. A. Mackintosh at Cambrai in November 1917. Like Rosenberg, T. P. Cameron Wilson was killed during the spring retreat in 1918, and Henry L. Simpson by sniper fire in August 1918. Had some of these writers survived, they might have significantly altered the evolution of poetry in Britain later in the century. Edward Thomas, in particular, might have renewed pastoral idioms in the way Blunden anticipated, resisting or reshaping the metropolitan influences of modernism in the years that followed the war.

As well as enumerating writers' problems in 'War Books', Gurney nevertheless indicates ways war poetry succeeded despite its difficulties—even because of them—when he goes on to talk of writing 'our world's death songs, ever the best'. In one way, a 'world's death' and 'war's worst anger' can be seen as challenges fierce enough to have enforced—in Owen's case especially—unusually rapid development beyond any element of juvenilia evident in early writing. In another way, as Gurney's idea of a 'world's death songs' suggests, war poetry could lay claim to an unusual, even unique historical significance—momentous enough, for later generations, to make its evaluation strictly as literature or 'wrought art' seem superfluous or insensitive. Even if Great War poets *are* considered 'occasional', in other words, the occasion concerned is more than sufficiently significant to guarantee lasting importance for their work. The poet Donald Davie is one of several later commentators to elaborate this idea, claiming in the 1960s that the value of some of Sassoon's writing has little to do with what he calls its 'very dubious status as poetic art', and that some 'pieces by Rosenberg and Owen are not poems at all, but something less than that and more; they are first-hand and faithful witnesses to a moment in the national destiny... high-water marks in the national psychology'.[152]

In apparently renouncing interest in poetic art, Owen came close in 1918 to anticipating the alternative values Davie assigned his work nearly fifty years later. 'These elegies are to this generation... in no sense consolatory', Owen remarks in his Preface, 'they may be to the next'.[153] In many ways, they were. For later generations, war poetry increasingly took on the conventionally consolatory functions of elegy, shaping and distancing feelings of loss, and allowing a 'world's death' gradually to acquire a familiar, settled place within the national psychology. As Davie suggests, entering national psychology and configuring national destiny so decisively is a formidable achievement for any poetry. Paradoxically, though, it may not be one which guarantees full appreciation either of the writing concerned or of the historical pressures it sought to confront. War poetry has instead been a victim of its own success. The more successfully poets settle the Great War's place in national psychology, the less either their work or the war itself may require fresh thought or concern. Geoff Dyer highlights this problem in his travelogue *The Missing of the Somme* (1994), remarking that 'before we have even settled down to read the first stanza of Owen's "Dulce et Decorum Est", we are already murmuring to ourselves the old mantra, "the horror of war"'. This 'old mantra', in his view, 'has become so automatic... that it conveys none of the horror it is meant to express'.[154] Instead, it deflects thought almost as comprehensively as the old lies it was intended to supplant. 'Automatic' responses of this sort threaten to consign writing by Owen and other war poets to the kind of role occupied by Brooke's poetry around 1916— as a thoroughly compelling, but undisturbing, expression of ideas already familiar and acceptable to the reader.

None of this is the war poets' fault, of course. Questions Dyer highlights are not about the value or faithfulness of their witnessing, but about how its full potential can continue to be realized. One way of doing so, suggested above, is to stress, contrary to critics like Crawford or Davie, how extensively poets concerned can be valued for the manner as well as the content of their witnessing—for formal changes immediately

[152] Donald Davie, 'In the Pity', *New Statesman*, 28 Aug. 1964, 68(1746), 282.
[153] Owen, *Complete Poems*, II: 535.
[154] Geoff Dyer, *The Missing of the Somme* (London: Phoenix, 1994), 27.

responsive to the pressures of war, but influential long afterwards in communicating its experience, and in shaping the work of later generations of poets. Another strategy, followed throughout this chapter, lies in broadening the cohort of writers examined. Considering minor as well as canonical war poetry not only highlights the strengths of the latter, but also the particularity of its values—not necessarily inevitable or universal ones, but part of a wider range of responses to the war. Some of this range, of course, is evident even through comparison of canonical writers themselves. Though these poets have much in common, there are obvious differences between Sassoon the satirist and Rosenberg the metaphysician, and neither writer, nor Ivor Gurney, is focused as unremittingly as Owen on the pity of war. Poetry by Brooke and Grenfell indicates how thoroughly pity might be excluded altogether from visions of the war, and the long-sustained public enthusiasm for their work suggests how far early idealism survived into later, disillusioned years. The range of responses is still fuller if less well-known poets such as E. A. Mackintosh, R. E. Vernède, or Gilbert Frankau are included in it. Each was ready to regret aspects of war, or ways it was presented to civilians, yet committed to its continued conduct, and even ready to relish some of the experiences it offered.

Another lesser known writer, Edward de Stein, offers a further alternative to horror in 'Envoi'. His poem almost regrets the end of 'wonderful, terrible days' of war, made more tolerable by good comradeship and by 'facing the world that was not too kind with a jest and a song'.[155] Values 'Envoi' celebrates are further evidenced in many of the poems in Vivian Noakes's anthology *Voices of Silence* (2006). These values are also stressed in her introduction, which praises poetry 'written by soldiers to raise the spirits of their comrades and make more bearable the shared tragedy of their suffering'. In doing so, poets concerned often relied on elements of jest—'what man's humour said to man's supreme distress', in Blunden's phrase in '"Trench Nomenclature"'—ones which Noakes considers too often overlooked in later accounts of war writing. As she acknowledges, humorous verse was often only ephemeral, or 'juvenile jollity'.[156] Yet as any edition of the *Wipers Times* confirms, humour and even juvenile jollity usually offered brisk resistance to official discourse, often exploiting

---

[155] Gardner (ed.), *Up the Line*, 147.
[156] Noakes (ed.), *Voices*, xii; Blunden, *Poems*, 173.

the alternative vision implicit in colloquial or vernacular language. Humour, too, as de Stein remarks, could offer some alternative to the grimness of war more generally, or simply fulfil the need, as Owen puts it in 'Apologia Pro Poemate Meo', 'to laugh... | Where death becomes absurd and life absurder'.[157] Several poets develop these potentials extensively, sometimes within a wider repertoire of attitudes and tones. A. P. Herbert was one of these. 'Untitled' offers thoroughgoing 'juvenile jollity', expressed with verbal dexterity anticipating his later career as a comic author. Yet Herbert could also write as bitterly as Sassoon, pillorying pompous generals in 'After the Battle', or as sadly and sonorously as Owen, in surveying a 'sullen mile of mud' in 'Beaucourt Revisited' and in imagining conversations with former comrades buried beneath it.[158]

A comparable expanse of feeling, extending from humour to horror, extends throughout *Voices of Silence*. Subtitled *The Alternative Book of First World War Poetry*, Noakes's anthology is one of several ranging well beyond the work of the canonical war poets. Similar breadth appears in Dominic Hibberd and John Onions's *The Winter of the World* (2007), also distinguished by a chronological arrangement which allows assessment of how far, between 1914 and 1918, war poets replaced rhetoric with realism, idealism with disillusion. A much earlier collection, Brian Gardner's *Up the Line to Death* (1964), continues to offer a particular interest by including fragments of popular wartime song—described by the editor as 'the instinctive poetry of the troops themselves'. Wallace Stevens defines modern poetry generally as 'the mind in the act of finding | What will suffice'.[159] Each anthology demonstrates how many and how varied were the acts of mind required to find anything sufficient to the experience of the Great War. Each invites in this way a less narrowed, numbed, or habitual response to its horrors. These are described vividly, painfully, and directly in much of the poetry included. But their immediacy is heightened by an expanded awareness of loss—of men constrained by no single outlook, but capable of such varied, imaginative vision, ranging from inviolate stars to rotting corpses, from Brooke's idealism to Owen's frozen sense of futility. Engagement with this varied

---

[157] Owen, *Complete Poems*, I: 124.

[158] Hibberd and Onions (eds), *Winter*, 179.

[159] Gardner (ed.), *Up the Line*, xxiii; Wallace Stevens, 'Of Modern Poetry', *The Collected Poems of Wallace Stevens* (London: Faber and Faber, 1955), 239-40.

vision—with jest and popular song, as well as 'death songs'—indicates how profoundly the war impacted on the language of an age still so much under the sway of the rhythms and tricks of verse. It may also make less distant—less occluded by old lies or old mantras—the vanished life of soldiers who once swung and sang, in shade or sun, on their wearying way through Picardy. Through Picardy to hell.

| 4 |

Unforgettable War

> The 'Somme Offensive' in 1916 is ancient history now: a thing of Staff-maps and war-diaries, of barren paper and profitless arguments, flat as the faked film of it men once sold for profit in the market-place... What remains of it today? Only memories, bitter memories that waken men o'nights.

Neither the Somme, nor the Great War generally, has ever faded into 'ancient history' in the way Gilbert Frankau suggests above—in a passage from his novel *Peter Jackson*, completed in 1919.[1] A century later, the Great War is still remembered as a central influence on the emergence of the modern world. Writing immediately afterwards, in describing the Somme remaining *only* in memories, Frankau underestimates the huge pressure of remembrance weighing on the years following the armistice. Jay Winter describes the settling of a 'cloud of grief' over these years—a sense of recent mass death which left survivors as if 'perched on a mountain of corpses'. The dead remained, Winter sug-

---

[1] Gilbert Frankau, *Peter Jackson: Cigar Merchant: A Romance of Married Life* (London: Hutchinson, 1920), 283.

gests, still 'living among the living'. In the 'private thoughts and dreams' of the bereaved, in particular, they remained as vividly present as anyone who had survived.[2] Even fifteen years after the war, familiar, busy city streets could seem only 'long boulevards where the ghosts walk now', as May Cannan describes in her poem 'Perfect Epilogue: Armistice Day 1933'. The dominance of the war, in thinking of recent history, inclined a whole generation and its authors, and not only the bereaved, to share Cannan's feeling that 'Time's no mender of hearts but only | ... the divider of Light and Darkness'.[3]

For ex-combatants, the war's darkness often remained especially intense, in the kind of nightmare memories Frankau mentions. Ten years after its end, 65,000 victims of shell shock and similar disorders still remained in hospital. Even for those less obviously traumatized, there remained 'strange hells within the minds war made', as Ivor Gurney remarked in 1922. His poem 'Strange Hells' goes on to suggest how former soldiers often struggled, when returning to ordinary civilian life, 'on state-doles, or showing shop patterns', to 'keep out of face' their memory of 'hell's thunders'.[4] Much as Gurney describes, a *Guardian* article in July 1919 records a 'very far-away look' on a shop assistant's face as he recommends 'one of our very newest designs in voile, madam' during that year's summer sales. The look disguises—just—his recollection that a year previously he had been fighting against the remnants of the German spring offensive, with the Lancashire Fusiliers, in the trenches at Givenchy.[5] In the 1920s, and for some time thereafter, for ex-combatants especially, 'hell's thunders' rumbled on, barely suppressed beneath the banal surface of everyday life.

Memory and Memorial

The war could not be forgotten, but means of remembering or commemorating it were much discussed—naturally in the years following

[2] Jay Winter, *Sites of Memory, Sites of Mourning: The Great War in European Cultural History* (Cambridge: Cambridge University Press, 1995), 17, 144.
[3] Vivien Noakes (ed.), *Voices of Silence: The Alternative Book of First World War Poetry* (London: Sutton, 2006), 386.
[4] *Collected Poems of Ivor Gurney*, ed. P. J. Kavanagh (Oxford: Oxford University Press, 1982), 140–1.
[5] 'From Givenchy to the Sales', *Manchester Guardian*, 18 July 1919, 6.

the armistice, but also earlier, during the conflict itself. The intensities of Great War experience seemed to demand *immediate* remembrance, as Henry Williamson describes in *A Chronicle of Ancient Sunlight*. His protagonist is intrigued to encounter the term 'souvenir', describing it as 'a new word picked up from the regulars' in the first months of the war.[6] Though long used in English, 'souvenir' rapidly gained wider currency at the time—sometimes even as a verb—among soldiers collecting curios from the battlefields, or purchasing them from shrewd French tradesmen. Regimental badges, shell nose-caps, and the Germans' spiked, leather 'Pickelhaube' helmets were in particular demand among British soldiers, as presents for families or memorabilia of their own. As the war went on, it often manoeuvred them into other strangely souveniring roles. A year after the Battle of the Somme, John Masefield's *The Old Front Line* (1917) provided thorough, topographic descriptions of the battlefield, detailed almost as a tourist destination. Another year later, the German spring offensive forced many soldiers to re-encounter the area almost in this way, as Herbert Read's *In Retreat* (1925) describes. Retreat across the shattered landscape of the Somme revived intense memories of the fighting there, and of long-dead comrades—ones who sometimes seemed, as Chapter 2 described, to return as ghostly auxiliaries among the beleaguered armies of 1918.

By that time, or even earlier, many soldiers were anticipating more conventional forms of tourism developing after the war. In *The Red Horizon* (1916), Patrick MacGill thinks ahead to a time when 'holidays to the scene of the great war become fashionable', with souvenirs widely on sale. David Jones's *In Parenthesis* (1937) describes crawling wounded from one of the Somme's actions, abandoning a rifle likely to be found one day by the 'Cook's tourist to the Devastated Areas' he recalls imagining in 1917. In a poem published a year later, 'High Wood', Philip Johnstone assumes the voice of a future tour guide, pointing out features on one of the Somme's bloodiest battlefields, and the merits of souvenirs available in the tour company's shop. These expectations were soon realized. H. M. Tomlinson's *All Our Yesterdays* (1930) describes two ex-combatants who return to the area of High Wood, shortly after the war, encountering a 'large party...looking for souvenirs'. Chattering and

[6] Henry Williamson, *How Dear is Life* (1954; rpt. London: Arrow, 1985), 290.

cheerful, the tourists descend from a motor charabanc, barely listen to their guide, and seem to the ex-soldiers scarcely aware of the battle-field and 'what it all means'.[7] In *The Wet Flanders Plain* (1929), Henry Williamson describes similar insouciance in an American tourist encountered in Ypres, anxious only to complete an itinerary of estab-lished sights as quickly as possible. A more pensive, respectful visit to a 'neat restored trench', six years after the armistice, appears in F. Scott Fitzgerald's *Tender is the Night* (1934).[8]

Other visits to the battlefields were differently motivated. By 1919, organizations had been established to assist the bereaved to travel to war zones, in France and elsewhere, and to visit the cemeteries which were steadily consolidated by the Imperial War Graves Commis-sion[9] throughout the 1920s. Kipling's short story 'The Gardener' (1925) describes the breath-taking scale of these cemeteries, their 'merciless sea' of crosses making a guide—perhaps a divine one, the story sug-gests—almost essential for visitors.[10] The work of the War Graves Commission profoundly shaped experiences of bereavement and remembrance in other ways. Each cross in that merciless sea was inscribed only with the dead soldier's name, number, age, date of death, regiment and regimental insignia. Anything further, up to a limit of 66 characters, had to be paid for by the bereaved, at a rate of 3¼d per char-acter.[11] Though the charge was often waived, its challenge to textual and emotional economy was taken up in less than 50 per cent of cases. Mourners were further distanced and silenced by a decision taken even before the War Graves Commission was set up in 1917—that with very few exceptions, the bodies of the dead, even if they could be found on the battlefields, were not to be returned to Britain. Without the closure offered by local funerals and interments, memories of the dead persisted

---

[7] Patrick MacGill, *The Red Horizon* (London: Herbert Jenkins, 1916), 282; David Jones, *In Parenthesis* (1937; rpt. London: Faber and Faber, 1978), 186; Brian Gardner (ed.), *Up the Line to Death: The War Poets 1914–18* (1964; rpt. London: Methuen, 2007), 157; H. M. Tomlinson, *All Our Yesterdays* (London: William Heinemann, 1930), 538.

[8] F. Scott Fitzgerald, *The Bodley Head Scott Fitzgerald* (London: Bodley Head, 1959), II: 131.

[9] Later renamed the Commonwealth War Graves Commission.

[10] Rudyard Kipling, *Debits and Credits* (1926; rpt. Harmondsworth: Penguin, 1987), 286.

[11] Less than 1½p, though messages of any length would have entailed a significant outlay at that time.

all the more vividly, for their families and the population more generally. This focused attention on other kinds of local commemoration—frequently, on the construction of public war memorials. An Imperial War Museum database records the eventual existence of more than forty thousand of these throughout Britain. Winter's *Sites of Memory, Sites of Mourning* discusses some of the styles of monumental architecture devised for them, during the 1920s and later. Contemporary fiction sometimes reflects dissatisfaction with the results. The second volume of Lewis Grassic Gibbon's *Scots Quair* trilogy, *Cloud Howe* (1933), offers a view of 'the War Memorial of Segget toun', described as an ornate angel in a 'stone night-gown...like a constipated calf'. Not surprisingly, neither this 'trumpery flummery' nor the Armistice Day service held beside it much appeal to Segget's former soldiers, already disillusioned by the outcome of their war service, followed in many cases by unemployment and 'state-dole' during the depressed 1920s.[12]

The flummery angel is also criticized, implicitly, by comparison with another memorial—one as straightforward and austere as a casualty list, and described in the first volume of *A Scots Quair*, *Sunset Song* (1932). The names of the village's dead are in this case simply carved into ancient standing stones on the edge of moors nearby. The service inaugurating this modest memorial describes the dead as 'the Last of the Peasants, the last of the Old Scots folk', their loss marking 'the sunset of an age and an epoch'. This provides a moving conclusion for Gibbon's account of the war's effects on a rural community, and on its perennial struggle with the harsh landscape surrounding it.[13] It also shares a vision of the war long present in English fiction. An early example appears in Hugh de Selincourt's description in *The Cricket Match* (1924) of a village still struggling to recover from its losses, during the post-war years. The same period, and the same sense of loss, continue to figure much later, in Laurie Lee's *Cider with Rosie*, published in 1959. Throughout Britain, and throughout Europe, the war memorials set up in almost every community marked not only the death of individuals, but the sunset of an entire outlook and way of life, one still remembered and regretted long afterwards.

[12] Lewis Grassic Gibbon, *A Scots Quair: Sunset Song, Cloud Howe, Grey Granite* (1932-4; rpt. Edinburgh: Canongate, 1995), 44-5.

[13] Ibid. 255-6.

Similar concerns figure in Christopher Isherwood's *The Memorial* (1932), particularly in the second section's account of the inauguration of a cross of remembrance in 1920. Like Gibbon's characters, Isherwood's are concerned about their memorial's ornate design, comparing it uneasily with 'granite atrocities they were putting up in the neighbouring villages'. They also worry more generally about the loss, harshness, and sorrow of post-war life, and *The Memorial* is especially significant for the form in which these wider concerns are presented. Isherwood's central character, widowed in the war, returns repeatedly to memories of an altogether different age before its outbreak—to 'a beautiful, happy world, in which next summer would be the same, and the next and the next'.[14] Similarly recursions into memory figure throughout *The Memorial*, its chronology further disrupted by division into four parts, headed 1928, 1920, 1925, 1929. Non-sequential construction of this kind appears elsewhere in 1930s fiction. Aldous Huxley's *Eyeless in Gaza* (1936) is divided into sections variously dated between 1902 and 1935, including one describing a disastrous betrayal of innocence in the summer of 1914. A comparable sense of loss shapes George Orwell's *Coming up for Air* (1939). Throughout its second part, Orwell's narrator George Bowling returns in memory to an innocent, idyllic rural childhood in the pre-war years—'a good time to be alive', lost irrevocably in the 'unspeakable idiotic mess' after 1914.[15]

Fractured chronologies in these novels extend tactics evident earlier, in 1920s fiction. They confirm that the war affected literary imagination not only in introducing the 'alteration of time' or 'war time' discussed in Chapter 2, disrupting steady, hourly progression through the mornings, afternoons, and evenings of daily life. The war also dislocated any broader faith in an evolving, coherent history, advancing steadily through the months and years. John Dos Passos recalls this faith surviving as a 'quiet afterglow of the nineteenth century' in the early years of the twentieth—still confident that 'industrial progress meant an improved civilisation, more of the good things of life all round, more

---

[14] Christopher Isherwood, *The Memorial* (1932; rpt. St Albans: Triad/Panther, 1978), 66, 58.

[15] George Orwell, *Coming up for Air* (1939; rpt. Harmondsworth: Penguin, 1962), 102, 123.

freedom, a more humane and peaceful society'.[16] Dos Passos is one of many authors, including Henry James, quoted in the Preface, who considered this confidence in an ever-improving future—generally sustained since the Enlightenment in the late eighteenth century—to have been shattered in 1914. Thereafter, uncertainties about the present and the future tended to draw imagination backward into the past instead, towards remembrance of the stability and allure of the pre-war years. Rebecca West's *The Return of the Soldier* (1918) offers a paradigm of this tendency. Its hero's response to shell shock in 1916 takes the form of a complete mental reversion to an idyllic period fifteen years earlier, described throughout the novel's third chapter.

This direction was followed in one way or another by many modernist novels published in the 1920s. Written between 1914 and 1921, James Joyce's *Ulysses* (1922) meticulously recreates the life and geography of Dublin in 1904—partly destroyed in the Easter Rising of 1916—further escaping the 'nightmare' of history through deeper recursions into memory in the novel's concluding section. At the beginning of his *Parade's End* tetralogy (1924–8), Ford Madox Ford looks back regretfully at the 'perfectly appointed...luxuriant, regulated...admirable' pre-war world, charting its decay and loss throughout the thousand pages that follow.[17] In *Mrs Dalloway* (1925), and in the third section of *To the Lighthouse* (1927), Virginia Woolf shapes almost every paragraph around the thoughts of characters who are drawn away from the present towards recollections of a more congenial pre-war world. 'Remembrance of Things Past' was the title C. K. Scott Moncrieff chose for the translations of Marcel Proust's *À la recherche du temps perdu* (1913–27) he began publishing in 1922, rather than the more literal 'In Search of Lost Time'. Like Proust, modernist writers in English in the twenties were particularly attracted to remembrance of lost times and the 'feeling of security...of continuity' Orwell and others ascribe to the summery, sunlit years before 1914. In terms May Cannan's poem suggests, 1920s and 1930s novels often emphasize, formally, contemporary views of time as 'no mender of hearts', and of the war itself as a 'divider of Light and Darkness'. The 'breach...with

---

[16] John Dos Passos, Preface (1945) to *One Man's Initiation: 1917: A Novel* (1920; rpt. Ithaca, NY: Cornell University Press, 1969), 36.

[17] James Joyce, *Ulysses* (1922; rpt. Harmondsworth: Penguin, 1992), 42; Ford Madox Ford, *Parade's End* (1924–8; rpt. Harmondsworth: Penguin, 1982), 3.

the course of history' Henry James envisaged as its result can be traced in the structure of all the novels mentioned above, most clearly in the tri-partite division of *To the Lighthouse* into pre-war, wartime, and post-war sections.[18] Lasting commemoration of the Great War, in other words, appears not only in the many public monuments constructed in the years that followed. It also figures in the fractured forms and favourings of memory appearing in much fiction in the interwar years—from *The Return of the Soldier* in 1918 to *Coming up for Air* in 1939.

Recollection and Revision

'Before the war!', Bowling remarks in *Coming up for Air*, 'how long shall we go on saying that, I wonder? How long before the answer will be "Which war?" '[19] Much as he foresees, within three months of the publi-cation of *Coming Up for Air* a second war had intervened, further dis-tancing memories of the period before the first. The Second World War also shaped recollection of the previous conflict in other ways, consoli-dating more firmly some views which had been developing since the 1920s. As earlier chapters outlined, during that decade versions of the war delivered by newspapers, propaganda, and official histories were gradually replaced by ex-combatants' much less affirmative accounts of their experience. Disillusion and regret, central to the new wave of Great War publishing at the end of the 1920s, also extended into the next dec-ade, and expanded still further in consequence of popular perceptions of renewed conflict with Germany. However appalling its losses, a war against Nazism appeared a just and necessary struggle, especially at its end, following revelations about the concentration camps. Any worth-while causes the Great War might have served seemed obscure by comparison, encouraging the view that its griefs and losses were as unjustifiable as they were appalling. As the historian Gary Sheffield suggests, 'viewed through the lens of the "Good War" of 1939–45 the struggle of 1914–18 seemed to be a very bad war indeed'.[20]

---

[18] Orwell, *Coming up for Air*, 107; James, letter of 18 June 1915 to Compton Mackenzie, *The Letters of Henry James*, ed. Percy Lubbock (London: Macmillan, 1920), 493.

[19] Orwell, *Coming up for Air*, 35.

[20] Gary Sheffield, *Forgotten Victory: The First World War: Myths and Realities* (London: Review, 2002), xix.

In the late 1940s and the 1950s, this recent 'Good War' naturally dominated the attention of writers, historians, and the public generally. Interest in the Great War resurfaced strongly in the 1960s, heightened by the fiftieth anniversary of its outbreak, in 1964, and by publications and media productions marking the occasion. In the previous year, Theatre Workshop combined documentary material, contemporary song, and satiric views of war as 'political and economic necessity' into a production popular enough to transfer from their Stratford East theatre to London's West End—*Oh What a Lovely War*, later adapted for the cinema, in 1969.[21] Throughout 1964, BBC2 broadcast the twenty-six episodes of *World War 1: The Great War*, a documentary series sombrely narrated by Michael Redgrave and drawing on film archives and the reminiscences of the many veterans still alive at the time. Interest generated by theatre and television was extended by publication or republication of Great War material, on a scale almost matching the much-expanded output at the end of the 1920s. Over 200 new books on the Great War appeared during the 1960s and early 1970s. Novels reissued at the time included Aldington's *Death of a Hero*, Frederic Manning's *The Middle Parts of Fortune*, and Cecil Lewis's *Sagittarius Rising*. Wilfred Owen's poetry appeared in a new edition in 1963, edited by C. Day Lewis, with a memoir by Edmund Blunden, and also figured substantially in new anthologies published at the time. Brian Gardner's *Up the Line to Death* (1964), introduced by Blunden, and I. M. Parsons's *Men who March Away* (1965) were soon followed by two further collections for use in schools. Growing interest among critics and teachers was reflected in studies such as J. H. Johnston's *English Poetry of the First World War*, published in 1964, followed by Bernard Bergonzi's *Heroes' Twilight* in the next year, with Paul Fussell's influential *The Great War and Modern Memory* following in 1975.

This renewed interest was shaped and extended by contemporary conflict in Vietnam, involving increasing numbers of US troops as the 1960s went on. Graphically reported daily on television, the Vietnam War provoked growing public antipathy, including violent street protests in cities throughout Europe and America later in the decade and in the early 1970s. In this context, the Great War acquired a strongly renewed

---

[21] Theatre Workshop and Charles Chilton, *Oh What a Lovely War* (1965; rpt. London: Methuen, 1998), 61.

relevance. Regret for its terrible losses, along with the obscurity of any purpose they might have served, offered the perfect paradigm for contemporary determinations to resist war in general. Emotive power and immediate contemporary relevance helped to make Great War literature readily teachable. By 1968, Owen and the War Poets had become part of the A-level syllabus in England, and of English teaching throughout the UK. Generations of schoolchildren since the 1960s continued to encounter the Great War principally through its literature, almost always poetry. As Gary Sheffield remarks, it has generally been 'teachers of English, not history, who have had the greatest impact on the shaping of views on the First World War'. Given the pressures of the school curriculum, and of popular memory more generally, this 'shaping' inevitably inclined towards readily assimilated, easily shared views, contributing to what Samuel Hynes outlines in *A War Imagined* (1990) as a settled set of assumptions about 'what the war was and what it meant'. Hynes stresses that this 'collective narrative' is 'not a falsification of reality', but an imaginative or simplified version of it, a 'Myth of the War'.[22] As he explains, this 'Myth' generally shares the emphases of *Oh What a Lovely War*, envisaging a generation of idealistic young men disillusioned and betrayed by their elders—by stupid generals, cynical politicians, and profiteering businessmen, who ensured they were slaughtered needlessly, in vast numbers, for no valid purpose.

Though widely accepted during the later twentieth century, and since, this 'Myth' or 'collective narrative' also attracted amendment and revision. Particularly during the 1980s and 1990s, commentators sought to focus less exclusively on a generation of young men, exploring instead women's experiences, and the changes the Great War wrought more generally on life and work within Britain. Further, fundamental reappraisals of Hynes's 'Myth' appeared in the work of revisionist historians early in the twenty-first century. In *Forgotten Victory: The First World War: Myths and Realities* (2001), Gary Sheffield offers a representative and vigorously argued version of the revised views involved. Rather than the futile, wasteful, dispiriting conflict of the 'Myth', *Forgotten Victory* describes the Great War in terms of necessary, worthwhile, and eventually well-organized resistance to German military aggression. Contrary

[22] Sheffield, *Forgotten Victory*, 18; Samuel Hynes, *A War Imagined: The First World War and English Culture* (1990; rpt. London: Pimlico, 1992), ix–x.

to the 'limited and skewed view' he ascribes to war literature, Sheffield envisages a war fought by soldiers mostly convinced of its justice, and led by staff officers and generals who scarcely deserve their dismissal as incompetents—even, in some accounts of the war, as donkeys. After the disasters of 1915, he argues, their work exhibited instead a 'bloody learning curve'—one leading on through the turning-point of the Somme towards the well-marshalled victory of 1918.[23]

Resistance to disillusioned or 'mythic' collective views is not unique to the twenty-first century. It is almost as long-standing as the negative views themselves. In 1930, Cyril Falls's *War Books: A Critical Guide* and Douglas Jerrold's *The Lie about the War: A Note on Some Contemporary War Books* each strongly criticized the disillusionment prevailing in the war narratives published in growing numbers at the time. For Jerrold, 'lies' about the war could best be avoided by ignoring these accounts— mostly personal, or fictional—in favour of official histories and generals' memoirs. Official accounts, in Jerrold's view, helped to confirm that the war seemed 'neither futile nor avoidable' to those fighting it, allowing 'the agonies, the ardours, and the endurances' of their service to be accorded properly 'tragic and heroic dignity'. Cyril Falls, a staff officer himself, particularly regretted that contemporary emphases on the miseries of the trenches obscured the real variety of military life, which included periods of rest and recreation and 'hundreds of games of football... played every day on the Western Front'.[24]

Both Falls and Jerrold help eliminate some misconceptions about the war. As Falls feared, Great War soldiers are often assumed to have been tortured without respite in the trenches, whereas periods of duty there were rarely of more than a week, and often briefer. In his memoir *A Subaltern's War* (1929), Charles Edmonds explains the various locations and demands entailed in a year's duties, probably including around 65 days in front-line trenches, 36 spent nearby, 120 in reserve, 73 at rest, and—for officers at any rate—some time spent on leave. Serving soldiers were as various in their attitudes as in their activities, and as Jerrold suggests, far from universally sceptical. This is amply evident even in some of the

---

[23] Sheffield, *Forgotten Victory*, 19, xvii.

[24] Douglas Jerrold, *The Lie About the War: A Note on Some Contemporary War Books* (London: Faber and Faber, 1930), 29, 23; Cyril Falls, *War Books: A Critical Guide* (London: Peter Davies, 1930), xi.

books he criticized. Authors characterized as the war's fiercest adversaries can usually be seen to offer a wider and subtler range of responses. In *Memoirs of an Infantry Officer* (1930), Sassoon acknowledges that the war 'had a sombre and unforgettable fascination', despite its insufferable loss and destruction. He also records 'wonderful moments' when 'the idea of death made everything seem vivid and valuable' and 'the flavour of life... doubly strong'. Acts of courage, he adds, regularly highlighted 'the power of the human spirit' or showed men 'glorified by the thing which sought to destroy them'. Robert Graves recalls experiencing 'new meanings of courage, patience, loyalty and greatness of spirit' alongside 'discomfort, grief, pain, fear and horror'. Like Sassoon, in *A Passionate Prodigality* (1933) Guy Chapman mentions 'compelling fascination' or 'a subtler, even a vile attraction' in the war—one acknowledged, he suggests, by 'every writer of imagination who has set down in honesty his experience'.[25] Many authors record the antidotes to discomfort, grief, or horror to be found in laughter, comradeship or song. Even in describing 'strange hells' and 'the racket and fear guns made' in the poem quoted earlier, Gurney explains that these were not always as terrible as might have been expected. As an example, he recalls a time when his company outlived and even out-roared a bombardment through thunderous renditions of ' "Après la guerre fini" '—sung 'beyond all dreads', uproariously, 'till hell all had come down'.[26]

Attitudes to the war were obviously further diversified simply by differences of outlook, temperament, or experience among individuals involved. As H. M. Tomlinson suggests in *All Our Yesterdays*, 'the Great War was almost as many different wars as there were men who were in it'. Some of the men in it would certainly have gone further than the equivocal comments quoted above, sharing instead the views of a character in Somerset Maugham's play *For Services Rendered* (1932) who simply remarks 'I had the time of my life in the war'. Patrick Miller's central figure in *The Natural Man* (1924) considers that he 'enjoyed every hour of

[25] Siegfried Sassoon, *The Complete Memoirs of George Sherston* (1937; rpt. London: Faber and Faber, 1972), 462, 636, 418, 319; Graves, Introduction to Frank Richards, *Old Soldiers Never Die* (1933; rpt. London: Faber and Faber, 1964), 1; Guy Chapman, *A Passionate Prodigality: Fragments of Autobiography* (1933; rpt. London: Buchan and Enright, 1985), 226.

[26] Gurney, *Collected Poems*, 140–1.

it', finding army service, like many soldiers, a liberation from the tedium of civilian life. In *Gallipoli Memories*, Compton Mackenzie likewise describes the war as a 'holiday' from the demands of authorship—one particularly enlivened, for an enthusiast for classical literature, by his first encounters with the 'legend-haunted world' of Greece and the Aegean.[27] This spectrum of views, affirmative or equivocal, helps develop the 'collective narrative' Hynes outlines into a fuller picture of 'what the war was and what it meant'. Understanding of what it meant to those involved is not helped, nor their lives and deaths accorded the dignity they deserve, by assuming they encountered *only* horror and futility, rather than a range of experiences and attitudes, including commitment and loyalty demanding new levels—'new meanings'—of courage. As Chapter 3 suggested, conclusions about the war's horror and futility are more persuasive when recognized as ones reached by writers otherwise so various and vivid in the range of their vision and experience. Much as Gurney continued singing under a bombardment, Sassoon and Owen continued to fight bravely while writing poetry excoriatingly critical of the conflict. Criticism and courage, horror at the war alongside continued commitment to its cause, all gain in conviction, for later readers, when seen as interrelated, and as parts of a full and varied set of contemporary reactions.

Though helpful in indicating this variety, Jerrold, Falls, and later revisionist historians are less convincing in claims about the 'limited and skewed' outlook of Great War literature. Such claims have gathered force since the 1980s, when Fussell was often accused of concentrating the analysis of *The Great War and Modern Memory* on writing by officers—usually members of a well-educated middle class, narrow and particular in their views of the war. There are even commentators, such as Martin Stephen, who suggest that war writers somehow had no alternative to membership of this class. Stephen's *Never Such Innocence* (1988) is one of several anthologies to have usefully expanded the range of readily available Great War poetry. Yet his preface continues to claim that when this writing was *not* produced by an officer class, it nevertheless originated in

[27] H. M. Tomlinson, *All Our Yesterdays* (London: William Heinemann, 1930), 389; W. Somerset Maugham, *The Collected Plays of W. Somerset Maugham* (London: William Heinemann,1931), III: 165; Patrick Miller, *The Natural Man* (1924; rpt. London: Richards, 1930), 69; Compton Mackenzie, *Gallipoli Memories* (London: Cassell, 1929), 180, 400.

a 'middle-class mind which happened to be serving in the ranks'.[28] This is unnecessarily patronizing, or pessimistic. Stephen may identify a 'skewing' evident generally in literature, perhaps always biased towards the views of a middle class equipped with greater leisure to write and read. Yet any such bias is probably less than usually evident in the period of the Great War, which forced into articulacy writers who were various in social background and belonged exclusively neither to an officer class nor to its mindset. Poets discussed in Chapter 3 were far from uniformly middle class in origin, and the 'hurricane' of poetry produced at the time by no means exclusively the work of officers. Both Gurney and Rosenberg wrote about the war from their perspective as privates. So did narrative authors such as Frank Richards, Frederic Manning, Patrick MacGill, and, in some of his work, Henry Williamson. Len Smith's dextrously illustrated journal, *Drawing Fire* (2009), offers further evidence of an ordinary soldier pressed into extraordinary expressiveness by the war. Views these writers communicate do not differ sufficiently from those of officer-authors to suggest that the latter were particularly limited or unusual in their views.

Revisionist history is no more convincing in looking at the higher echelons of the army, or at the overall justice of Britain's cause in the war. Britain's readiness to confine military aggression to distant parts of the world—rather than directing it, as Germany did, on European neighbours—hardly constitutes a morally superior position. Any claims on such a position would require more analysis of the nineteenth-century expansion of empires than studies such as *Forgotten Victory* have scope to provide—in particular, of what Sheffield describes as Britain's picking up colonies 'almost from force of habit'.[29] Regarding the High Command, few historians have attempted to defend the generals responsible for the disasters of 1915. Though they might be seen to have gained in efficiency thereafter, describing the improvement as a 'learning curve' raises awkward questions. Why did so much learning have to be undertaken during the war, and at such cost, when the military technologies involved had in many cases been developed a decade or more before 1914? Might the generals' 'learning curves' have been sharper and less bloody had

[28] Martin Stephen (ed.), *Never Such Innocence: Poems of the First World War* (1988; rpt. London: Dent, 2003), xiv.
[29] Sheffield, *Forgotten Victory*, 63.

those undertaking them been sharper themselves? Sheffield and others persuasively dismiss the idea of Great War generals as donkeys. Yet the abilities concerned may in only a few cases have exceeded those of the perfectly brave, determined, hard-working, ambitious but not especially bright figure—resembling Haig—whom C. S. Forester describes in his novel *The General* (1936). A 'learning curve', moreover, may be too generous a metaphor for the improvements involved, implying steadier progress than really occurred in the latter years of the war, marked by the huge losses at Passchendaele and in early 1918. Any overall progress at the time might be better envisaged as a gradual, oft-interrupted upward incline, or a game of snakes and ladders in which the generals eventually grew better at deploying ladders and avoiding snakes.

Another question—considered later, in assessing tactics required in any description of the war—concerns the depths of suffering underlying those metaphors above, whether of learning, incline, ladder, or snake. Hundreds of thousands of men died or were mutilated in the course of any progress achieved, a scale of loss imperilling any conclusions about victory, gain, or affirmative experience of the war generally. Cyril Falls's views might in this way be particularly swiftly qualified. All those football games and recreations near the Front can be put in a very different perspective by Frank Richards's recollection, in *Old Soldiers Never Die* (1933), that only three members of a twelve-man tug-of-war team remained alive a few days after a competition. Or by the fate of the sixteen members of the first-team squad at Heart of Midlothian—comfortably at the top of the Scottish football league at the time—who had enlisted in the 2nd Edinburgh City Battalion by November 1914. Not surprisingly, the battalion's football team remained undefeated until July 1916. But three Hearts players died on the first day of the Somme, and of the nine who eventually returned from the war, few were able to play again. The team's fate was a real-life enactment of the loss and mutilation envisaged in Sean O'Casey's *The Silver Tassie* (1928)—one of the most powerful plays of the war, tracing the fate of a football hero paralysed by injuries in the trenches.

Revisionist history cannot be accused of ignoring the war's loss and mutilation. *Forgotten Victory* is regularly attentive to the 'the callous arithmetic of battle' and the 'butcher's bill' that resulted. Yet Sheffield also suggests at one stage that the Canadians' capture of Vimy Ridge in 1917 was achieved 'with relatively little difficulty, although at the cost of

11,000 casualties'. Such remarks cast doubt on his promise of 'analysis based on a firm grasp of the facts'.[30] Avoidance of difficulty, even relatively, at the cost of 11,000 casualties, is not a fact but an interpretation—the kind of interpretation generals were apt to make themselves, often without even the concession of that 'although'. Haig, for example, remarked that losses on the first day of the Somme, underestimated at 40,000, should not, in the circumstances 'be considered severe'.[31] In its views of Vimy Ridge, and more generally, Sheffield's analysis is less persuasively fact-based than simply another illustration of the pattern outlined above—of a war interpreted, as H. M. Tomlinson suggests, very variously at the time, and diversely remembered and reinterpreted ever since. Even when so determined, in 1930, to show contemporary writing presenting 'a picture of war which is fundamentally false', Douglas Jerrold sensibly acknowledges that 'there is no such thing as "the truth about war"'.[32] From Jerrold to Sheffield, revisionist views help resist the imposition on the Great War of any single, simplified 'truth' or 'Myth'. They can revitalize in this way the reading of war literature, challenging habitual responses, in terms of 'the old mantra, "the horror of war"', discussed in Chapter 3. Yet there is little reason to think that revisionist history in the twenty-first century will—or should—do more than qualify the 'collective narrative' that had emerged by the end of the twentieth. The scale of its losses suggests that if the Great War is remembered as a victory at all, it is likely to be only as a Pyrrhic one.

Gender and Class

Other forms of revisionist history might still offer alternatives to this conclusion. One of these is suggested in a study published at the height of the 1960s revival of interest—Arthur Marwick's *The Deluge: British Society and the First World War* (1965). Marwick's study is much less concerned with military action than with the possibility that the huge changes war enforced left Britain 'in the inter-war years... "a better place

[30] Ibid. 103, 244, 195, x.
[31] Quoted in Malcolm Brown, *The Imperial War Museum Book of the Somme* (London: Pan Books in Association with the Imperial War Museum, 1996), 119.
[32] Jerrold, *Lie about the War*, 9.

to live in" than it had been in 1914'.[33] This possibility scarcely seemed promising as those years began. In 1920, in *Realities of War*, Philip Gibbs describes instead a thoroughly Pyrrhic victory, one 'gained at the cost of nearly a million dead, and a high sum of living agony, and all our wealth, and a spiritual bankruptcy worse than material loss'. In terms of lost wealth, Gibbs pointed to an increase in the national debt from £645m in 1914 to £7800m in 1919. Looking back on that year, the historian Adrian Gregory calculates that, without the war, Britain 'could have built new universities in every major city, hundreds of advanced hospitals, thousands of schools', generally increased welfare and childcare and still kept taxes lower than they were in 1919.[34] Yet Marwick's interests are less in the nation's wealth and resources than in the war's influence on the structure of British society: in particular, on engrained restrictions of gender and class. Early in *Testament of Youth* (1933), Vera Brittain confirms how influential gender hierarchies remained, before the war, when she records 'suffering, like so many women in 1914, from an inferiority complex'.[35] She goes on to record several developments in the next few years which removed some of the causes of such feelings. Principal among these was the passing, early in 1918, of the Representation of the People Bill. As well as enfranchising male householders over the age of twenty-one, the Bill at last fulfilled some of the suffrage movement's long-held ambitions by giving the vote to women of property over thirty years of age. Late the following year, it was followed by the Sex Disqualification (Removal) Bill, intended to open all professions and civil or judicial careers to women, as well as allowing them to take university degrees.

Just as influential on women's lives were the shifting social and economic conditions which had virtually forced the government into making these legislative changes. Even politicians previously hostile to female suffrage—including the former Prime Minister Herbert Asquith—had to acknowledge the key role of women's labour within a beleaguered wartime economy, in armament manufacturing particularly. As Marwick

[33] Joanna Bourke, Preface to Arthur Marwick, *The Deluge: British Society and the First World War*, reissued 2nd edn (London: Macmillan, 2006), [ix].

[34] Philip Gibbs, *Realities of War* (London: William Heinemann, 1920), 296, 453; Adrian Gregory, *The Last Great War: British Society and the First World War* (Cambridge: Cambridge University Press, 2008), 2.

[35] Vera Brittain, *Testament of Youth: An Autobiographical Study of the Years 1900–1925* (1933; rpt. London: Virago, 2004), 84.

notes, almost a million women were employed in munitions factories in Britain by the end of the war, nearly a fivefold increase compared to 1914. New opportunities in this and other areas allowed many women to escape the drudgery of domestic service—poorly paid, but one of their few chances of employment before the war. Numbers working in this area had declined by around 400,000 by 1918, leading to a permanent shift in the organization of many households. Virginia Woolf identified the occasional appearance in the living room of a cook—rising from the household's 'lower depths'—as a marker of radical changes one of her essays ascribes to the year 1910.[36] By 1919, as Somerset Maugham suggests in a play produced that year, *Home and Beauty*, cooks were scarce enough to be able not only to demand use of the living room, but to dictate almost any employment terms they chose. In other areas, as conscription removed more and more men from the labour force after 1916, women had steadily filled the vacant places, with numbers entering munitions manufacturing matched by the total finding employment in sectors ranging from transport or industry to entertainment. In an odd reversal of Elizabethan convention, Sybil Thorndike found herself playing several of Shakespeare's leading male characters in an Old Vic season in 1916. Emblematically, she was also cast as Everyman in the medieval play of that name. Many roles once thought exclusive to everyman were opened, during the war, to everywoman, too. Even the anti-suffragist Mrs Humphry Ward had to acknowledge, in her novel *Missing* (1917), that the war had opened up a 'world of the new woman—where are women policemen, women engineers, women in khaki, women in overalls and breeches, and many other strange types'.[37]

Not every woman benefited, of course, either during the war or in its aftermath. As Vera Brittain notes, women were often quickly displaced from new occupations after the armistice—ironically, just at the moment the new legislation was passing through Parliament. Yet the war had allowed women at least a vision, and often direct experience, of new forms of independence, financial autonomy, and self-determination. This naturally had lasting effects on life and literature, too wide-ranging to be considered in more than outline here. As H. G. Wells anticipated in

[36] Virginia Woolf, 'Character in Fiction' (1924), rpt. in *The Essays of Virginia Woolf*, ed. Andrew McNeillie and Stuart N. Clarke (London: Hogarth Press, 1986–2011), III: 422.

[37] Mrs Humphry Ward, *Missing* (London: Collins, 1917), 341.

Mr. Britling Sees It Through (1916), the war altered 'the proportions of the sexes for a generation, bringing women into business and office and industry... flooding the world with strange doubts and novel ideas'.[38] For male authors, strange doubts often predominated, evident in the frequent appearance of femme fatale figures in their work, indicative of new anxieties about female empowerment. During the war, these figures range from the relatively innocent nurse, attracting competing desires in Hugh Walpole's *The Dark Forest* (1916), to the more wayward heroine of Stephen McKenna's popular *Sonia* (1917), brought back towards conventional behaviour through a plot resembling Shakespeare's in *The Taming of the Shrew*. Similarly challenging figures appear throughout 1920s fiction, in novels directly concerned with the war, including Ford Madox Ford's *Parade's End* (1924–8), or R. H. Mottram's *Spanish Farm* sequence (1924–7). They also turn up in many others, such as Aldous Huxley's, which examine new social conditions the war helped to create. Sexual behaviour was often a central interest of these novels. In *Death of a Hero* (1929), Richard Aldington's narrator may be claiming too much for recent behavioural changes when he suggests that 'the simple process of dissociating sex life from the philoprogenitive instinct was performed by the War Generation'.[39] Sexual relations in their extramarital forms at any rate figured with new explicitness in fiction at the time. As well as featuring in novels mentioned above, they were also daringly explored in Arnold Bennett's account of intimate relations in *The Pretty Lady* (1916), and in John Galsworthy's description of an extramarital wartime pregnancy and its consequences in *The Saint's Progress* (1919).

Women writers naturally explored 'novel ideas' of female autonomy with more enthusiasm, and often a ready familiarity. Ideas of women's independence were after all not entirely novel. Early volumes of Dorothy Richardson's *Pilgrimage* sequence (1915–67), for example, follow the 'New Woman' fiction, popular in the late nineteenth and early twentieth centuries, in describing new social and behavioural possibilities opening up for women at that time. Women writers were also increasingly aware of the need for an independent style, sharing Woolf's later conclusion, in *A Room of One's Own* (1929), that 'it is useless to go to the great men writers for help'. In the fourth volume of *Pilgrimage, The Tunnel*

[38] H. G. Wells, *Mr. Britling Sees It Through* (London: Cassell, 1916), 257.
[39] Richard Aldington, *Death of a Hero* (1929; rpt. London: Hogarth Press, 1984), 171.

(1919), Richardson likewise suggests that no woman can reveal 'even the fringe of her consciousness' within established linguistic or artistic conventions, generally shaped and dominated by 'the achievements of men'.[40] Moves towards new styles and subjects, though in evidence before 1914, gained greatly in momentum during the years of the war, sometimes through direct experience of its violence and destruction. In her account of ambulance work in *A Journal of Impressions in Belgium* (1915), for example, May Sinclair stresses that, in war as in peacetime, 'the modern woman does not ask to be protected, does not want to be protected'.[41] In a novel partly reflecting her recent Belgian experiences, *Tasker Jevons* (1916), Sinclair goes on to present a heroine firmly committed to this principle, and in one of her best-known works, *Mary Olivier* (1919), to explore more fully the struggles for independence it entails.

Many women writers endured wartime experiences more disturbing than those described in Sinclair's *Journal*—at times almost touristic in its account of the war's early weeks. In some contexts, pain and shock women experienced matched or exceeded anything encountered by men. Agonies of loss, finished in an instant for dying soldiers, sometimes extended across a lifetime for those they left bereaved. This is the theme of May Cannan's poem, quoted earlier, and several others in Catherine Reilly's anthology of Great War women's verse, *Scars Upon my Heart* (1981). Long-lasting consequences of wartime bereavement are also movingly explored in W. Chetham-Strode's play, *Sometimes Even Now* (1933). Stresses could likewise be intense and long-sustained for the many women working in the hospital services—as regular nurses, or, like Vera Brittain, in the Voluntary Aid Detachment (VAD), 80,000 strong by the war's end. Soldiers endured spells of terrifyingly violent action, but often separated by weeks of boredom, while stationed in areas of relative safety. Even when working in hospitals well away from the Front, nurses were confronted unremittingly, daily and hourly, with mutilated bodies and the dismembered human wreckage of battle. Some of the effects on writers involved were identified in Chapter 2, in

---

[40] Virginia Woolf, *A Room of One's Own* (1929; rpt. Harmondsworth: Penguin, 1975), 76; Dorothy Richardson, *The Tunnel* (1919), in *Pilgrimage* (1915–67; rpt. London: Virago, 1979), II: 210, 222.

[41] May Sinclair, *A Journal of Impressions in Belgium* (London: Hutchinson, 1915), 236.

discussing the supposedly artless 'collection of fragments' Mary Borden offers in *The Forbidden Zone* (1929). Similar effects appear in the fragmented, reticent style of *A Diary without Dates* (1918), an account of VAD work in London by Enid Bagnold, later a friend of modernist writers including Katherine Mansfield. Like some of the patients she describes, Bagnold seems to 'watch without curiosity, speak no personalities, form no sets, express no likings, analyse nothing'.[42] Her abbreviated paragraphs and restless shifts of attention are comparable to the flickering, unsettled synecdochies often marking male authors' descriptions of the Front. Like Ernest Hemingway's prose, Bagnold's suggests a mind profoundly committed to direct, authentic representation of wartime experience, yet painfully recoiling from the terrible realities it is forced to present. Like Hemingway, or Ford Madox Ford, both Borden and Bagnold suggest close connections between experience of the war and some of the innovative styles developed in the next decade. As Woolf shows in *Mrs Dalloway*, 'this late age of world's experience had bred in...all men and women, a well of tears', leaving fractured styles, scars upon heart and mind, another of the war's memorials, or legacies, in writing by both genders.[43]

Wartime changes Marwick identifies in Britain's class structure were at least as influential as those affecting gender hierarchies. Britain in 1914 remained a rigorously class-structured country, with a 'great and accepted gulf', as Marwick calls it, separating the lower orders from the rest of society.[44] The armed forces could scarcely have continued fighting as they did without long-engrained allegiances and deferences still sharply stratifying British life. The armies of most other warring nations eventually engaged in substantial forms of mutiny. Yet apart from a brief rebellion around Étaples in 1917, ordinary British soldiers generally continued faithfully to follow their officers' orders, despite regularly encountering good reasons to doubt their wisdom. These included the inexperience, compared to some of the ordinary soldiers themselves, of many of the officers immediately commanding them. Especially at the start of the war, officers often obtained commissions not on the grounds of military experience or aptitude, but on the basis of class, education, or

---

[42] Enid Bagnold, *A Diary without Dates* (London: William Heinemann, 1918), 64.

[43] Virginia Woolf, *Mrs Dalloway* (1925; rpt. Harmondsworth: Penguin, 1975), 12.

[44] Marwick, *The Deluge*, 60.

convenient connections within the army staff. In *Peter Jackson*, Frankau's semi-autobiographical hero is offered a commission simply because he has been to Eton. In *A Subaltern's War*, Edmonds describes acquiring his as a result of getting his uncle to 'pull some strings'.[45] Once posted to the Front, officers did share most of the dangers and privations endured by ordinary soldiers, but not all. Some in senior positions took a servant with them to the trenches. Most had a private soldier to cook for them and to look after their kit. In moving location around the Front, officers could often travel on horseback, and have their belongings carried on transport wagons, while ordinary soldiers had to slog along beneath heavy packs, for mile after mile, through blistering sunshine or teeming rain. In practice, officers were sometimes ready to forego their privileges, helping weary men by carrying an extra pack or rifle, and sometimes more than one. In any case, as George Coppard records in his memoir *With a Machine Gun to Cambrai* (1968), potentially inflammatory instances of class privilege were usually just accepted by ordinary soldiers as 'the natural order of things'—parts of the 'accepted gulf' Marwick emphasizes in British life in 1914.[46]

As the war continued, though, it did much to challenge and reshape this 'natural order'. High attrition rates among officers enforced greater openness in their selection. By 1918, nearly a quarter of a million new officers had been commissioned. Around half of these 'temporary gentlemen' were former privates, and more than a third were men who had come from working-class or lower middle-class occupations. Officers who considered themselves longer established or more authentic gentlemen were often grudging in their acceptance of newcomers, as Henry Williamson describes in *A Fox Under my Cloak* (1955). An expanded officer class nevertheless helped ensure, as MacGill records in *The Amateur Army* (1915), that 'men of all classes, who had been as far apart as the poles in civil life' were likely to find themselves, sooner or later, 'knit together in the common brotherhood of war'.[47] Many effects followed from these new proximities. Recent studies have suggested that for some officers—Owen and Sassoon in particular—an admiring, affectionate

---

[45] Charles Edmonds, *A Subaltern's War* (1929; rpt. London: Anthony Mott, 1984), 21.

[46] George Coppard, *With a Machine Gun to Cambrai* (1980; rpt. London: Macmillan, 1986), 17.

[47] Patrick MacGill, *The Amateur Army* (London: Herbert Jenkins, 1915), 63–4.

concern for soldiers under their command inclined towards the homoerotic, or carried into the trenches some of the sexual habits acquired in all-male English public schools. Proximity with ordinary soldiers probably had more significant linguistic and political consequences, either in introducing some Great War writers to a range of possibilities offered by slang and the vernacular, as earlier chapters discussed, or simply in suggesting the need for social change. Lt Col E. W. Hermon, for example, strongly registers this need in his letters from France. Late in 1916, he describes attending a dinner organized exclusively for ex-Etonian officers—seventy-three of them, serving close to the Front at the time. Yet in the same week he records being impressed enough by the conduct of a soldier under his command—and far beneath his social rank—to conclude that 'there's no doubt that a lot of our social ideas are rot'.[48]

Writing for the *Spectator*, Donald Hankey considered that by 1915 'a national ideal had proved stronger than class prejudice', ensuring 'all classes were at one ... in the new citizen Army' and that the war in general had proved a successful 'experiment in democracy'.[49] Many authors expected this experiment to continue into the post-war years. In a play produced in 1917, but set after the war, *The Foundations*, John Galsworthy records the hope that 'class hatred' might be succeeded by 'wonderful unity'. Galsworthy continues to tease at conventional social boundaries in *Windows* (1922), and J. M. Barrie considers them more whimsically in his play *A Kiss for Cinderella* (1920), hoping that the war may have 'mixed things up till we forget how different we are'. Virginia Woolf sounds a less progressive but probably more realistic note in her diary in 1918, mentioning 'the horrible sense of community which the war produces, as if we all sat in a third class railway carriage together'.[50] As she suggests, new brotherhood and 'wonderful unity' were not necessarily approved universally, nor guaranteed to outlast the war. In *For*

---

[48] Lieutenant Colonel E. W. Hermon, *For Love and Courage: The Letters of Lieutenant Colonel E. W. Hermon from the Western Front 1914–1917*, ed. Anne Nason (London: Preface, 2009), 312.

[49] Donald Hankey, *A Student in Arms* (1916; rpt. London: Andrew Melrose, 1917), 25.

[50] John Galsworthy, *The Plays of John Galsworthy* (London: Duckworth, 1929), 465; J. M. Barrie, *The Plays of J. M. Barrie* (London: Hodder and Stoughton, 1930); 452; Virginia Woolf, diary entry for 7 June 1918, *The Diary of Virginia Woolf*, ed. Anne Olivier Bell (London: Hogarth Press, 1977–85), I: 153.

Services Rendered, Somerset Maugham suggests the affluent classes tended once again to close ranks after the war, to the detriment of 'temporary gentlemen'. As with gender roles, the war might be considered to have created a new vision of social mobility, rather than achieving comprehensive or lasting change.

Officers' admiration for their soldiers' fortitude—so often recorded in Great War writing—indicates in other ways an urgent need for social change. 'What the devil made the men stick it? They were unbelievable', Ford's hero Tietjens ponders in *Parade's End*.[51] Some answers to his question can be found in the conditions endured by a majority of the British population early in the twentieth century. Nostalgia for the Edwardian years in novels such as *The Memorial* is in one way genuinely 'skewed'— biased towards the experience of the upper and middle classes, for whom a 'safe, happy, world' was much more accessible than for those less well-off. Though *Coming up for Air* claims that a sense of security and continuity informed the Edwardian period generally, and at a profound level, Orwell also acknowledges—like Grassic Gibbon in *Sunset Song*—the frequent misery of ordinary daily life at the time. 'It isn't that life was softer then than now', Orwell's George Bowling explains, 'actually it was harsher. People on the whole worked harder, lived less comfortably, and died more painfully.'[52] Historians such as Marwick and Adrian Gregory thoroughly endorse this view. As Gregory points out, even after the war industrial injuries were still running at a rate of around half a million annually. As well as dangerous and gruelling factory conditions, the working classes endured overcrowded, insanitary housing, and an infant mortality rate of at least 25 per cent.

For ordinary soldiers, largely drawn from these classes, dangers and privations at the Front may have been more 'stickable' because they were far from wholly unfamiliar. Wilfred Owen suggests as much in one of the few poems he published during the war, 'Miners'. Writing in January 1918, in response to a Welsh colliery disaster which had killed 150 men and boys, Owen regrets that a complacent public easily forgets 'us poor lads, | Left in the ground', whether in the mines or the trenches. In *Goodbye to All That* (1929), Robert Graves points to much the same equivalence, describing former miners sufficiently 'accustomed to death' to

[51] Ford, *Parade's End*.
[52] Orwell, *Coming up for Air*, 106.

remain cheerful even while under fire in the front line.[53] Other authors even consider that the army offered working men improved conditions during the war. In *The Red Horizon* (1916), Patrick MacGill suggests that service in France might be construed as 'the poor man ... having his first holiday on the Continent', though also 'perhaps his last'. One of Vernon Bartlett's characters even finds that 'war means ... safety', as regular army pay allows him and his family 'enough to eat for the first time in our blooming lives'. In *All Our Yesterdays*, Tomlinson likewise notes that soldiers had 'no job to hold down, no fear of the sack, no landlord' and could at least rely confidently on being fed and clothed.[54]

Both Marwick and Gregory demonstrate how far the Great War extended similar confidence on the Home Front. Increased demand for labour guaranteed virtually full employment for unskilled as well as skilled workers, also allowing those employed casually or seasonally to find permanent jobs. Wage rates doubled for skilled labour, and tripled for the unskilled, while the working week's reduction from 55 to 48 hours offered more opportunities for overtime, often further enhanced by productivity bonuses. In this way, though prices doubled during the war, wages generally more than kept pace with them. There were other gains, too, for working people, including legislation to improve housing and education, and a nationwide imposition of rent controls following Red Clydeside agitation in 1915–16. Soldiers returning after the armistice generally did not find 'homes fit for heroes', nor in some cases homes or jobs at all. But they did find that the need to involve the whole population in the war effort had forced the government towards greater attention to the welfare of the country generally. Many returning soldiers also found themselves newly empowered, like women at the time, through the acquisition of the vote. Recollections of service in what MacGill describes as 'an army which outshone its figureheads' added further to a sense of democratic achievement at the time.[55]

---

[53] *Wilfred Owen: The Complete Poems and Fragments*, ed. Jon Stallworthy (London: Chatto and Windus, Hogarth Press, and Oxford University Press, 1983), I: 136; Robert Graves, *Goodbye to All That*, rev edn (1929; rpt. Harmondsworth: Penguin, 2000), 97.

[54] MacGill, *Red Horizon*, 25–6; Vernon Bartlett, *No Man's Land* (London: George Allen and Unwin, 1930), 174–5; Tomlinson, *All Our Yesterdays*, 448.

[55] Patrick MacGill, *The Great Push: An Episode of the Great War* (London: Herbert Jenkins, 1917), 134.

Might this social and material progress allow the Great War to be considered a 'forgotten victory' after all? Support for this possibility was often expressed in official histories and memoirs appearing in its immediate aftermath. In a *Gallipoli Diary* published in 1920, the Allied commander Sir Ian Hamilton suggests that '*there is no other way* of progress' than through war, and that 'only by intense sufferings can the nations grow'.[56] Yet such equations of progress and destruction, questionable at any time in history, seem particularly hard to justify in relation to the Great War. Given the political agitation gathering pace under Liberal governments in the Edwardian years, more decisive social change might have ensued had the war *not* intervened. The intensity of suffering in the Great War, in any case, once again seems disproportionate to improvements in material circumstances it might have produced, especially as many of them—like those glimpses of shifting class and gender hierarchies—faded from view as depression and unemployment ravaged the 1920s. There were, moreover, many commentators, at the time and earlier, who saw emphases on wages, commerce, and commodities—on materialism generally—as among the factors that had allowed war to break out, further constraining everyday life in the years that followed.

Materialism and Mechanism

Philip Gibbs reflected this view in 1920, in his concern that losses in spiritual terms outweighed any material considerations. Something of this loss had been anticipated by D. H. Lawrence, even two weeks after the war's outbreak, in an article published in the *Guardian* under the pseudonym 'H. D. Lawrence'. Forecasting 'what war would be like', Lawrence predicts that those involved will be merely 'a part in some iron insensate will, our flesh and blood, our soul and intelligence shed away, and all that remained of us a cold, metallic adherence to an iron machine'. The war, he considers, will be 'an affair entirely of machines, with men attached to the machines, as the subordinate part thereof'.[57] Lawrence draws on a set of antitheses—between man and machine, soul or spirit

---

[56] General Sir Ian Hamilton, *Gallipoli Diary* (London: Edward Arnold, 1920), I: 34.
[57] D. H. Lawrence ['H.D. Lawrence'], 'With the Guns', *Manchester Guardian*, 18 Aug. 1914, 10.

and materiality—developed in *Women in Love* (1921), written during the war, and evidently already familiar enough to the general population, by 1914, to have been quickly taken up in wartime propaganda. Though Lawrence discusses modern warfare generally, it was probably convenient for his article's appeal that it recalls Bavarian army manoeuvres— ones he had witnessed a year previously. Patriotic and propagandist writing was usually much more specific, construing the kind of mechanization and soullessness Lawrence fears as deliberate aspirations of German—usually Prussian—militarism and statecraft. In his propagandist study, *When Blood Is Their Argument* (1915), Ford Madox Ford firmly equates 'Prussianism, materialism, militarism, and the mania for organization', complaining that German 'Kultur' is committed to 'perfecting already too perfect machines'. In a Preface to his anthology *The Spirit of Man* (1916), Robert Bridges likewise ascribes corrupt faith in 'material force' specifically to the Germans, insisting instead that 'man is a spiritual being' with a responsibility to 'conquer the material aspects of the world'. His views are extended in Hereward Carrington's *Psychical Phenomena and the War* (1918), as much propaganda as spiritualist enquiry. Locating the origins of the war in 'strife for material power and gain' Carrington claims of the Germans that 'materialism has laid hold upon them, as a nation; their mechanistic conception of the universe has led to the complete disregard of the higher, spiritual values and powers'.[58] Antitheses of this kind also shaped French propaganda early in the war. In *The Meaning of the War: Life and Matter in Conflict* (1915), Henri Bergson describes the Germans as direct adversaries of the *élan vital* and creative evolution long advocated in his own philosophy. Instead of the 'spiritualization' sought by the rest of humanity, Bergson accuses Prussia of having 'plotted an inverse experience for mankind', involving 'the mechanisation of spirit instead of the spiritualization of matter'. Guilty of invoking 'powers of death . . . against life', Germany perversely intends, in his view, that 'mechanical forces . . . take possession of man in order to make his nature material as their own'.[59]

[58] Ford Madox Ford, *When Blood is Their Argument: An Analysis of Prussian Culture* (London: Hodder and Stoughton, 1915), xi, 294; Robert Bridges, *The Spirit of Man*, (London: Longmans, Green, 1916), [i–ii]; Hereward Carrington, *Psychical Phenomena and the War* (New York: Dodd, Mead, 1918), 102, 8.

[59] Henri Bergson, *The Meaning of the War: Life and Matter in Conflict*, trans. H. Wildon Carr (London: T. Fisher Unwin, 1915), 35–6, 38.

As the war went on and early idealism faded, soulless materialism and 'mania for organisation' began to seem characteristics harder to ascribe solely to Germany. They seemed instead—much as Lawrence had predicted—inevitable adjuncts of all modern warfare. In *Gallipoli Memories*, Compton Mackenzie recalls reluctantly reaching this view while witnessing 'a system crash to pieces...the deathbed of an old order' during the unsuccessful landings in 1915 at Suvla Bay. Their failure, he considered, made inevitable 'the murderous folly of the Somme' in the following year, and ensured that 'the war would last now until we had all turned ourselves into Germans to win it'. His conviction was widely shared, Lawrence also suggesting that 'it was in 1915 the old world ended'.[60] As Chapter 2 described, many commentators considered—like Sassoon, in *Memoirs of an Infantry Officer*—that it was not only the Somme, in the summer of 1916, but the introduction of conscription earlier in the year that had ended an old world and left military organization 'undisguisedly mechanical and inhuman'. Even the changing appearance of soldiers seemed to confirm a hardening inhumanity at the time. For Sassoon, gas masks issued early in 1916 turned his company into 'grotesque, goggle-faced creatures', an 'omen' of the harsher conditions that would develop during that year (Fig. 11). For Edmund Blunden, the introduction of steel helmets later in 1916 symbolized 'the change that was coming over the war, the induration from a personal crusade into a vast machine of violence'. New headgear and the demise of the old leather 'Pickelhaube' seemed similarly indicative on the German side, Ernst Jünger describing the first steel-helmeted soldier he encounters as 'the denizen of a new and far harsher world'.[61]

War could obviously change appearance much more radically, forcing wounded soldiers to rely on devices more disfiguring than gas masks or helmets. George Ramage's journal for July 1916 indicates the huge range of artificial limbs and prosthetic devices needed by amputees in the army's rehabilitation centre at Roehampton. In *One Man's Initiation*, Dos Passos describes a wounded soldier whose nose has been replaced by 'a triangular black patch that ended in some mechanical contrivance with

---

[60] Mackenzie, *Gallipoli Memories*, 373; D. H. Lawrence, *Kangaroo* (1923; rpt. London: Heinemann, 1974), 220.

[61] Sassoon, *Complete Memoirs of George Sherston*, 382, 257; Edmund Blunden, *Undertones of War* (1928; rpt. Harmondsworth: Penguin, 1986), 53; Ernst Jünger, *Storm of Steel* (1920/1961/1978), trans. Michael Hofmann (Harmondsworth: Penguin, 2004), 92.

FIG 11 Gas masks worn by British soldiers in the trenches in Salonika in 1917.
© Imperial War Museums (Q 60966).

shiny little black metal rods that took the place of the jaw'.[62] Hemingway's short story 'In Another Country' (1928) gives a sceptical account of medical machinery designed to restore destroyed muscles or fractured limbs. David Jones's *In Parenthesis* envisages doctors in their 'clinical shrines' giving soldiers 'glass eyes to see | and synthetic spare parts to walk in the Triumphs'.[63] Though inevitably more acute for the wounded, some of this awareness of body parts and the vulnerable, mutable nature of the human frame was inescapable for all serving soldiers. Concerns that war's 'insensate will' might leave iron in the soul were obviously less immediate than the threat that many forms of hurtling metal might invade the body. George Coppard recalls being 'permanently conscious that [he] was made with a brain-box, heart, lungs and stomach', each utterly defenceless against bullet or shell. As Walter Benjamin remarks,

[62] Dos Passos, *One Man's Initiation*, 54.
[63] Jones, *In Parenthesis*, 175–6.

'under the open sky...in a field of force of destructive torrents and explosions, was the tiny, fragile human body', susceptible at any moment to dismembering, shattering reduction into the mere components Coppard lists.[64] Few combatants could avoid witnessing such shattering. Remarque describes 'men living with their skulls blown open...with their two feet cut off...without mouths, without jaws, without faces'. Edmund Blunden recalls a trench strewn with 'gobbets of blackening flesh, the earth-wall sotted with blood, with flesh, the eye under the duckboard, the pulpy bone'. Hospital workers such as Mary Borden inevitably encountered 'heads and knees and mangled testicles... stumps where legs once were fastened...parts of faces—the nose gone, or the jaw...things, but no men'. 'It is impossible to be a woman here', Borden adds of her hospital work, describing herself as 'another machine' instead (Fig. 12).[65]

Borden's remarks indicate that Bergson had good reason to construe 'the meaning of the war' as 'life and matter in conflict'. But like many of the comments quoted above, describing wartime reductions of men and women to things and machines, her views suggest that Bergson may have been wrong to assume that life would assuredly prevail over matter. Chapter 3 discussed authors who were far from believing in the triumph of life or spirit—poets, such as Owen, in 'À Terre', who suggest that dissolutions into 'thing' or inert matter may have been less to be feared than welcomed. Shortly after the war, thinking of this kind was codified and extended by a theorist more influential on the early twentieth century even than Bergson, though in this case directly opposed to his views— Sigmund Freud. Whereas Bergson favoured 'spiritualisation of matter', in *Beyond the Pleasure Principle* Freud envisages the spirit, or life generally, attracted inevitably towards matter's inertness. Based around observation of traumatic neuroses the war had caused, Freud's study outlines a new drive—an urge towards 'lifelessness', counterbalancing sexual and life-advancing instincts described in his earlier writing. '*The goal of all life is death*', Freud now stresses, emphasizing that '*the inanimate was*

[64] Coppard, *With a Machine Gun to Cambrai*, 40; Walter Benjamin, 'The Storyteller' (1936), rpt. in *Illuminations*, ed. Hannah Arendt, trans. Harry Zohn (New York: Schocken Books, 1969), 84.
[65] Erich Maria Remarque, *All Quiet on the Western Front* (1929), trans. A. W. Wheen (London: Mayflower, 1963), 91; Blunden, *Undertones of War*, 46; Mary Borden, *The Forbidden Zone* (London: William Heinemann, 1929), 60, 64.

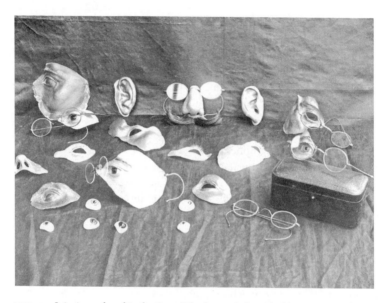

FIG 12   Injuries endured in the Great War demanded rapid advances in prosthetics and plastic surgery, as Thomas Pynchon describes in the fourth chapter of his novel *V.* (1963). The kind of prosthetic devices illustrated began to be produced in quantity by institutions such as the 3rd London General Hospital.

© Imperial War Museums (Q 30460)

there before the animate' and that there is '*a tendency innate in living organic matter impelling it towards reinstatement of* [this] *earlier condition*'. Freud's theory views fatalistically in this way the development of all life: the entire 'evolution of our earth, and its relations to the sun'. First published in German in 1920, it seems a desolate extension of Owen's vision in 'Futility', written two years earlier—of 'fatuous sunbeams' stirring 'the clays of a cold star' into an aimless interlude between two phases of inanimacy.[66] One of Freud's most arcane studies, *Beyond the Pleasure Principle* might be read not only for what it offers psychoanalysis. It can also be seen to project towards myth, or intellectual fable,

[66] Sigmund Freud, *Beyond the Pleasure Principle* (1920), trans. C. J. M. Hubback (London/Vienna: International Psycho-Analytical Press, 1922), 54, 47, 44, 46—Freud's italics; Owen, *Complete Poems*, I: 158.

the destructiveness of the period immediately preceding its publication—one extending to new depths the perennial struggle between animate and inanimate, exacerbated at this time by modernity's expanding emphases on materialism and the machine.

Modernism and War

More affirmative responses obviously remained possible, and necessary. As Max Plowman concludes in *A Subaltern on the Somme* (1928), 'art lives by all that war destroys'.[67] What history disturbs, culture seeks to restore. Values most challenged in any historical period are often, naturally enough, the ones imagination most vigorously attempts to sustain or repair. Even Owen's 'À Terre' finds a vestigial affirmation in the fertility offered by decaying corpses. For other authors, intensified wartime awareness of the materiality of the human frame—as thing or machine—often provokes reciprocal re-emphasis of the *non*-physical, or of the body's relative insignificance compared to mind, soul, or spirit. In *No Man's Land*, Bartlett remarks of a corpse that it 'lay so stiff, so deprived of will or mind or soul, that one could hardly believe it had ever been more than a puppet'. For Isaac Rosenberg in 'Dead Man's Dump', soldiers' corpses seem merely 'their soul's sack'. For Ernest Raymond, in *Tell England* (1922), they likewise appear as no more than 'some empty crate', offering no reason to think 'in terms of matter instead of in terms of spiritual realities'. Even in describing the burial of forty rotting corpses on a pitch-black night—one of the direst duties mentioned in his letters—Lieutenant Colonel Hermon finds the experience convinces him only that 'the soul of man must be so to speak "detachable"'.[68]

For Raymond—or for Robert Bridges, quoted earlier—emphasis on 'spiritual realities' was exalted and more or less religious in nature. Yet as Hermon's comment suggests, it could also be almost practical, or mundane. The 'spirit' which Bergson envisages resisting matter, mechanism,

---

[67] Max Plowman ['Mark VII'], *A Subaltern on the Somme: in 1916* (1927; rpt. New York: E. P. Dutton, 1928), 220.

[68] Bartlett, *No Man's Land*, 162; Isaac Rosenberg, *The Poems and Plays of Isaac Rosenberg*, ed. Vivien Noakes (Oxford: Oxford University Press, 2004), 140; Ernest Raymond, *Tell England: A Study in a Generation* (1922; rpt. London: Cassell, 1929), 247; Hermon, *For Love and Courage*, 117.

and materialism was in any case not explicitly religious, but a property instead of the continuous, creatively evolving vitality his philosophy ascribes to individual consciousness. Working in the wake of the Great War, modernist writers were often inclined to follow this kind of thinking. In 'Modern Novels'—an essay first published a few months after the armistice, demanding new priorities for fiction—it is significant that Virginia Woolf chooses the term 'spiritual' to describe one of the emerging writers whose work she recommends, James Joyce. Her choice is all the more striking as her essay goes on to complain about Joyce's difficulty, unpleasantness, and even indecency. Psychology, mentioned on the next page of her essay, might have offered a term more obviously appropriate in defining the quality she most admires in Joyce's work—its determination 'to reveal the flickerings of that innermost flame which flashes its myriad messages through the brain'. Yet labelling Joyce as 'spiritual' is in other ways thoroughly helpful for Woolf's argument. It highlights preferences for Joyce 'in contrast to those whom we have called materialists'—principally an older generation of novelists, including Arnold Bennett, John Galsworthy, and H. G. Wells, whom she seeks to consign to a pre-war period superseded by the changefulness of the war. Defining this generation as materialists insufficiently concerned with 'mind and spirit' also allows her, ironically, to dismiss these writers in terms widely exploited during the war in the kind of propaganda they had been much involved in producing themselves.[69]

Later critics have pointed out that Woolf's criticisms are in one way obviously unfair. Bennett, Galsworthy, and Wells were each committed to social reform in the years before the war, and critical—directly and explicitly—of materialism and commercialism advancing at the time. Yet Woolf is not arguing only about the subject of fiction. In her view, the work of this older generation was covertly complicit with advancing materialism at the level of style, through its meticulous descriptive concentration on an external, everyday, material world. Joyce's 'innermost flame' illumines instead an inner domain of individual consciousness potentially detached from this world, and freer of the shadows cast upon it by the Great War. Woolf went on to explore this potential in her own fiction throughout the 1920s. In *Mrs Dalloway*, fluid transcriptions of her heroine's thoughts—and of memories of happier times in the

[69] Woolf, *Essays*, III: 34–5, 36.

past—lead away from the 'well of tears' left throughout contemporary life by the 'late age of world's experience'. The advantages of a detached, interior world—of 'losing consciousness of outer things'—are still more marked in *To the Lighthouse*. Interior consciousnesses explored throughout the novel's first and third parts lead away from the 'profusion of darkness' described in the second, set during the war years, and from the hostilities of a physical, external world so painfully evident at that time.[70]

Adding this account of Woolf's fiction to analyses of narrative and poetry in Chapters 2 and 3—and of time and memory earlier in this chapter—might confirm the Great War as a principal influence on the evolution of modernist writing in the 1920s. Further evidence could be advanced in support of this view. The sense of a corrupted language discussed in Chapter 1—of 'words...cancelled'—offered a strong incentive to remake literature and culture. For Ezra Pound, in *Hugh Selwyn Mauberley* (1920), the war had revealed existing culture to be only 'a botched civilization'—one offering no more than 'two gross of broken statues, | ...a few thousand battered books'. In *All Quiet on the Western Front*, Remarque likewise suggests that a war hospital renders 'senseless...everything that can ever be written, done, or thought...the culture of a thousand years could not prevent this stream of blood being poured out, these torture-chambers'.[71] In the general terms each suggests, the Great War profoundly challenged established authority and traditions, in culture as in life more widely, encouraging the kind of demands for change Woolf began making so promptly after its conclusion. Yet it is the year 1910, and not 1914 or 1916, that Woolf's essays identify as the key moment that made a new art so necessary. Pound himself had been complaining about a 'botched civilization' ever since he arrived in London in 1908, urging any authors and artists who would listen to him to 'make it new'. Wyndham Lewis had needed no persuading, enlisting Pound's help in producing his journal *Blast*, vehemently committed to revolution in art and writing. Significantly, its first number appeared in late June 1914, six weeks before the war broke out. Regretting later how quickly his journal had been overtaken by 'a bigger *Blast*', Lewis stressed

---

[70] Virginia Woolf, *To the Lighthouse* (1927; rpt. Harmondsworth: Penguin, 1973), 181, 143.

[71] Ezra Pound, *Hugh Selwyn Mauberley* (1920), rpt. in *Selected Poems*, ed. T. S. Eliot (1948; rpt. London: Faber and Faber, 1973), 176; Remarque, *All Quiet*, 172–3.

how closely war and art had seemed to 'dovetail into each other', and how extensively 'sound and fury' had characterized the cultural world before August 1914. As his memoir *Blasting and Bombardiering* (1937) suggests, *Blast* confirms that 'artists and men of letters had gone into action', in pursuit of new styles and interests 'prior to the Great Bloodletting'.[72]

Later commentators have generally confirmed this view—Jean-Michel Rabaté, for example, in his full-length study, *1913: The Cradle of Modernism* (2007). Most accounts of the period also acknowledge how extensively the changing conditions of modern life to which modernist art responded were already developing by 1914. As suggested earlier, the trenches sometimes seemed almost familiar to ordinary soldiers, already accustomed to the grimness of industrial life in the early years of the twentieth century. As D. H. Lawrence shows in *Women in Love*, principles of scientific management and early forms of production-line technology—not only technologized warfare—threatened throughout those years to reduce working men to things and machines. The Great War, in other words, occupied a central role in the development of modern literature and art, but sometimes only in rapidly accelerating towards maturity—or vexing towards nightmare—cradlefuls of initiatives already in vigorous infancy before 1914. In terms of the wider life of the times, the war might likewise be considered only an extension of processes already imposing on the early twentieth century an ever-changeful, ever-expanding modernity, increasingly technologized, industrialized, and reifying.

Literature and War

Further questions about literature's relation to its times are raised by modernist strategies discussed in this chapter, and in earlier ones. Modernist fiction, such as Woolf's, seeks some refuge from the stresses of the war years within memory and inner consciousness, or the distancing 'blue haze' and artistic vision that closes *To the Lighthouse*. Modernist poetry likewise moves from the anarchy and futility of contemporary life, as T. S. Eliot saw it, towards stable, distanced orders of art and myth.

---

[72] Wyndham Lewis, *Blasting and Bombardiering* (1937; rpt. London: John Calder, 1982), 4, 35, 85.

In each case, modernist writing might simply be admired for new imaginative ingenuities, transcending new scales of loss and destruction in recent history. More sceptical views might nevertheless suggest themselves. Earlier chapters identified a widespread disposition, during and after the war, to replace straightforward accounts of terrible events with consolatory, mythic, or mendacious versions of them—through spiritualism, for example, or simply through the sanitized, affirmative reporting of newspapers and propaganda. The Angels of Mons, or the 'hosts of angels' envisaged in Hereward Carrington's spiritualism[73]—or even that trumpery angel on the Segget war memorial—all offer apt emblems of this evasiveness. Could it be seen to reappear, in another form, in modernist literature's attempts to escape or transcend the shock of recent history? Several authors in the twenties saw this as a possibility not confined to modernist writing, but potentially affecting *all* literature and art. C. E. Montague's war novel *Rough Justice* (1926) worries that 'books...those assistant-teachers of the art of living' might be 'perverted into screens for a soft mind to hold between all the harsh winds of life and itself'. In *No Man's Land*, Vernon Bartlett suggests that 'most fiction, most cinema films, most plays, were false'—merely drops in 'the ocean of narcotics' required by a population that 'refused to face the truth'. In his fantasy *The Dream* (1924), H. G. Wells attempts distanced objectivity by describing the war from a point supposedly 2,000 years in the future. Yet he still worries that 'always literature has told people what their minds were prepared to receive, searching for what it should tell rather in the mind and expectation of the hearer or reader...than in the unendowed wildernesses of reality'.[74]

Such concerns might extend even further, encompassing any attempt to communicate chaotic war experience in narrative—in histories or supposedly factual accounts, as well as in fiction, play, or film. As the historiographer Hayden White suggests, part of the appeal of historical writing is that it 'endows...reality with form' and 'makes the real desirable' by imposing 'formal coherency' on the events represented. In *The Great War and Modern Memory*, Fussell worries still further about communicating experiences 'fierce beyond description'. In order to render

[73] See Chapter 2, p. 81.
[74] C. E. Montague, *Rough Justice* (1926; rpt. Chatto and Windus, 1969), 243; Bartlett, *No Man's Land*, 295; H. G. Wells, *The Dream: A Novel* (London: Jonathan Cape, 1924), 199.

such experience in language at all, he suggests, some compromise must be made between expectations that writing 'ought to be interesting and meaningful' and the 'cruel fact that much of what happens...is inherently without "meaning"'. All literary, linguistic, and rhetorical devices—even, in Fussell's view, 'sentence structures and connectives implying clear causality'—may misleadingly endow reality with 'coherency' possibly absent from the events concerned.[75] Remarque is one of several authors to raise this issue in Great War fiction. In *All Quiet on the Western Front*, his narrator invites Saussurean questioning of the gap between language and what it represents, remarking 'attack, counter-attack, charge, repulse—these are words, but what things they signify!' His reflection, a page or so later, that 'words...hold the horror of the world', seems more ambiguous than reassuring. Words hold horror up for readers to see, but may also hold it back, or hold it away—keeping events at a steady distance, even suppressing any urge to intervene in their terrible course.[76] 'Umschließen' and 'umfassen', the verbs in the original German, suggest similarly—if anything more strongly—some sense of enclosure or containment. Distancing or containment is after all a regular function of daily discourse, evident in the 'protective shield' Chapter 1 described soldiers finding in the inventions and euphemisms of the vernacular. A common—almost daily—usage of this kind was often noted by authors serving in France, including Charles Edmonds. Describing a particularly senseless fatal accident with a mortar bomb, Edmonds quotes one of the habitual responses of the French peasantry: 'Que voulez-vous? C'est la guerre; à la guerre comme à la guerre'.[77] (What do you expect? It's war: war is war.) Mostly empty of the meaning it pretends to proffer, the phrase if anything vindicates the war's nature as inevitable, suppressing any urge to protest against it.

Obviously, not all words about the war worked in this way. Many authors deliberately set out to dispel euphemisms, evasions, or suppressions, communicating the war's shocks as directly as possible. Questions nevertheless remain about the effectiveness of what they achieved.

[75] Hayden White, *The Content of the Form: Narrative Discourse and Historical Representation* (Baltimore/London: Johns Hopkins University Press, 1987); 20–1; Paul Fussell, *The Great War and Modern Memory* (Oxford: Oxford University Press, 1975), 172.

[76] Remarque, *All Quiet*, 88, 90.

[77] Edmonds, *Subaltern's War*, 27.

In *No Enemy: A Tale of Reconstruction* (1929), mostly written in 1919, Ford Madox Ford's central character hopes that the recent 'Armageddon' might exercise an 'educative' effect for decades to come.[78] Similar hope survived at least as far as the enthusiasm for Great War writing in the 1960s. Yet any survey of the century following the Great War is bound to show how comprehensively it disappointed the hopes Ford records, or the optimism H. G. Wells expressed in 1914 in *The War That Will End War*. Contemporary pessimism proved far more prescient. Even a few months before the war began, in 'Channel Firing', Thomas Hardy was already wondering 'will the world ever saner be' and describing guns audible as far inland as 'Camelot, and starlit Stonehenge'.[79] Writers in the years that followed obviously found the world no saner, indicating instead, like Hardy, an unceasing, everlasting aspect in war and conflict. A. P. Herbert's characters in *The Secret Battle* (1919) are intrigued to discover that their base at Gallipoli allows them a view of 'the wide green plain' of Troy, site of the struggles of 'Achilles and Hector and Diomed and Patroclus and the far-sounding bolts of Jove'. In *Gallipoli Memories*, Mackenzie records equivalent excitement at looking over 'the wide green hollow land of Troy...thinking that Diomed and Odysseus might have stared across the water like this'.[80] Soldiers on the Western Front were sometimes similarly aware of proximity to the battlefields of Crécy or Waterloo. Throughout David Jones's *In Parenthesis*, descriptions of the Great War are interwoven with references to a huge range of earlier conflicts, actual and mythical. These stretch back through Arthurian or Roman times to the Trojan War, even extending to the war in heaven described in Milton's *Paradise Lost*.

In *The Silence of Colonel Bramble* (1919), André Maurois's pessimistic doctor looks back no further than the Romans. He is nevertheless able to calculate that wars have accounted for an average of nineteen million deaths every century—enough to 'feed a fountain of blood running 700 litres an hour from the beginning of history'. He naturally concludes that war is 'eternal and unalterable...men will always have passions,

---

[78] Ford Madox Ford, *No Enemy: A Tale of Reconstruction* (1929; rpt. Manchester: Carcanet, 2002), 48.

[79] Thomas Hardy, *The Complete Poems of Thomas Hardy*, ed. James Gibson (1976; rpt. London: Macmillan, 1991), 306.

[80] A. P. Herbert, *The Secret Battle* (1919; rpt. Oxford: Oxford University Press, 1982), 10; Mackenzie, *Gallipoli Memories*, 189–90.

and . . . will never cease to go for one another at regular intervals with the most energetic means which the science of their time can procure for them'.[81] Thinking about modern military science in the second issue of *Blast*—its 'War Number', published in 1915—Wyndham Lewis wonders if technology might one day 'arrive at such a point of excellence that two-thirds of the population of the world could be exterminated with mathematical precision in a fortnight'.[82] Thirty years later, that day had more or less arrived, with the first use of the atom bomb—also anticipated by H. G. Wells, in *The World Set Free* (1914). On this evidence, 'educative' effects derived from the Great War and its literature might seem no more promising than Sassoon's notion—during a period of leave spent with his aunt—of 'trying to teach Popsy the parrot how to say "Stop the War"'.[83] Maurois's fountain has if anything increased its flow since 1919—seeming still a 'stream of blood', as Remarque suggests, which 'the culture of a thousand years could not prevent'. What then can Great War writing still offer its readers? Might its remembered grief not be allowed after all to fade into 'ancient history', reaching—as Julian Barnes's story 'Evermore' (1995) speculates—'some point in the first decades of the twenty-first century, one final moment, lit by the evening sun, before the whole thing [is] handed over to the archivists'?[84]

Unforgettable War

Barnes's 'final moment' nevertheless seems some distance away, and the Great War's continuing presence, in the twenty-first century, perhaps not even a matter of choice. Like the troubled mind of a trauma patient, the conscience of later ages continues to return repeatedly to the Great War, simply because its events were too deranged and desolate—too far beyond the destructiveness even of earlier conflicts—ever to have been fully contained in mind or conscience. Questions the Great War raises

[81] André Maurois, *The Silence of Colonel Bramble*, trans. Thurfrida Wake (1919; rpt. Harmondsworth: Penguin, 1940), 143, 103–4.

[82] Wyndham Lewis, 'A Super-Krupp—Or War's End', *Blast*, 2 (July 1915), 14.

[83] Sassoon, *Collected Memoirs of George Sherston*, 492.

[84] Julian Barnes, 'Evermore' (1995), rpt. in Barbara Korte and Anne-Marie Einhuas (eds), *The Penguin Book of First World War Stories* (Harmondsworth: Penguin, 2007), 361.

about the capacities of language, literature, and culture to contain experience—to 'hold the horror of the world', to prevent catastrophe, or to communicate effectively its nature when it occurs—remain thoroughly troubling, and perhaps ultimately unanswerable. For that reason alone, the Great War and its literature cannot be allowed to fade into any twilight of historical inattention, or of critical unconcern.

Many other factors further confirm the Great War's continuing importance for imagination and modern or postmodern memory. One of these is simply the extent to which later decades continued to live, and write, in ways the war shaped, remaining troubled by stresses in the modern world it first made inescapably evident. In Max Plowman's summary, what made the war 'so ghastly' was that in its 'power of organisation' and of press opinion, as well as its technologies, it appeared to be 'machine-made'. A technologized, industrialized modern age was already developing before 1914, but it still seemed progressive in much of its achievement and potential. 'Technical war', as Jünger calls it, with 'machines...playing an ever greater part on the battlefield', vigorously demonstrated the lethal as well as progressive powers of technology, as authors such as Henry James and John Dos Passos recognized.[85] Particularly after the 'old world ended' in 1915, soldiers and many civilians had to confront mechanization and rationalization in other ways, too—in the regimentation of life and death in the armed forces, and in the growing intrusion of state power into daily life. Accounts such as Manning's, of the 'mechanical operation' of army command, or Owen's, of an automated fate in 'The Send-Off', retain a unique significance for later ages, reflecting a much-accelerated phase in the advance of modernity, and deepening doubts about its consequences. As the historian Dan Todman suggests, Great War writing represents, in this way, an early and uniquely direct encounter with 'many of the archetypal tensions of the modern world'.[86] As discussed earlier, new awareness of these tensions also contributed to a period of much-accelerated development in literary forms and styles. Modernism had many roots already stirring earlier than 1914, but nothing before, or since, matched the efflorescence of the 1920s, with the war a key factor in its development.

---

[85] Plowman, *Subaltern*, 162; Jünger, *Storm of Steel*, 261.
[86] Dan Todman, *The Great War: Myth and Memory* (London: Hambledon Continuum, 2005), 223.

'Archetypal tensions' are encapsulated in other ways in Great War writing, adding further to its hold on memory and imagination. Some of these derive from the peculiar conditions of the fighting, on the Western Front particularly. Fussell's *The Great War and Modern Memory* has been accused of concentrating too exclusively on this area of operations. Yet there are reasons for this bias—one shared by many other studies, including to an extent the present one, and evident even in contemporary accounts of the war. In 1917, Francis Brett Young offered in *Marching on Tanga* (1917) an outstandingly vivid account of campaigns in East Africa, yet acknowledged that fighting there was only a 'side-show' compared to 'the root of the whole tragedy, at home in Europe'.[87] Relative to other theatres of war, much more was written about the Western Front, not only because it seemed the centre of the tragedy, but because it involved more army personnel, probably including greater numbers of well-educated volunteers, and hence more numerous potential authors. Trench warfare also offered peculiarly profound challenges to imagination. As one soldier remarked of his first experience of trench life (though in Gallipoli rather than the Western Front) 'there was an utter utterness about it'.[88] Enemy soldiers mostly remained invisible, in another, hostile world of their own. Yet in many cases this was no more than a hundred yards away—sometimes only thirty—across a patch of ground utterly uninhabitable except, perilously, during the hours of darkness. Many accounts of trench fighting seek to define this weird adjacency of absolute otherness, hostility, and mortal danger. Patrick Miller's hero in *The Natural Man* envisages the trenches as a 'meeting line of two worlds ... the base line of a vertical, impalpable plane that cut from heaven to earth'. 'Just beyond this last line', Miller adds, there was 'something else, not men, not individuals, not parts of any known world—but yet figures of men, like them, but things no one could go near, fatal, ready to kill.' MacGill's fiction likewise describes duty in the most forward positions as 'isolated from the whole world': distanced from quieter sectors to the rear, and from uncomprehending civilians at home, while 'over the parapet of the trench was the Unknown with its mysteries deep as those of

[87] Francis Brett Young, *Marching on Tanga: With General Smuts in East Africa* (1917; rpt. Gloucester: Alan Sutton, 1984), 75.

[88] W. H. Lench, 'The Evacuation of Suvla Bay', in C. B. Purdom (ed.), *True World War I Stories: Sixty Personal Narratives of the War* (1930; rpt. London: Robinson, 1999), 299.

the grave'. In Owen's 'Spring Offensive', soldiers occupy a space only yards and dwindling minutes away from 'the end of the world'—the area, 'sheer to infinite space', of an attack certain to leave many of them in the grave.

In *Blasting and Bombardiering*, Lewis defines the front-line trench simply as the point where 'civilisation ended'. Beyond it, he adds, lies only 'nothingness... arid and blistering vacuum'.[89] In these accounts and many others, trench warfare appears 'utter' not only in military but in existential terms, involving extreme confrontations between self and other, being and nothingness, life and extinction, mind and 'unendowed wilderness'. These confrontations, moreover, were not always as brief as those experienced by Owen's soldiers, but could extend instead over hours and days in front-line trenches, all the more tensely if an attack was anticipated. Such sustained entrapment—within a landscape so finely delineated in its separations of life and death—had scarcely figured earlier in the history of warfare, and was hardly to occur again. Even by early 1918, entrenched defences had begun to succumb regularly to new forms of coordinated assault. Mobile forms of warfare continued to develop up until the armistice, and again in later conflicts.

Peculiar in its challenge to imagination, and in its role in the advance of modernity, the Great War also occupies a highly particular place in the history of literature, even in the history of the English language itself. The war marked a key stage in transitions between the long-standing dominance of literature and the written word, and the use instead of cinema and the visual image as the principal means of bringing the world and its events to an audience. In no later conflict would writing and reporting retain the central roles—though already diminishing—that they occupied in communicating the events of the Great War. This contemporary predominance was emphasized by C. F. G. Masterman's immediate co-opting for propaganda work, in September 1914, of most of the established authors of the time. Their efforts, and government propaganda generally, had lasting effects on language and communication. As well as questioning the reliability of language generally, as Chapter 1 explained, a particular consequence was in widening gaps between official discourse and individual witness. As Chapters 2 and 3

---

[89] Miller, *Natural Man*, 42, 281–2; MacGill, *Red Horizon*, 86; MacGill, *Great Push*, 38; Owen, *Complete Poems*, I: 192; Lewis, *Blasting and Bombardiering*, 131.

described, many Great War authors shared a principal commitment to realism—to providing accounts of the war more faithful to what they had witnessed than those offered by newspapers, during the conflict, or by official histories in the years that followed. The eventual result was a decisive shift and refocusing in the vision of war, perhaps even in public discourse generally, in ways Douglas Jerrold summed up quite accurately, though dismissively, in 1930. As he suggests, the numerous official histories and memoirs published early in the 1920s continued to concentrate—like most writing about previous wars—on 'the conflict of *armies*', and on the aims and achievements of military and political leaders in charge of them. In the profusion of publishing towards the end of the decade, these official accounts were steadily supplanted by writing which was instead, in Jerrold's summary, 'always and continuously from the standpoint of the individual'.[90]

Use of this standpoint was neither as unprecedented nor nearly as limiting—in the view of most later readers—as Jerrold suggests in *The Lie about the War*. Private views of war—literally, privates' views—had appeared fairly regularly during the nineteenth century. In his description of campaigns against Napoleon, *Twenty-Five Years in the Rifle Brigade* (1833), for example, William Surtees begins by recounting his experiences as a private soldier, and an introduction to a modern edition of his memoir mentions several similar accounts. Yet literary responses to the Great War generally differ from this writing in at least two respects. The first concerns scale and perspective. A higher level of literacy and education made written propaganda a more essential and effective tool than ever before, for the government, but it also ensured that many more ordinary citizens had the ability to produce their own alternative accounts of their experience. The rapid establishment of a huge army— much bigger than any Surtees would have known—ensured large numbers of these educated and literate citizens soon found themselves in or near the front line. As a result, for perhaps the first time in history, a war was extensively described, almost literally, from below rather than above—by 'lads | Left in the ground', in trenches and shell-holes, rather than generals aloofly surveying the field.

Another, related, consequence—another difference from the retrospection of memoirists such as Surtees, or of official histories—was a

---

[90] Jerrold, *Lie About the War*, 17, 22.

huge gain in immediacy. Great War poetry was sometimes written at or close to the Front. Even when composed elsewhere, it generally offers a direct, eyewitness description of events. A similarly restless, disturbing immediacy figures in many prose accounts of the war. These are also usually communicated with the conviction of personal experience, their immediacy often heightened, in some of the best accounts, by use of the present tense. Characteristic of so much Great War literature, these qualities suggest that the army of 1914–18 not only 'outshone its figure-heads', but eventually outwrote them as well. As Wells recognized in 1927, the 'undistinguished multitude, caught in the machine...has found a voice in this war, as it has never found a voice in any preceding convulsion'.[91] Never before, and never since, during an age increasingly allegiant to the image, has war been described so vividly in literature, and as it affected so many of those involved—muddy, grounded individuals, distant from the heroic, legend-haunted world of Diomed and Patroclus; closer in status to James Joyce's hero in *Ulysses* (1922) than to Homer's original view of Odysseus. In its own age, this down-to-earth, diversified vision offered a literary extension of democratizations discussed earlier in social and political terms. For later generations, it offers a vision still political in some of its potentials. Blood continues to flow through history apparently eternally and unstoppably, in conflicts evidently without end. The unromantic, unillusioned, un-Homeric witnessing of Great War authors at least offers later ages the fullest available opportunity to imagine what such conflicts, at their worst, are really like.

Yet claims that literature can communicate what the Great War was 'really like' obviously re-open a problem considered earlier, concerning the elusiveness of 'truth about the war', inevitably screened through perspectives, rhetorics, 'narcotics', and the inapposite orderliness of language itself. There is no complete solution to this problem. There is no zero degree of writing: no words that can touch or wholly hold 'the horror of the world' and carry it over, raw and complete, to readers. The 'bridge...over an ontological impossibility' Santanu Das hopes for—somehow putting readers into unmediated contact with the experience of the Great War—can never be constructed out of the materials of

---

[91] H. G. Wells, Preface to A. D. Gristwood, *The Somme: Including Also The Coward* (1927; rpt. Columbia: University of South Carolina Press, 2006), 10.

language, or, probably, in any other way.[92] This limitation concerned authors at the time, often contributing to their choice of writing strategies, and it continues to have implications for ways Great War writing may be read in later ages. In their various effects and degrees of immediacy, literary strategies in the war years and the 1920s might be conveniently figured in terms of the topography of the Front, and in particular the significantly named 'communication trenches' that ran across the area. Dug at right angles to the firing line, these led back from advanced positions—those directly in the face of the enemy—through reserve and support trenches towards the safer areas in the rear. Some of the modernist writing discussed earlier can be thought of as following this direction, employing new literary strategies to lead readers away from the 'blistering vacuum' of war towards blue distances and the orderly imaginative spaces of art itself. This need not be considered merely another version of the flight represented by the Angels of Mons. Modernist writing is concerned not with events that did not or could not have taken place, but with finding imaginative means of distancing and dealing with ones that did.

Yet as Chapter 2 concluded, this ambition contributes to priorities very different from those shared by writers who had witnessed the war directly, generally determined to take their readers in an opposite direction, through communications bringing them as close as possible to the experience of the Front. Commitment to the most direct, honest communication—often heightened by disgust at the mendacities of propaganda and newspaper reporting—naturally made these authors wary of rhetoric and of complex literary strategies or potentially falsifying artistic orderliness. Like Herbert Read, many of them 'wanted the events to speak for themselves unaided by any art'.[93] Suspicions of art and artifice expressed by Wilfred Owen, Mary Borden, and Edmund Blunden were mentioned in earlier chapters, and consequences for Borden's own writing style discussed in this one. Similar scepticisms are recorded in a preface Charles Edmonds added later to *A Subaltern's War*. This describes a dislike of 'belles-lettres' and of 'aesthetical impact', recalling that he sought simply to record events while 'adding nothing and omitting noth-

[92] Santanu Das, *Touch and Intimacy in First World War Literature* (Cambridge: Cambridge University Press, 2005), 227.

[93] Herbert Read, *In Retreat* (London: Hogarth Press, 1925), 7.

ing'. Admitting that some 'literary flourishes' survived nonetheless, he suggests that he might 'now prefer the rough drafts, if they had survived'. He particularly regrets losing an account of the first day of the Somme, written 'in a front-line dug-out, that very evening when the fighting had died down'.[94] Both Graves and Sassoon did incorporate journals written in the trenches within their memoirs, much as Edmonds proposes. For later readers, such tactics might suggest an inversion of conventional literary or aesthetic valuations, where Great War writing is concerned, and a particular valorization of certain genres. If authenticity, directness, and fullness of knowledge are the principal values sought from this writing, then journals and diaries—likely to be freer of literary artifice—may have more to offer than poetry, fiction, or even autobiography and memoir. Or, in this estimation, a poem such as E. J. L. Garstin's 'Lines written between 1 and 2.30 a.m. in a German Dugout' might be highly valued for its immediacy, even although—or because—its author obviously lacked scope for much artistic polish. Accidental oddities of spelling and grammar in Pte H. E. Beaven's letter, quoted at the start of Chapter 2, might likewise offer immediacies unavailable to writers more concerned with belles-lettres or aesthetic impact.

Yet even Private Beaven is not immune to rhetoric. The end of his letter is phrased consolingly, shaped by idealisms widely shared in 1914. Nor, obviously, can he be free of the linguistic 'structures and connectives' Fussell mentions. As Edmonds discovered, 'literary flourishes' and elements of artifice cannot be eliminated altogether from accounts of the war. Nor should they be ignored by modern readers. To do so would be to fall into the habit criticized in Chapter 3—of admiring Great War writers only for their subject matter; for what they wrote about rather than how they wrote about it. There is good reason to value instead the strategies of writing which—despite enormous contemporary challenges to language and representation—managed to render experience potentially 'fierce beyond description' so vividly into words, allowing it to remain so powerfully, and for so long, in the consciousness of later readers. But the unique historical and political significance of Great War writing, and its challenges to literature and art, nevertheless demand from its readers particular—doubled—forms of attention, keeping in

---

[94] Edmonds, *Subaltern's War*, 9, 10.

view a kind of two-way traffic in the channels of communication concerned. As always, tactics of artistically representing experience—means
of making 'the real desirable', in Hayden White's terms—remain a focus
of literary evaluation, but it is the 'unendowed... reality' of the experience itself, as far as this can be recovered, which may offer the principal
power and interest of Great War writing. Representational tactics may
therefore be appreciated mostly for the ways in which they assist this
recovery. Identification of them—of the means through which experience was mediated—may be most valuable if in looking *at* tactics concerned, readers are also encouraged to look beyond them, towards the
original experience itself. As a result, unusually in literary study, aesthetic evaluation of Great War writing may often be assigned a subsidiary role, and content—'the real'—valued over form, or to an extent, if
possible, even detached from it.

Sebastian Faulks indicates a measure, or method, of this detachment
in *Birdsong*, published in 1993, nearly eighty years after the Great War
broke out. Disinterment figures as a central interest of his novel, in various forms. One of these is literal—the story of his central character's
miraculous escape from entombment in the tunnelling operations both
sides used to undermine each other's trenches. Another unearthing,
though, is metaphoric—the story of how the truth about this character's
experience emerges, decades later, as his granddaughter works out ways
of decrypting the codes he used in writing his journals. A century or so
after the Great War, readers may need to practise similar decoding.
Reading between the lines may help recover experience in and between
the lines—in the trenches and in that unknown and unendowed wilderness confronting soldiers looking out over No Man's Land. On the other
hand, decoding or decrypting may be overly elaborate metaphors for
what readers achieve just by recognizing literary strategies, and their
effects, and exercising imagination about what they are used to represent. Awareness of the outlook and idealism of 1914, for example, obviously clarifies any reading of Rupert Brooke, or for that matter of Private
Beaven. Knowledge of the conventions—or 'codes'—of pastoral writing
likewise contextualizes grand illusions, and disillusions, through which
poets tried to contain their experience of the war.

This awareness of outlooks, textual tactics, and conventions is what
the present volume has sought to supply, in accord with authors' determination to communicate their experience as directly as possible, and to

maintain contact with what Edmund Blunden describes as 'the soul of the war'. For Blunden, this could not be reached by denoting 'armies in coloured inks on vast maps'—any more than, for Frankau, it could be found in 'barren paper' or 'faked film'. It involves instead drawing aside the 'paper curtain' of representations of the war, and looking beyond consoling coherences of form, containment, or desire they may offer. Blunden wants to take his readers instead towards 'some poor jaw-dropping resting sentry, under the dripping rubber sheet, balanced on the greasy fire-step, a fragment of some rural newspaper...beside him'; towards 'men achingly asleep in narrow chilly firetrenches'; towards deadly 'malignity' in No Man's Land beyond. Twenty-first-century readers cannot enter those chilly trenches, or look by any means directly into those aching, deadly spaces. Since the last surviving combatant died in 2009, there is no one any longer alive who witnessed them, or who endured their appalling uproar, obscene stenches, unimaginable visions. The Great War can never now—perhaps could never ever—be wholly known or imagined. Yet readers may still find some way up the communication trenches war writing provides, reaching as nearly as possible toward those dark and archetypal modern experiences. Duly prepared, we can still follow Blunden's instruction—'I would have you see...date yourself 1916, and come.'[95]

[95]   Blunden, *Undertones of War*, 141, 83.

BIBLIOGRAPHY

Adams, Bernard, *Nothing of Importance: A Record of Eight Months at the Front with a Welsh Battalion: October, 1915, to June, 1916* (London: Methuen, 1917).

Aldington, Richard, *The Complete Poems of Richard Aldington* (London: Alan Wingate, 1948).

——, *Death of a Hero* (1929; rpt. London: Hogarth Press, 1984).

——, H.D., John Gould Fletcher, F. S. Flint, D. H. Lawrence, Amy Lowell, *Some Imagist Poets: An Anthology* (Boston/New York: Houghton Mifflin, 1915).

Allatini, Rose ['A. T. Fitzroy'], *Despised and Rejected* (1918; rpt. London: GMP, 1988).

Armstrong, Tim, *Modernism, Technology and the Body: A Cultural Study* (Cambridge: Cambridge University Press, 1998).

Arthur, Max, *The Faces of World War I* (London: Cassell Illustrated, 2007).

——, *Forgotten Voices of the Great War* (London: Ebury Press, 2003).

——, *Last Post: The Final Word from our First World War Soldiers* (London: Weidenfeld and Nicholson, 2005).

Auden, W. H., *Collected Shorter Poems* (1966; rpt. London: Faber and Faber, 1971).

Ayres, Ruby M., *Richard Chatterton VC* (London: Hodder and Stoughton, 1915).

Bagnold, Enid, *A Diary without Dates* (London: William Heinemann, 1918).

——, *The Happy Foreigner* (London: William Heinemann, 1920).

Baldrick, Chris, *Literature of the 1920s: Writers among the Ruins* (Edinburgh: Edinburgh University Press, 2012).

——, *The Modern Movement: Oxford English Literary History*, vol. 10: 1910–1940 (Oxford: Oxford University Press, 2004).

Barbusse, Henri, *Le Feu (Journal d'une Escouade)* (Paris: E. Flammarion, 1916).

——, *Under Fire* (1916), trans. Robin Buss (Harmondsworth: Penguin, 2003).

Barclay, Florence, *My Heart's Right There* (1914; rpt. London: G. P. Putnam's Sons, 1916).

Barker, Pat, *The Regeneration Trilogy: Regeneration, The Eye in the Door, The Ghost Road* (London: Viking, 1996).

Barnes, Julian, 'Evermore' (1995), rpt. in Barbara Korte and Anne-Marie Einhaus (eds), *The Penguin Book of First World War Stories* (Harmondsworth: Penguin, 2007).

Barrie, J. M., *The Plays of J. M. Barrie* (London: Hodder and Stoughton, 1930).

Bartlett, Vernon, *Mud and Khaki: Sketches from Flanders and France* (London: Simpkin, Marshall, Hamilton, Kent, 1917).

——, *No Man's Land* (London: George Allen and Unwin, 1930).

Baudrillard, Jean, *Simulations*, trans. Paul Foss, Paul Patton, and Philip Beitchman (New York: Semiotext(e), 1983).

Beaver, Patrick (ed.), *The Wipers Times: A Complete Facsimile of the Famous World War One Trench Newspaper, Incorporating the 'New Church' Times, the Kemmel Times, the Somme Times, the B.E.F. Times, and the 'Better Times'* (London: Macmillan, 1973).

Benjamin, Walter, *Illuminations*, ed. Hannah Arendt, trans. Harry Zohn (New York: Schocken Books, 1969).

Bennett, Arnold, *Lord Raingo* (London: Cassell, 1926).

——, *Over There: War Scenes on the Western Front* (London: Methuen, 1915).

——, *The Pretty Lady* (1918; rpt. Leek, Staffordshire: Churnet Valley Books, 2009).

Bergonzi, Bernard, *Heroes' Twilight: A Study of the Literature of the Great War* (1965; rpt. Manchester: Carcanet, 1996).

Bergson, Henri, *The Meaning of the War: Life and Matter in Conflict*, trans. H. Wildon Carr (London: T. Fisher Unwin, 1915).

——, *Time and Free Will: An Essay on the Immediate Data of Consciousness* (1889), trans. F. L. Pogson (London: George Allen and Unwin, 1971).

Berkeley, Reginald, *The White Château* (London: Williams and Norgate, 1925).

Bishop, Major, *Winged Warfare: Hunting the Huns in the Air* (London: Hodder and Stoughton, 1918).

Bloch, Marc, *Memoirs of War, 1914–15 (1969)*, trans. Carole Fink (Ithaca, NY: Cornell University Press, 1988).

Blunden, Edmund, *The Poems of Edmund Blunden* (London: Cobden-Sanderson, 1930)

——, *Undertones of War* (1928; rpt. Harmondsworth: Penguin, 1986).

Booth, Allyson, *Postcards from the Trenches: Negotiating the Space between Modernism and the First World War* (Oxford: Oxford University Press, 1996).

Borden, Mary, *The Forbidden Zone* (London: William Heinemann, 1929).

Brereton, Capt. Frederick S., *Under French's Command: A Story of the Western Front from Neuve Chapelle to Loos* (London: Blackie and Son, 1915).

——(ed.), *An Anthology of War Poems* (London: W. Collins Sons, 1930).

Bridges, Robert (ed.), *The Spirit of Man: An Anthology in English and French from the Philosophers and Poets made by the Poet Laureate in 1915* (London: Longmans, Green, 1916).

Brittain, Vera, *Chronicle of Youth: War Diary 1913–1917*, ed. Alan Bishop with Terry Smart (London: Victor Gollancz, 1981).

——, *Testament of Youth: An Autobiographical Study of the Years 1900–1925* (1933; rpt. London: Virago, 2004).

Brooke, Rupert, *The Complete Poems* (1932; rpt. London: Sidgwick and Jackson, 1945).

Brophy, John, and Eric Partridge, *The Long Trail: What the British Soldier Sang and Said in the Great War of 1914–18* (London: Andre Deutsch, 1966).

Brown, Malcolm, *The Imperial War Museum Book of the Somme* (London: Pan Books in Association with the Imperial War Museum, 1996).

Buchan, John, *The Battle of the Somme: First Phase* (London: Thomas Nelson, 1916).

——, *Greenmantle* (1916; rpt. Oxford: Oxford University Press, 1993).

Buitenhuis, Peter, *The Great War of Words: British, American and Canadian Propaganda and Fiction, 1914–1933* (Vancouver: University of British Columbia Press, 1987).

Cannan, Gilbert, 'The Drama: A Note in War Time', *Poetry and Drama*, 2(7) (Sept. 1914), 307–8.

Cannan, May, and Bevis Quiller-Couch, *The Tears of War: The Love Story of a Young Poet and a War Hero*, ed. Charlotte Fyfe (Upavon: Cavalier, 2000).

Carrington, Hereward, *Psychical Phenomena and the War* (New York: Dodd, Mead, 1918).

Cecil, Hugh, *The Flower of Battle: British Fiction Writers of the First World War* (London: Secker and Warburg, 1995).

Chapman, Guy, *A Passionate Prodigality: Fragments of Autobiography* (1933; rpt. London: Buchan and Enright, 1985).

Chapman, Stuart, *Home in Time For Breakfast: A First World War Diary* (London: Athena Press, 2007).

Chetham-Strode, W., *Sometimes Even Now: A Play in Three Acts* (London: Victor Gollancz, 1933).

Childers, Erskine, *The Riddle of the Sands: A Record of Secret Service Recently Achieved* (London: Smith, Elder, 1903).

Churchill, The Rt. Hon. Winston S., *The World Crisis: 1911–1918* (London: Odhams Press, 1950), 2 vols.

Cobley, Evelyn, *Representing War: Form and Ideology in First World War Narratives* (Toronto: University of Toronto Press, 1993).

Coppard, George, *With a Machine Gun to Cambrai* (1980; rpt. London: Macmillan, 1986).

Corcoran, Neil, *English Poetry since 1940* (London: Longman Group, 1993).

Coward, Noël, *Post-Mortem: A Play in Eight Scenes* (London: William Heinemann, 1931).

Crawford, Fred D., *British Poets of the First World War* (London: Associated University Presses, 1988).

Cummings, E. E., *The Enormous Room* (1922; rpt. New York/London: Liverwright, 1978).

Das, Santanu, *Touch and Intimacy in First World War Literature* (Cambridge: Cambridge University Press, 2005).

Davie, Donald, 'In the Pity', *New Statesman*, 68(1746) (28 Aug. 1964), 282–3.

Davis, Wade, *Into the Silence: The Great War, Mallory and the Conquest of Everest* (London: Bodley Head, 2011).

Dickens, Charles, *David Copperfield* (1849–50; rpt. Harmondsworth: Penguin, 1977).

Doolittle, Hilda ['H. D.'], *Bid Me to Live* (1960; rpt. London: Virago, 1984).

Dos Passos, John, *One Man's Initiation: 1917: A Novel* (1920; rpt. Ithaca, NY: Cornell University Press, 1969).

——, *Three Soldiers* (1921; rpt. New York: Sun Dial Press, 1937).

——, *U.S.A.* (1932–6; rpt. Harmondsworth: Penguin, 1973).

Duhamel, Georges, *The New Book of Martyrs* (1917), trans. Florence Simmonds (London: William Heinemann, 1918).

Dyer, Geoff, *The Missing of the Somme* (London: Phoenix, 1994).

Edmonds, Charles, *A Subaltern's War* (1929; rpt. London: Anthony Mott, 1984).

Edmonds, Brigadier-General Sir James E., *History of the Great War: Based on Official Documents: By Direction of the Historical Section of the Committee of Imperial Defence: Military Operations: France and Belgium,* (London: Macmillan/Shearer, 1922–47), 26 vols.

Eliot, T. S., *Collected Poems: 1909–1962* (1963; rpt. London: Faber and Faber, 1974).

——, *The Waste Land: A Facsimile and Transcript of the Original Drafts Including the Annotations of Ezra Pound*, ed. Valerie Eliot (London: Faber and Faber, 1971).

Emden, Richard van, and Steve Humphries, *All Quiet on the Home Front: An Oral History of Life in Britain during the First World War* (London: Headline, 2003).

Falls, Cyril, *War Books: A Critical Guide* (London: Peter Davies, 1930).

Farrar, Martin J., *News from the Front: War Correspondents on the Western Front: 1914–18* (Stroud: Sutton, 1999).

Faulks, Sebastian, *Birdsong* (1993; rpt. London: Viking, 1994).

Ferenczi, S., Karl Abraham, Ernst Simmel, and Ernest Jones, *Psychoanalysis and the War Neuroses*. Introduction by Professor Sigmund Freud (London/Vienna/New York: International Psycho-Analytical Press, 1921).

Fitzgerald, F. Scott, *The Bodley Head Scott Fitzgerald* (London: Bodley Head, 1959), vol. II.

Ford, Ford Madox, 'A Day of Battle', *The Ford Madox Ford Reader*, ed. Sondra J. Stang (London: Paladin, 1987).

——, *The Good Soldier: A Tale of Passion* (1915; rpt. Harmondsworth: Penguin, 1977).

——, *No Enemy: A Tale of Reconstruction* (1929; rpt. Manchester: Carcanet, 2002).

——, *Parade's End* (1924–8; rpt. Harmondsworth: Penguin, 1982).

——, *When Blood Is Their Argument: An Analysis of Prussian Culture* (London: Hodder and Stoughton, 1915).

Forester, C. S., *The General* (London: Michael Joseph, 1936).

Forster, E. M., *A Passage to India* (1924; rpt. Harmondsworth: Penguin, 1967).

Frankau, Gilbert, *Peter Jackson: Cigar Merchant: A Romance of Married Life* (London: Hutchinson, 1920).

Freud, Sigmund, *Beyond the Pleasure Principle* (1920), trans. C. J. M. Hubback (London/Vienna: International Psycho-Analytical Press, 1922).

Fussell, Paul, *The Great War and Modern Memory* (Oxford: Oxford University Press, 1975).

Galsworthy, John, *The Burning Spear: Being the Experiences of Mr John Lavender in Time of War: Recorded by A.R.P-M* (London: Chatto and Windus, 1919).

——, *The Plays of John Galsworthy* (London: Duckworth, 1929).

——, *Saint's Progress* (London: William Heinemann, 1919).

Gardner, Brian (ed.), *Up the Line to Death: The War Poets 1914–1918: An Anthology* (1964; rpt. London: Methuen, 2007).

Gibbon, Lewis Grassic, *A Scots Quair: Sunset Song, Cloud Howe, Grey Granite* (1932–34; rpt. Edinburgh: Canongate, 1995).

Gibbs, Philip, *Realities of War* (London: William Heinemann, 1920).

Gibson, Wilfrid Wilson, *Battle* (London: Elkin Matthews, 1916).

Glass, Loren, 'Modernism and Dirty Words', *Modernism and Modernity*, 14(2) (Apr. 2007), 209–23.

Goux, Jean-Joseph, *The Coiners of Language* (1984), trans. Jennifer Curtiss Gage (Oklahoma/London: Oklahoma University Press, 1994).

Graves, Robert, *But it Still Goes On* London: Jonathan Cape, 1930).

——, *Fairies and Fusiliers* (London: William Heinemann, 1919).

——, *Goodbye to All That*, rev edn (1957; rpt. Harmondsworth: Penguin, 2000).

——, *Over the Brazier* (1916; rpt. London: St. James Press, 1975).

Gregory, Adrian, *The Last Great War: British Society and the First World War* (Cambridge: Cambridge University Press, 2008).

Gristwood, A. D., *The Somme: Including also The Coward* (1927; rpt. Columbia: University of South Carolina Press, 2006).

Gurney, Ivor, *Collected Poems of Ivor Gurney*, ed. P. J. Kavanagh (Oxford: Oxford University Press, 1982).

Haig, Field-Marshall Sir Douglas, Papers, *c.*1859–195?, National Library of Scotland, Acc. 3155, no. 144.

Hamilton, General Sir Ian, *Gallipoli Diary* (London: Edward Arnold, 1920), 2 vols.

Hammond, Mary, and Shafquat Towheed, *Publishing in the First World War: Essays in Book History* (London: Palgrave, 2007).

Hankey, Donald, *A Student in Arms* (1916; rpt. London: Andrew Melrose, 1917).

Hanley, James, *The German Prisoner: A Reflection of Those Unspoken Times during the First World War* (1930; rpt. Holstein, Ontario: Exile Editions, 2006).

Harari, Yuval Noah, 'Military Memoirs: A Historical Overview of the Genre from the Middle Ages to the Late Modern Era', *War in History*, 14(3) (2007), 289–309.

Hardy, Thomas, *The Complete Poems of Thomas Hardy*, ed. James Gibson (1976; rpt. London: Macmillan, 1991).

Haste, Cate, *Keep the Home Fires Burning: Propaganda in the First World War* (London: Allen Lane, 1977).

Hay, Ian, *The First Hundred Thousand* (1915; rpt. London: Corgi, 1976).

Hemingway, Ernest, *The Essential Hemingway* (London: Panther, 1977).

——, *A Farewell to Arms* (1929; rpt. London: Vintage, 2005).

Herbert, A. P., *The Secret Battle* (1919; rpt. Oxford: Oxford University Press, 1982).

Hermon, Lieutenant Colonel E. W., *For Love and Courage: The Letters of Lieutenant Colonel E.W. Hermon from the Western Front, 1914–1917*, ed. Anne Nason (London: Preface, 2009).

Hibberd, Dominic, *The First World War* (London: Macmillan, 1990).

——(ed.), *Poetry of the First World War: A Casebook* (London: Macmillan, 1981).

——and John Onions (eds), *The Winter of the World: Poems of the First World War* (London: Constable, 2008).

Hodson, J. L., *Grey Dawn—Red Night* (London: Victor Gollancz, 1929).

Hollis, Matthew, *Now All Roads Lead to France: The Last Years of Edward Thomas* (London: Faber and Faber, 2011).

Holton, Robert, *Jarring Witnesses: Modern Fiction and the Representation of History* (Hemel Hempstead: Harvester Wheatsheaf, 1994).

Hunt, Violet, and Ford Madox Hueffer, *Zeppelin Nights* (London: John Lane, 1916).

Huxley, Aldous, *Eyeless in Gaza* (1936; rpt. London: Vintage, 2004).

Hynes, Samuel, *A War Imagined: The First World War and English Culture* (1990; rpt. London: Pimlico, 1992).

Isherwood, Christopher, *The Memorial* (1932; rpt. St Albans: Triad/Panther, 1978).

James, Henry, *Henry James on Culture: Collected Essays on Politics and the American Social Scene*, ed. Pierre A. Walker (Lincoln/London: University of Nebraska Press, 1999).

——, *The Letters of Henry James*, ed. Percy Lubbock (London: Macmillan, 1920), 2 vols.

——, *Within the Rim and Other Essays 1914–15* (London: W. Collins Sons, 1918).

James, William, *The Principles of Psychology* (London: Macmillan, 1890), 2 vols.

Jerrold, Douglas, *The Lie about the War: A Note on Some Contemporary War Books* (London: Faber and Faber, 1930).

Johns, Capt. W. E., *Biggles: Pioneer Air Fighter* (London: Dean and Sons, 1961).

Jones, David, *In Parenthesis* (1937; rpt. London: Faber and Faber, 1963).

Joyce, James, *Ulysses* (1922; rpt. Harmondsworth: Penguin, 1992).

Jünger, Ernst, *Storm of Steel* (1920/1961/1978), trans. Michael Hofmann (Harmondsworth: Penguin, 2004).

Keegan, John, *The Face of Battle* (London: Jonathan Cape, 1976).

——, *The First World War* (London: Hutchinson, 1998).

Kendall, Tim, *Modern English War Poetry* (Oxford: Oxford University Press, 2006).

Kern, Stephen, *The Culture of Time and Space: 1880–1918* (Cambridge, MA: Harvard University Press, 1983).

Kerr, Douglas, *Wilfred Owen's Voices: Language and Community* (Oxford: Clarendon Press, 1993).

Kipling, Rudyard, *Debits and Credits* (1926; rpt. Harmondsworth: Penguin, 1987).

——, *A Diversity of Creatures* (1917; rpt. Harmondsworth: Penguin, 2008).

Korte, Barbara, and Anne-Marie Einhaus (eds), *The Penguin Book of First World War Stories* (Harmondsworth: Penguin, 2007).

Kosok, Heinz, *The Theatre of War: The First World War in British and Irish Drama* (London: Palgrave Macmillan, 2007).

Kreisler, Fritz, *Four Weeks in the Trenches: The War Story of a Violinist* (Boston/New York: Houghton Mifflin, 1915).

Kyle, Galloway (ed.), *Soldier Poets: Songs of the Fighting Men* (London: Erskine Macdonald, 1916).

Larkin, Philip, *The Whitsun Weddings* (London: Faber and Faber, 1964).

Lawrence, D. H., *Kangaroo* (1923; rpt. London: Heinemann, 1974).

——, *Lady Chatterley's Lover* (1928; rpt. Harmondsworth: Penguin, 1960).

——, *Women in Love* (1921; rpt. Harmondsworth: Penguin, 1971).

——, ['Lawrence H. Davison'], *Movements in European History* (1921; rpt. Oxford: Oxford University Press, 1971).

Lawrence, D. H., ['H. D. Lawrence'], 'With the Guns', *Manchester Guardian*, 18 Aug. 1914.

Lawrence, T. E., *Seven Pillars of Wisdom* (1935; rpt. Hertfordshire: Wordsworth, 1997).

Le Queux, William, *The Invasion of 1910: With a Full Account of the Siege of London* (London: Eveleigh Nash, 1906).

Lee, Laurie, *Cider with Rosie* (London: Hogarth Press, 1959).

Leed, Eric J., *No Man's Land: Combat and Identity in World War I* (Cambridge: Cambridge University Press, 1979).

Lewis, Cecil, *Sagittarius Rising* (1936; rpt. London: Warner, 1998).

Lewis, Wyndham, *Blasting and Bombardiering* (1937; rpt. London: John Calder, 1982).

——, *The Childermass* (London: Chatto and Windus, 1928).

——, 'A Super-Krupp—Or War's End', *Blast*, 2 (July 1915).

Lloyd George, David, *War Memoirs* (1934; rpt. London: Odhams Press, 1938), 2 vols.

Longley, Edna, *Poetry in the Wars* (Newcastle: Bloodaxe Books, 1986).

Lynch, E. P. F., *Somme Mud: The Experiences of an Infantryman in France, 1916–1919* (London: Bantam Books, 2006).

Macaulay, Rose, *Non-Combatants and Others* (1916; rpt. London: Hodder and Stoughton, 1986).

MacDiarmid, Hugh, *Complete Poems*, ed. Michael Grieve and W. R. Aitken (Manchester: Carcanet, 1994).

MacGill, Patrick, *The Amateur Army* (London: Herbert Jenkins, 1915).

——, *The Great Push: An Episode of the Great War* (London: Herbert Jenkins, 1917).

——, *The Red Horizon* (London: Herbert Jenkins, 1916).

Mackay, Robert L., The War Diary of Lieut. R. L Mackay, 11th and later 1st/8th Battalion, Argyll and Sutherland Highlanders, September 1916 to January 1919. National Library of Scotland, Acc. 12350/18.

McKenna, Stephen, *Sonia: Between Two Worlds* (1917; rpt. London: Methuen, 1920).

Mackenzie, Compton, *Gallipoli Memories* (London: Cassell, 1929).

——, *Sinister Street* (1913–14; rpt. Harmondsworth: Penguin, 1983).

Mackinlay, George A. C., *Poems* (Glasgow: Lyon, 1919).

Mackintosh, E. A., *A Highland Regiment* (London: John Lane, Bodley Head, 1917).

——, *War, the Liberator and Other Pieces* (London: John Lane, Bodley Head, 1918).

MacNeice, Louis, *Collected Poems* (1966; rpt. London: Faber and Faber, 1979).

——, *Selected Literary Criticism of Louis MacNeice*, ed. Alan Heuser (Oxford: Clarendon Press, 1987).

McNeile, H. C. ['Sapper'], *Men, Women and Guns* (London: Hodder and Stoughton, 1916).

——, *Sapper's War Stories* (London: Hodder and Stoughton, 1930).

Machen, Arthur, *The Angels of Mons. The Bowmen and Other Legends of the War* (London: Simpkin, Marshall, 1915).

Malleson, Miles, *'D' Company and Black 'Ell: Two Plays by Miles Malleson* (London: Henderson, 1916).

Mann, Thomas, *The Magic Mountain* (1924), trans. H. T. Lowe-Porter (Harmondsworth: Penguin, 1999).

Manning, Frederic, *The Middle Parts of Fortune: Somme and Ancre, 1916* (1929; rpt. London: Peter Davies, 1977).

Marsh, Edward (ed.), *Georgian Poetry: 1913–1915* (1915; rpt. London: Poetry Bookshop, 1918).

Marwick, Arthur, *The Deluge: British Society and the First World War*, 2nd edn (1991; rpt. London: Macmillan, 2006).

Masefield, John, *The Old Front Line: or, the Beginning of the Battle of the Somme* (London: William Heinemann, 1917).

Maugham, W. Somerset, *The Collected Plays of W. Somerset Maugham* (London: William Heinemann, 1931), 3 vols.

Maurois, André, *The Silence of Colonel Bramble*, trans. Thurfrida Wake (1919; rpt. Harmondsworth: Penguin, 1940).

[Meynell, Wilfred], *Aunt Sarah & the War: A Tale of Transformations* (London: Burns and Oates, 1914).

Middlebrook, Martin, *The First Day on the Somme: 1 July 1916* (1971; rpt. Harmondsworth: Penguin, 2001).

Miller, Patrick, *The Natural Man* (1924; rpt. London: Richards, 1930).

Milne, A. A., *First Plays* (London: Chatto and Windus, 1927).

Monkhouse, Alan Noble, *War Plays* (London: Constable, 1916).

Montague, C. E., *Disenchantment* (London: Chatto andWindus, 1922).

——, *Fiery Particles* (London: Chatto and Windus, 1923).

——, *Rough Justice* (1926; rpt. London: Chatto and Windus, 1969).

Mottram, R. H., *The Spanish Farm Trilogy* (New York: The Dial Press, 1927).

——, *Ten Years Ago: Armistice and Other Memories: Forming a Pendant to 'The Spanish Farm Trilogy'* (London: Chatto and Windus, 1928).

Murry, John Middleton, *The Evolution of an Intellectual* (London: Richard Cobden-Sanderson, 1920).

Musil, Robert, *The Man without Qualities* (1930–42), trans. Eithne Wilkins and Ernst Kaiser (1954; rpt. London: Picador, 1979), 4 vols.

Nichols, Robert, *Ardours and Endurances: Also a Faun's Holiday and Poems and Phantasies* (1917; rpt. London: Chatto and Windus, 1918).

Nietzsche, Friedrich, *Human, all too Human: A Book for Free Spirits* (1880), trans. R. J. Hollingdale (Cambridge: Cambridge University Press, 1986).

Noakes, Vivien (ed.), *Voices of Silence: The Alternative Book of First World War Poetry* (Stroud: Sutton, 2006).

O'Casey, Sean, *Three More Plays: The Silver Tassie, Purple Dust, Red Roses for Me* (1928, 1940, 1942; rpt. London: Macmillan, 1980).

O'Flaherty, Liam, *Return of the Brute* (1929: rpt. Dublin: Wolfhound Press, 1998).

Orwell, George, *Coming up for Air* (1939; rpt. Harmondsworth: Penguin, 1962).

——, *Nineteen Eighty-Four* (1949; rpt. Harmondsworth: Penguin, 1969).

Osborn, E. B. (ed.), *The Muse in Arms: A Collection of War Poems for the Most Part Written in the Field of Action, by Seamen, Soldiers, and Flying Men Who are Serving, or Have Served, in the Great War* (London: John Murray, 1917).

Oudit, Sharon, *Fighting Forces, Writing Women: Identity and Ideology in the First World War* (London: Routledge, 1994).

Owen, Wilfred, *The Poems of Wilfred Owen: A New Edition Including Many Pieces Now First Published, and Notices of his Life and Works*, ed. Edmund Blunden (London: Chatto and Windus, 1931).

——, *Wilfred Owen: Collected Letters*, ed. Harold Owen and John Bell (London: Oxford University Press, 1967).

——, *Wilfred Owen: The Complete Poems and Fragments*, ed. Jon Stallworthy (London: Chatto and Windus, Hogarth Press, and Oxford University Press, 1983), 2 vols.

Oxenham, John, *'All's Well!': Some Helpful Verse for These Dark Days of War* (London: Methuen, 1915).

Panichas, George A. (ed.), *Promise of Greatness: The War of 1914–1918* (New York: John Day, 1968).

Parfitt, George, *Fiction of the First World War: A Study* (London: Faber and Faber, 1988).

Parsons, I. M. (ed.), *Men Who March Away: Poems of the First World War* (London: Chatto and Windus, 1965).

Pinter, Harold, *Plays: One* (London: Eyre Methuen, 1976).

Plowman, Max ['Mark VII'], *A Subaltern on the Somme: in 1916* (1927; rpt. New York: Dutton, 1928).

Potter, Jane, *Boys in Khaki, Girls in Print: Women's Literary Responses to the Great War 1914–1918* (Oxford: Clarendon Press, 2005).

Pound, Ezra, *Selected Poems*, ed. T. S. Eliot (1948; rpt. London: Faber and Faber, 1973).

Price, Evadne ['Helen Zenna Smith'], *Not so Quiet…: Stepdaughters of War* (1930; rpt. New York: Feminist Press, 1989).

Priestley, J. B., *Literature and Western Man* (London: Heinemann, 1960).

——, *Margin Released: A Writer's Reminiscences and Reflections* (London: Heinemann, 1962).

Proust, Marcel, *Remembrance of Things Past* (1913–27), trans. C. K. Scott Moncrieff and Terence Kilmartin (Harmondsworth: Penguin, 1983), 3 vols.

Purdom, C. B. (ed.), *True World War I Stories: Sixty Personal Narratives of the War* originally published as *Everyman at War* (1930; rpt. London: Robinson, 1999).

Quinn, Patrick J., and Steven Trout (eds), *The Literature of the Great War Reconsidered* (London: Palgrave, 2001).

Rabaté, Jean-Michel, *1913: The Cradle of Modernism* (Oxford: Blackwell, 2007).

Ramage, George. 'The Rather Tame War Experiences in Flanders 1915 of Lance Corporal George Ramage, 1st Battalion Gordon Highlanders', 4 vols. National Library of Scotland MS944–7

Raymond, Ernest, *Tell England: A Study in a Generation* (1922; rpt. London: Cassell, 1929).

Read, Herbert, *Collected Poems* (London: Faber and Faber, 1966).

——, *In Retreat* (London: Hogarth Press, 1925).

Reilly, Catherine W. (ed.), *Scars upon My Heart: Women's Poetry and Verse of the First World War* (1981; rpt. London: Virago, 2009).

Remarque, Erich Maria, *All Quiet on the Western Front* (1929), trans. A. W. Wheen (London: Mayflower, 1963).

——, *Im Westen Nichts Neues* (Berlin: Verlag, 1929).

Richards, Frank, *Old Soldiers Never Die* (1933; rpt. London: Faber and Faber, 1964).

Richardson, Dorothy, *Pilgrimage* (1915–67; rpt. London: Virago, 1979), 4 vols.

Romains, Jules, *Verdun: The Prelude to Battle* (1938), trans. Gerard Hopkins (New York: Alfred A. Knopf, 1939).

Rosenberg, Isaac, *The Collected Works of Isaac Rosenberg: Poetry, Prose, Letters, Paintings and Drawings*, ed. Ian Parsons (London: Chatto and Windus and Hogarth Press, 1984).

——, *The Poems and Plays of Isaac Rosenberg*, ed. Vivien Noakes (Oxford: Oxford University Press, 2004).

Royle, Trevor, *The Flowers of the Forest: Scotland and the First World War* (Edinburgh: Birlinn, 2007).

——(ed.), *In Flanders Fields: Scottish Poetry and Prose of the First World War* (Edinburgh: Mainstream, 1990).

Sanders, M. L., and Philip Taylor, *British Propaganda during the First World War, 1914–18* (London: Macmillan, 1982).

Sassoon, Siegfried, *Collected Poems: 1908–1956* (London: Faber and Faber, 1961).

——, *The Complete Memoirs of George Sherston* [*Memoirs of a Fox-Hunting Man, Memoirs of an Infantry Officer, Sherston's Progress*] (1937; rpt. London: Faber and Faber, 1972).

Sassoon, Siegfried, *Siegfried's Journey: 1916-1920* (London: Faber and Faber, 1945).

Saunders, Max, *Ford Madox Ford: A Dual Life* (Oxford: Oxford University Press, 1996), 2 vols.

Saussure, F. de, *Course in General Linguistics* (1916), trans. Roy Harris (London: Duckworth, 1983).

Sayers, Dorothy L., *The Unpleasantness at the Bellona Club* (1928; rpt. London: Hodder and Stoughton, 2003).

Selincourt, Hugh de, *The Cricket Match* (London: Jonathan Cape, 1924).

Service, Robert, *The Collected Poems of Robert Service* (1940; rpt. New York: G. P. Putnam's Sons, 1993).

Shaw, George Bernard, *Common Sense about the War* (London: Statesman Publishing, 1914).

——, *The Complete Plays of Bernard Shaw* (London: Paul Hamlyn, 1965).

——, *Heartbreak House* (1919; rpt. Harmondsworth: Penguin, 1977).

Sheffield, Gary, *Forgotten Victory: The First World War: Myths and Realities* (London: Review, 2002).

Sherriff, R. C., *Journey's End* (1929; rpt. Harmondsworth: Penguin, 2000).

Sherry, Vincent (ed.), *The Cambridge Companion to the Literature of the First World War* (Cambridge: Cambridge University Press, 2005).

——, *The Great War and the Language of Modernism* (Oxford: Oxford University Press, 2003).

Silkin, Jon (ed.), *The Penguin Book of First World War Poetry* (Harmondsworth: Penguin, 1981).

Sinclair, May, *A Journal of Impressions in Belgium* (London: Hutchinson, 1915).

Sitwell, Osbert, *After the Bombardment* (1926; rpt. Harmondsworth: Penguin, 1938).

Smith, Angela K., *The Second Battlefield: Women, Modernism and the First World War* (Manchester: Manchester University Press, 2000).

Smith, Private Len, *Drawing Fire: The Diary of a Great War Soldier and Artist* (London: Collins, 2009).

Sorley, Charles Hamilton, *The Collected Letters of Charles Hamilton Sorley*, ed. Jean Moorcroft Wilson (London: Woolf, 1990).

——, *The Collected Poems of Charles Hamilton Sorley*, ed. Jean Moorcroft Wilson (London: Woolf, 1985).

Stephen, Martin, *The Price of Pity: Poetry, History and Myth in the Great War* (London: Leo Cooper, 1996).

——(ed.), *Never Such Innocence: Poems of the First World War* (1988; rpt. London: Dent, 2003).

Stevens, Wallace, *The Collected Poems of Wallace Stevens* (London: Faber and Faber, 1955).

Strachan, Hew (ed.), *The Oxford Illustrated History of the First World War* (Oxford: Oxford University Press, 1998).

Strang, Herbert, *With Haig on the Somme: A Story of the Great War* (Oxford: Oxford University Press, 1918).

Surtees, William, *Twenty-Five Years in the Rifle Brigade* (1833; rpt. London: Greenhill Books, 1996).

Sylvaine, Vernon, *The Road of Poplars: A Play in One Act* (London: H. F. W. Deane, 1930).

Tate, Trudi, *Modernism, History and the First World War* (Manchester: Manchester University Press, 1998).

Theatre Workshop and Charles Chilton, *Oh What a Lovely War* (1965; rpt. London: Methuen, 1998).

Thomas, Edward, *The Annotated Collected Poems*, ed. Edna Longley (Northumberland: Bloodaxe, 2008).

——, *The Collected Poems of Edward Thomas*, ed. R. George Thomas (Oxford: Oxford University Press, 1981).

——, 'War Poetry', *Poetry and Drama*, 2(8) (Dec. 1915), 341–5.

Todman, Dan, *The Great War: Myth and Memory* (London: Hambledon Continuum, 2005).

Tomlinson, H. M., *All Our Yesterdays* (London: William Heinemann, 1930).

Trotter, David, *The English Novel in History 1895–1920* (London: Routledge, 1993).

Trotter, Lieutenant Nigel, Letters of Lieutenant Nigel Trotter to his family concerning military training and the first weeks of the Great War. National Library of Scotland, Acc. 6614.

Tuchman, Barbara, *August 1914* (London: Constable, 1962).

Tylee, Claire M., *The Great War and Women's Consciousness: Images of Militarism and Womanhood in Women's Writings, 1914–64* (London: Macmillan, 1990).

Vaughan, Edwin Campion, *Some Desperate Glory: The World War I diary of a British Officer, 1917* (1981; rpt. New York: Henry Holt, 1988).

Waller, Philip, *Writers, Readers and Reputations: Literary Life in Britain 1870–1918* (Oxford: Oxford University Press, 2008).

Walpole, Hugh, *The Dark Forest* (London: Martin Secker, 1916).

Ward, Mrs Humphry, *Missing* (London: W. Collins Sons, 1917).

Watson, Janet S. K., *Fighting Different Wars: Experience, Memory and the First World War in Britain* (Cambridge: Cambridge University Press, 2004).

Wells, H. G., *Boon. The Mind of the Race, The Wild Asses of the Devil, and The Last Trump: Being a First Selection from the Literary Remains of George Boon, Appropriate to the Times: Prepared for Publication by Reginald Bliss: with An Ambiguous Introduction by H. G. Wells (Who is in Truth the Author of the Entire Book)* (1915; rpt. London: T. Fisher Unwin, 1920).

Wells, H. G., *The Dream: A Novel* (London: Jonathan Cape, 1924).

——, *Mr. Britling Sees It Through* (London: Cassell, 1916).

——, *Tono-Bungay* (1909; rpt. London: Ernest Benn, 1926).

——, *The War That Will End War* (London: Frank and Cecil Palmer, 1914).

——, *The World Set Free: A Story of Mankind* (London: Macmillan, 1914).

West, Arthur Graeme, *Diary of a Dead Officer: Being the Posthumous Papers of Arthur Graeme West* (1919; rpt. London: Greenhill Books, 2007).

West, Rebecca, *The Return of the Soldier* (1918; rpt. London: Virago, 2004).

Wharton, Edith, *The Marne: A Tale of the War* (London: Macmillan, 1918).

——, *A Son at the Front* (1923; rpt. DeKalb: Northern Illinois University Press, 1995).

White, Hayden, *The Content of the Form: Narrative Discourse and Historical Representation* (Baltimore/London: Johns Hopkins University Press, 1987).

Whitten, Wilfred, '"What the Soldier Said": Collecting the Slang of the Great War', *John O'London's Weekly*, 6(145) (14 Jan. 1922), 480.

Williamson, Anne, *Henry Williamson and the First World War* (Stroud: Sutton, 1998).

Williamson, Henry, *The Flax of Dream: A Novel in Four Books* (1921–8; rpt. London: Faber and Faber, 1936).

——, *A Fox under My Cloak* (1955; rpt. Stroud: Alan Sutton, 1996).

——, *The Golden Virgin* (1957; rpt. Stroud: Alan Sutton, 1996).

——, *How Dear is Life* (1954; rpt. London: Arrow, 1985).

——, *Love and the Loveless* (1958; rpt. Stroud: Alan Sutton, 1997).

——, *The Patriot's Progress* (1930; rpt. Stroud: Sutton, 2004).

——, *A Test to Destruction* (London: Macdonald, 1960).

——, *The Wet Flanders Plain* (1929; rpt. London: Faber and Faber, 2009).

Winter, Jay, *Remembering War: The Great War between Memory and History in the Twentieth Century* (New Haven, CT/London: Yale University Press, 2006).

——, *Sites of Memory, Sites of Mourning: The Great War in European Cultural History* (1996; rpt. Cambridge: Cambridge University Press, 1998).

Wolff, Leon, *In Flanders Field: The 1917 Campaign* (London: Longmans, Green, 1959).

Woolf, Virginia, *The Diary of Virginia Woolf*, ed. Anne Olivier Bell, assisted by Andrew McNeillie (London: Hogarth Press, 1977–85), 5 vols.

——, *The Essays of Virginia Woolf*, ed. Andrew McNeillie and Stuart N. Clarke (London: Hogarth Press, 1986–2011), 5 vols.

——, *Jacob's Room* (1922; rpt. London: Panther, 1976).

——, *Mrs Dalloway* (1925; rpt. Harmondsworth: Penguin, 1975).

——, *A Room of One's Own* (1929; rpt. Harmondsworth: Penguin, 1975).

——, *To the Lighthouse* (1927; rpt. Harmondsworth: Penguin, 1973).

——, 'Two Soldier Poets', *Times Literary Supplement*, 11 July 1918, 323.

Yeates, V. M., *Winged Victory* (London: Jonathan Cape, 1934).

Yeats, W. B. (ed.), *The Oxford Book of Modern Verse, 1892–1935* (Oxford: Clarendon Press, 1936).

Young, Francis Brett, *Marching on Tanga: With General Smuts in East Africa* (1917; rpt. Gloucester: Alan Sutton, 1984).

INDEX